JOHN GODDARD'S
TROUT-FISHING
TECHNIQUES

Trout Fly Recognition
Trout Flies of Stillwater
Big Fish From Saltwater
The Superflies of Stillwater
The Trout and the Fly (with Brian Clarke)
Stillwater Flies: How and When to Fish Them
Fly Fishing for Trout (with Brian Clarke)
John Goddard's Waterside Guide
Trout Flies of Britain and Europe

JOHN GODDARD'S
TROUT-FISHING
TECHNIQUES

JOHN GODDARD F.R.E.S.

ILLUSTRATED BY CHARLES JARDINE

Foreword by Lefty Kreh

THE LYONS PRESS
Guilford, Connecticut
An imprint of The Globe Pequot Press

The Lyons Press is an imprint of The Globe Pequot Press.

Printed in the United States of America

10 9 8 7 6 5 4 3 2 1

Text design and composition by Rohani Design, Edmonds, Washington

ISBN 1-58574-819-6

Library of Congress Cataloging-in-Publication data is available on file.

CONTENTS

ACKNOWLEDGMENTS

T HIS BOOK COVERS A LONG PERIOD going back to the early sixties when I first became a dedicated fly fisher. I would therefore like to thank those fly fishers, many of them well known in the angling world, who have given so generously their time, expertise, and invaluable help over this long period. Very regrettably such giants of the angling world as Dick Walker, Major Oliver Kite, David Jacques, and my old buddies Leslie Moncrieff, Cliff Henry, Frank Fortey, and Jimmy Handley are no longer with us. I should also like to acknowledge the great assistance and help I have received from the following with whom I have fished on so many occasions over the years, most of whom are good friends of long standing: Preben Torp Jacobsen, Dr. Ivan Tomka, John Veniard, Taff Price, Dermot Wilson, Peter Lapsley, Charles Jardine, Stewart Canham, Fred J. Taylor, David and Kay Steuart, John Ginnifer, Conrad Voss Bark, and John Ketley. In addition I must also include the many good friends I have made in America over the years who have provided so much information on American waters, fishing methods, and fly patterns: Gary Borger, Mel

Krieger, Dick Talleur, Ron Cordes, Larry Solomon, Darrel Martin, John Betts, Leonard Wright, Craig Mathews, and last but not least my old buddy Bernard Lefty Kreh.

These acknowledgments would be incomplete without also mentioning my particular fishing buddies with whom I have spent so many happy hours on so many different waters, discussing problems and tactics over half a lifetime: Max King, Bernard Cribbins, Ron Clark, Brian Clarke, Neil Patterson, and Norman Marsh, and Alan Simmons in New Zealand.

I should also like to thank all those very kind people who have granted me special access to the many lovely rivers I have fished and in particular must thank Herbert G. Wellington, Alan Mann, and Roy Darlington.

Finally, I must thank both Nick Lyons and Timothy Benn, publishers and great friends of many years, who are largely responsible for persuading me to write this book. Thanks are due also to Sandy Leventon, editor of *Trout & Salmon,* for permission to reproduce an article from the magazine.

FOREWORD

I HAVE BEEN LUCKY ENOUGH—during more than fifty years of trout fishing around the world—to fish with some of the finest practitioners of this wonderful sport. Many of them are superb casters and anglers, and a joy to be with. But without any doubt John Goddard is the best trout fisherman with whom I have spent time on the water. This is no idle compliment, since many famous fly rodders have shared their skills and time with me. John is the best.

More than that, so far as the readers of this book are concerned, John is a *total* fly fisherman. He has spent thousands of hours on the demanding chalkstreams of England; fished many of the most difficult trout streams in the United States; conquered the challenging, air-clear waters of New Zealand; and much more. But John is also a superb salt-water fly fisherman. He has caught everything from sailfish to bonefish on a fly. John Goddard is one of the best all-around fly fishermen who has ever lived.

There has been much written on trout senses. But Goddard's explanations and Charles Jardine's drawings are the most perceptive I have seen. Some ideas presented in this book that concern how a trout sees and how this applies to your approach and presentation I have not seen discussed anywhere. Eager trout fishermen will find extremely revealing his discussion on the effects of sight and smell as related to strikes, and his material on what factor noise plays in obtaining hook-ups is excellent.

Some years ago Vince Marinaro explored the different riseforms created by trout. Goddard delves much deeper into this, and Charles Jardine's illustrations are enlightening. Goddard also treats the subject of catching difficult trout better than anyone I know; he devotes an entire chapter to various casts to help you catch trout. If you are a serious trout fisherman and you study these sections, you will certainly catch more of those bigger, tough-to-fool trout.

One of the most important parts of this book is Goddard's treatment of how to fish lakes. American fly fishermen can be superb river technicians, but the English are the masters of stillwaters. Goddard discusses the totally different tackle used by English anglers; how to fish from shore (which we rarely do in the United States); and the complexities of using boats and tubes. For any lake fisherman this information is easily worth more than the price of the book.

As you digest the contents of this book, you will learn scores of things from the perceptive John Goddard, that took him more than fifty years to learn the hard way—on the water. This is not a book to be read lightly and put aside. *There is simply too much knowledge here to be absorbed in a single reading.* This is a superb manual on how to become a better trout fisherman. Even as your level of skill increases, rereading the book will give you insight into how to become an even better fly fisherman. Every trout fisherman I have ever met will want to thank John Goddard for this important book; it is the best on trout fly-fishing technique I have ever read.

—Lefty Kreh
Summer 1996

INTRODUCTION

A S A DEDICATED and fanatical fly fisherman, I often wonder which era I would have chosen to be born into, had I been given a choice: the late nineteenth century during the reign of the great F. M. Halford, when dry-fly fishing became *the* method; the early twentieth century, when nymph fishing was first introduced by that most innovative and forward thinking of fly fishers, G. E. M. Skues; the period between the two great wars, when progress was so slow despite the fact that there were so many opportunities for improvement; or the postwar period up to the present day, when we have seen so many revolutionary advances in tackle and fly-tying materials. In retrospect, I think I would have chosen to be where I am. In my lifetime I have experienced so many incredible advances in fishing methods—techniques and tackle—that I consider myself very fortunate.

I started fishing at the tender age of eight, like so many youngsters before me, with a small net and a jam jar. Minnows were my main quarry. Within a year or so I had acquired an old greenheart rod, brass reel, and some floats and had set my sights on larger quarry. We used to spend the school holidays at my grandfather's house on the river Thames not far from London. I well remember the first big fish that succumbed to my wriggling worm. He was a roach all of six inches in length. To me he was a monster compared with the tiny minnows I had been catching with the net. With his burnished silver scales and bright red fins he really fired my imagination, and from then on fishing was to become a large part of my life. By my late teens I had graduated from roach and dace to chub, bream, and pike, but the declaration of war in 1939 put a stop to all of this.

I was apprenticed as an engineer, joined the army in 1942, and was demobbed in 1947. During this time there were no opportunities to fish, so it was not until early 1948 that I was once again able to indulge in my favourite sport. This same year I entered the family business, started by my grandfather in 1908. Between the wars we manufactured a large range of garden furniture in our light engineering and sewing machine workshops. By 1950 competition in garden furniture had become so fierce we turned our attention to fishing and, towards the end of that year, launched a small range of angling luggage and accessories under the now wellknown brand name of EFGEECO (taken from the initials of the firm, which traded under the name of F. Goddard & Co.). This proved to be very successful and by the midseventies we were producing and wholesaling direct to the tackle shops over two hundred different items of fishing tackle. During the fifties and early sixties, I spent much of the time on the road, selling our products to the shops, which presented me with a unique opportunity to meet many of the great angling names of the time. Occasionally I was fortunate enough to be invited to fish with some of them.

During the early fifties I developed a keen interest in carp, often fishing through the night after finishing work on a Friday evening. In those days specialized carp fishing was in its infancy and few waters held fish of any size. The British record carp of forty-four pounds had been caught in 1952 by Richard Walker, whom I consider to be one of the greatest fishermen of this century. I felt very privileged to meet him soon after I took up carp fishing. Subsequently we became friends and on occasions I used to fish with him and the Taylor brothers, Fred and Ken, who were also big names in the sport at the time. We used to fish with heavy split-cane rods, the relatively new fixed-spool bait-casting reels, and homemade bite alarms. Our target in those heady days was to catch a carp over twenty pounds. I never achieved it although I came very close on several occasions.

It was not until 1955 that I took up trout fishing seriously. Like a lot of coarse fishermen, even today, my first trout-fishing expeditions were confined to stillwater. That summer I fished the newly opened Weir Wood Reservoir in Sussex, and had several nice bags of trout, both browns and rainbows. The largest was a lovely brown of just over four pounds. They were all taken on a Hardy nine-foot Model Perfect split-cane rod, a Kingfisher silk fly line—which, to keep it floating, had to be treated with a flotant several times each day—and one of the new nylon leaders and tippets that had just replaced the traditional silkworm gut leaders.

This proved to be a year that opened new horizons. During the summer I was thrilled to be invited by a very experienced river trout fisherman by the name of Frank Fortey to join him for a day on the little river Lambourne—a typical south-country chalkstream with crystal clear water running over bright golden gravel past vivid green patches of white-flowering rununculus. I fell in love with it immediately and, after a super day's dry-fly fishing, vowed that one day soon I would find a way to fish these chalkstreams on a regular basis.

During the same year I also spent some time down in the west country, deep-sea and shark fishing with some eminent anglers of the day—Bernard Venables, Bruce Ogden Smith, and Gurney Grice, who was managing director of the well-known fishing-reel manufacturer Grice & Young. In those days Looe in Cornwall was the major centre in England for shark fishing and on a good day it was not uncommon for a boat to bring back upwards of a dozen blue sharks. We caught many sharks of up to about a hundred pounds in weight, which, looking back, is most amusing, as we were using tackle capable of subduing fish of many times this weight. The rods were split-cane like broomsticks, mounted with huge centre-pin reels containing at least five hundred yards of the old Cuttyhunk or Ashaway braided line. We also enjoyed a couple days' wreck fishing for pollack and ling. I can still recall being totally exhausted at the end of the day, by which time we had boated nearly a thousand pounds of fish. My God, those were the days—today if you can find a wreck with any fish on at all, you are lucky.

That great American big-game fisherman Zane Grey had been my boyhood hero, so this little taste of deep-sea fishing proved to be the spark that ignited the flame. From then on I gradually progressed from deep-sea fishing around British shores to big-game fishing for tuna and marlin in many oceans throughout the world, mainly during the closed season for fly fishing. These big-game fishing expeditions eventually led to my being selected to fish for the English team in many of the European Big Game International Championships. They were also the source of many exciting adventures, outside the scope of a book on fly fishing.

It was around this time that I developed an interest in fly dressing and started to tie my own patterns. My first lesson was provided by the late Ivor Pickton, an elderly gentleman who ran a famous fishing tackle shop in the city of London that traded under the name of Peek's of Grays Inn Road. Ivor was a professional fly dresser and he tied most of the flies sold in the shop. During my frequent visits, I often watched him at his bench and eventually he persuaded me to spend an hour with him at the vise, where under his expert tuition I dressed my first fly. This was a simple dry fly, yet I can still vividly recall my amazement at the method used to wind the hackle to complete the fly. After this first lesson I was literally hooked.

I think it was in 1957 that I was invited by Frank Fortey to join the Piscatorial Society, one of the oldest fly-fishing societies in existence. In those days they leased some wonderful waters on the best chalkstreams. There were two stretches on the river Kennet, two on the lovely little Lambourne, one on the river Wylie, and they had also taken a fifteen-year lease on the famous Abbot's Barton Water on the Itchen, the same stretch that the great G. E. M. Skues had fished for most of his life. The river Itchen at Abbot's Barton proved to be a hard taskmaster. At that

time it was one of the most difficult and challenging waters for the fly
fisher in the country. Very slow and gin clear, and the trout had all the
time in the world to inspect your dry fly before accepting or, more often,
rejecting it. Matching the hatch was absolutely vital to achieve any sort
of success at all, which led to my lifelong interest in angling entomology
and macrophotography.

During my membership in the Piscatorials I twice won the Cup
or Spoon for the largest trout caught in a season, and it was with considerable regret that in 1972 I decided to resign. I strongly objected to
the newly appointed fishery officer's decision to stock each water at the
beginning of each season with trout in excess of twenty inches. For as
long as I had been a member, the policy had been to stock with trout
of between twelve and fourteen inches so the challenge always existed
of locating and catching a big trout. I am sure that most fly fishers
follow the same path. To start with you try to catch more trout than
any other fellow angler, you then progress to catching bigger trout
than anyone else, and eventually you are only happy trying to catch
those very difficult educated trout that have eluded all others. Having
passed through all those stages, I am now content just to be beside the
water and probably spend more time socializing with other fly fishers
than actually fishing. Since resigning from the Piscatorials I have had
a rod on most of the major chalkstream beats as well as fishing many
other famous rivers throughout the UK.

Throughout the fifties and sixties one of my constant fishing companions was the late Cliff Henry, one of the best stillwater fly fishers and
fly dressers whom it has been my privilege to know. Much of my knowledge of stillwaters has come from Cliff and from excursions I made with
him to the big reservoirs such as Chew, Blagdon, Grafham, and Rutland
Waters. In those early days a lot of our fly fishing was done from the
bank, starting before sunrise and continuing, with short breaks for lunch
and tea, until it was too dark to see.

As vice chairman of the Angling Trade Association and later also
chairman of the Angling Foundation, I was in a unique position to
meet and fish with many of the great anglers of the time. One of these,

the late Major Oliver Kite (Ollie to his friends), became a particular friend, and for many years I used to invite him to fish with me on the river Itchen several times a season. In return he invited me to fish with him on his stretch of the little river Wylie, mainly for grayling, which was great sport. An excellent dry-fly fisher, he was an absolute wizard with a nymph, having that very rare ability, almost a sixth sense, honed to a fine degree, of knowing when a fish had taken his nymph even when there was no visible sign or indication that he had. During the early sixties when I first started fishing with Ollie, he was a great buddy of Frank Sawyer, a river keeper on the river Avon who lived almost opposite to him in the little village of Netheravon in Wiltshire. Frank Sawyer was the genius who invented the now famous weighted Pheasant Tail Nymph and the induced-take method of fishing it, which was the forerunner of nymph fishing as we know it today. It is generally accepted that G. E. M. Skues was the first person ever to dress, fish, and popularize nymphs. Skues' nymphs were designed to fish just a few inches deep and were therefore quite useless for fishing to deep-lying trout, so it is to Sawyer that we must credit the more modern and effective methods of catching trout at all depths, and he was aided by Oliver Kite, a fact that few historians seem to accept. While Sawyer was a superb fly fisher and fly dresser, he was not a particularly accomplished writer, and without the literary skills of Kite I am very doubtful whether his patterns and methods would be so well known today. Kite, who was a great character, wrote regularly for the fishing press and also had his own television program, *Kite's Country,* which featured various aspects of fly fishing. Over a period of several years he promoted the Pheasant Tail Nymph and the induced-take method of fishing it, which eventually and sadly led to a rift between the two once great friends. Frank Sawyer's book *Nymphs and the Trout* and Oliver Kite's book *Nymph Fishing in Practice* are probably the two most important volumes in the history of this relatively new method of fly fishing.

Through my friendship with Ollie, I was introduced to one of Denmark's top fly fishermen, Preben Torp Jacobsen, who over the intervening years has also become a great friend. A keen angling entomologist, historian, and gifted fly dresser, he has been a mine of information on European fly-dressing and fishing techniques.

I started writing for the fishing press in the early sixties, which led to corresponding with fly fishers from the UK and America. Through this I have made friends and fished with some well-known American fly fishers, all experts in their own field, including Larry Solomon, Leonard Wright, Lee Wulff, Dick Talleur, Darrel Martin, Ron Cordes, Mel Krieger, Gary Borger, and, of course, Lefty Kreh, who is probably the greatest all-around fly fisher in the world today.

Since my first taste of saltwater fly fishing for bonefish in the Bahamas in 1975, I have become somewhat of a saltwater fly-fishing fanatic. I have fished most of the bonefishing hot spots, including Christmas Island in the Pacific, and have been lucky enough to catch several bonefish in excess of twelve pounds. More recently I have been pursuing permit and have to date caught eight of these most elusive fish on the fly. I have also caught over thirty other species of saltwater fish on the fly, including several sailfish, the largest of which was 128 pounds. Much as I still love my dry-fly fishing on the chalkstreams of England and the clearwater rivers of New Zealand and Montana, I think if I were given a choice I would be hard pressed to choose between dry-fly fishing on a sparkling stream and wading a gin-clear, silver sand flat for tailing bonefish.

Most of my previous books have been very technical, dealing with natural or artificial fishing flies, or in some cases both. This book is different. It is about the fly-fishing techniques I have developed or been shown on the many different waters I have fished over the last forty years all over the world. When writing on fishing, you cannot afford to be too dogmatic—the fish do not know the rules and are liable to change their behaviour without any warning or apparent reason. Do remember when reading this book that some of the advice or suggestions may not apply under certain circumstances. Fishing is fun, and even if you have a blank, you will at least have enjoyed a day in lovely surroundings. There are few days on a river or lake when one does not learn something new, even after a lifetime of experience. I hope that this book will appeal not only to those fly fishers who fish on chalkstreams or spring creeks but also to those who fish freestone or rain-fed rivers as well as lakes and reservoirs, and that the techniques and tips discussed will lead to a more fulfilling day on the next water you fish.

The Trout's Lifestyle

Senses, Habitat, Riseforms, Feeding Habits

TROUT, LIKE OTHER FISH, live in a mysterious, shadowy world in which they cannot rely upon sight alone. They also need their senses of hearing, smell, and, to a much lesser degree, touch and taste. Humans also rely upon these five senses but in very different ways. Let us deal with these senses in reverse order of importance.

TOUCH AND TASTE

It is generally accepted that fish do not have the same sensitivity of touch as humans do, but scientific research cannot yet tell us just how effectively fish use this sense. Certainly they react if you touch them, and bodily contact during spawning is important. When feeding, this sense must play some part, as trout will often take foreign matter into their mouths and very quickly eject it. The sense of taste is of more importance; trout feed upon a host of different insects, flies, and other aquatic fauna, and often develop a taste for one particular species over another. It is probably the sense of taste that accounts for selective feeding or the preoccupation of trout at certain times upon certain species to the exclusion of all others. A good example of this is the way that trout in rivers will often feed upon very small iron blue duns to the exclusion of other very similar upwinged species that are hatching at the same time.

SMELL .

Scientists in the latter half of this century have discovered many useful and fascinating facts about the fish's sense of smell. Extensive tests have demonstrated that many species can scent danger or food with incredible sensitivity. As a general rule, those fish that frequent muddy or turbid water or those that feed mainly at night have a much more highly developed sense of smell than those species that feed during the day in relatively clear water.

In some species, one or more of the senses may be developed to a much higher degree than the others. For example, we know that sharks have extremely poor eyesight, yet their sense of smell is incredibly good. We also know that salmon have excellent eyesight and a very highly developed sense of smell, which enables them to locate and return to the rivers of their birth through thousands of miles of open ocean. So far as trout are concerned, their sense of smell must be fairly well developed and probably assists in the location of food; during the spawning period it helps them to find the gravid females.

Take care when fly fishing to keep your hands reasonably clean to prevent possible fish-scaring odours from being transferred to the fly when you tie it onto your tippet. I learnt this the hard way many years ago during a trip to Alaska. At the time I was fishing for salmon with three companions and we were using wet flies. The river we were fishing was very clear and full of salmon and my companions were pulling fish out one after the other while I had not a bite. After a while I noticed that the fish were parting to let my fly past. When I mentioned this to one of my companions, his reply was caustic and very much to the point: "Idiot! I'll bet you transferred insect repellent from your hands to the fly when you tied it on." Of course he was quite right. After washing my hands and tying on a new fly, I was immediately into a fish.

Following on from this, it is interesting to note that in New Zealand, where the trout are very wild and extremely wary, none of the top guides will ever allow you to wet wade across a river in order to walk down and fish it up. If this is necessary, they will always insist that you put on chest waders, as they have discovered from long experience that the scent from your uncovered legs will travel many miles down a river and make the trout extra spooky.

HEARING

This is the trout's most versatile sense; even when his vision is all but totally obscured in highly coloured water or at night, his hearing remains acute. It is very much more highly developed than in humans, particularly through the medium of water, where he will hear sounds that would be completely inaudible to us. The trout's ears, like those of most other fish, are buried beneath the skin on either side of his head. In addition to these, he has a second sound-detecting organ in the form of a lateral line along his body, which is unique in the animal world. This lateral line extends from the head along the flank of the fish to the tail and is furnished at intervals with sound sensors, which are very sensitive to nearby low-frequency sounds. The ears pick up the farther-afield sounds, so the combination of these two systems provides the trout with a very comprehensive and acute sense of hearing. As fly fishermen, we must take this factor into account when seeking our quarry both in fresh water and in salt water.

As a parallel, consider saltwater fly fishing for barracuda on the gin-clear water of shallow sand flats in tropical climes. Barracuda have not only fantastic vision but also incredible hearing. These fish will often be observed lying motionless or moving very slowly. In shallow water they are very wary, so you should never cast too close; the relatively large fly hitting the water surface close to him would spook him off the flat. Cast the fly to land at least ten yards past and well to the side of the fish. If he is feeding, he will immediately launch himself in the direction of the sound. Barracuda move so incredibly fast that often they will intercept the fly before you have started your retrieve.

Likewise in trout fishing, splash a fly down onto the surface too close to a feeding fish and you will spook him, but splash that same fly several yards away and you will often attract him. This is a very useful ploy when an inaccessible trout is found feeding beneath a tree or bush. The sound of the fly hitting the surface will often lure him out.

Fortunately for the fisherman, sounds made in the air, such as normal conversation or even music from a radio, will not register to a fish as the water surface will reflect 99 percent of the sound. On the other hand, even the slightest of physical movements on the bank of a river or in the water or from a boat on the water will be picked up immediately by the fish. For this reason, when fishing from a boat on a lake or reservoir, try to keep any physical movements to an absolute minimum; when conditions allow, I remove my shoes. When bank fishing, lake or river, your approach to within casting distance should be made as stealthily as possible. On those occasions when it may be necessary to get into the water to cast a fish, do so as gently as possible. Finally, when wading out from the bank of a lake to cast to a fish or when wading up a stream or river looking for trout, go very slowly indeed so as not to form a bow wave in front of each leg as it is moved forward; at the same time, take care to feel carefully with each foot so as not to disturb any loose stones or boulders on the bottom.

SIGHT

How and what trout see is a subject that has always fascinated fly fishers. Over the years much research has been carried out, and while our knowledge is much greater than our forebears', there is still much to be learnt. But we cannot afford to be too dogmatic about any theories. Even when they are arrived at through personal observation of trout in their natural environment, we can never be sure how the trout's brain interprets any messages it receives through his eyes.

The Trout's Eye

Since the middle of the last century, many angling books have included sections on fish vision, but despite this the subject has not really received the coverage that it deserves. Early books were based on scientific knowledge that has since been superseded, and some later ones have perpetuated basic errors.

There are similarities between the human and the trout's eye: both have a cornea, a lens, an iris, and a retina carrying light-sensitive cells (rods and cones), which detect the images formed upon them. Both have an optic nerve to transfer visual information to the brain. (See figures 1 and 2.)

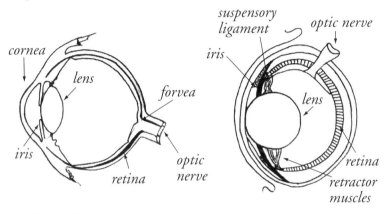

Figure 1. The human eye   Figure 2. The trout's eye

Beyond these similarities, they are very different—it would be surprising if eyes adapted to air and those adapted to water had not evolved differently. The major differences are the absence of eyelids on a trout's eye; the size and shape of its lens; the trout's ability to move the lens by using various muscles within the retina, to adjust its vision and focus; and of course the position of the eye. Trout, like most fish, have the eyes positioned laterally on the sides of the head, which, while resulting in more limited binocular vision, does give a much greater field of total vision.

Most reasonably experienced fly fishers will know roughly how and what a trout sees, but for those readers who would like more explicit and detailed information I recommend *The Trout and the Fly**, written by Brian Clarke and myself, which covers the whole subject of trout vision

* A&C Black, London, England; Lyons & Burford, New York, USA; 1980.

in great detail. Since writing the book with Brian, I have developed some interesting new theories that could have a bearing on how we present our flies and approach trout. The following is an extract from an article that I wrote for *Trout & Salmon* magazine, and is reproduced here with their kind permission.

> One of the most intriguing aspects of a trout's vision is the fish's ability to scan an arc of 160° or more on each side of his body while at the same time being able to observe objects ahead with binocular vision where the arcs of the eyes overlap. Obviously this area of binocular vision must be very important, particularly to a brown trout that spends a large percentage of his time searching for food on or near the surface. Would it not therefore be interesting from a fishing point of view, I asked myself, to find out the precise area that was covered by the fish's binocular vision? On referring to all the books in my library that cover the vision of fish, little seems to have been written about this aspect. The only reference, which most of them repeat, is that a trout has a narrow band of binocular vision some 45° dead ahead, where the arcs of the eyes overlap. Now it seems strange to me that a trout that spends much of his time searching the mirror or window overhead would only have binocular vision immediately ahead. I therefore decided to study the structure and position of the eye in the head of the trout. The first point I noticed—and one that seems to have escaped the attention of other researchers—was that not only do the eyes slope inwards slightly towards the nose, but they also slope inwards to the top of the head. In effect this means that the arcs of the eyes overlap not only immediately ahead but also over the top of the trout's head, so surely this should mean that the range of binocular vision is very much more extensive than previously suspected? To find out what area this covered I took a series of close-up photographs of the heads of many trout—both from directly in front and also from vertically overhead. I then measured the angles of the arcs formed by the inward angles of the eyes in front and overhead. While it was not possible with the equipment available to me to measure these angles precisely I am confident that they are probably accurate to within at least a

couple of degrees. To start with I found that the arc immediately in front was about 35° and not, as previously supposed, 45°. (See figure 3.) The arc overhead was a little less and seemed to be about 28°. (See figure 4.) Due to the fact that the two arcs (or more probably elongated cones) of binocular vision overlap considerably because of the two inwardly converging angles of the eyes, I assume that the overall area covered by binocular vision is about 125° from in front to overhead. I also assume that the trout's binocular vision at each end of this arc would be less acute, and that his most acute vision would occur where the cones or arcs overlap—which would probably be at an angle of between 35° and 40° from the horizontal in front of the trout's head. From many hundreds of subsequent personal observations of trout in their feeding lies, I noticed that most trout in a feeding lie seem to lie at a slight angle with their heads up. This in effect means that this optimum angle of acute binocular vision is probably nearer to 48° from the horizontal, which would enable the trout to observe not only the mirror above but also into the edge of his window, which we know occurs at an angle of 48.5°, which would certainly seem to make a lot of sense from the trout's point of view. During the latter stages of my

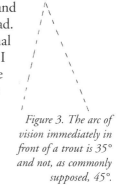

Figure 3. The arc of vision immediately in front of a trout is 35° and not, as commonly supposed, 45°.

research into the above, I contacted Professor W. R. A. Muntz in the department of biology at Stirling University. He is one of the world's leading authorities on fish vision and had been of considerable help to Brian Clarke and me when we were researching the fish vision section of our book.

This time I asked him if he could provide some detailed information on the structure of a trout's eye with particular reference to its binocular vision and focusing ability. The information he provided was most interesting, as he was able to provide accurate details of how a trout moves the lens in his eye by means of a large retractor muscle, to adjust its focus. When at rest in the retina, the lens is so positioned that anything in front and overhead is in close focus, which seems to confirm my research. This lentis muscle when retracted moves the lens both inward and toward the back of the retina in a straight line away from the nose, thereby providing focus to infinity directly in front and also to some degree above. As a matter of interest, during the research for our book we had established with the help of Professor Muntz that infinity occurred at about two feet in front of the trout. Having, I hope, established the approx-imate area of a trout's binocular vision I now wanted to establish, if possible, the width of water overhead and in front that this would cover. (See figure 5.) First of all we must take the two arcs first discussed: the one in front at 35° and the one overhead at 28°. A rough average would then be 32°. This means that if the trout's eyes were focused at less than infinity (two feet) he would be aware only of approaching food within a narrow arc no more than fifteen inches wide at most. Even with his eyes focused to infinity and concentrating on approaching food within his area of binocular vision, the band of water above and in front in which he would be able to see such small items as insects, even in pretty clear water, would be little more than forty inches wide at the maximum distance.

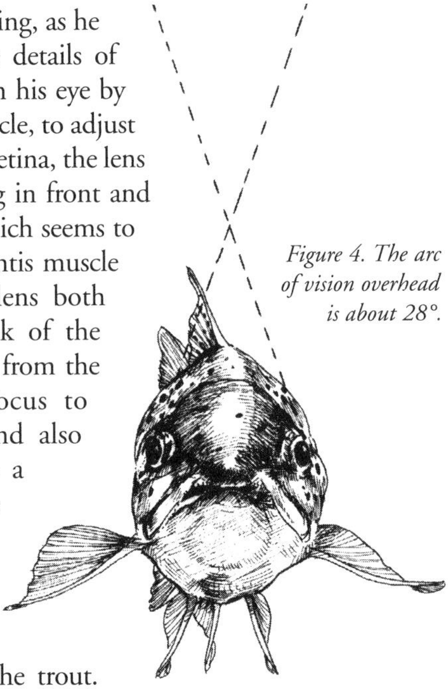

Figure 4. The arc of vision overhead is about 28°.

Seldom is one able to confirm theories by practical tests or observations in the field, but early the following season I was most fortunate to find a cooperative trout in a perfect lie in such a position that, with dense cover behind and partly above, I was able to lower a dry fly from directly above and place it very accu-

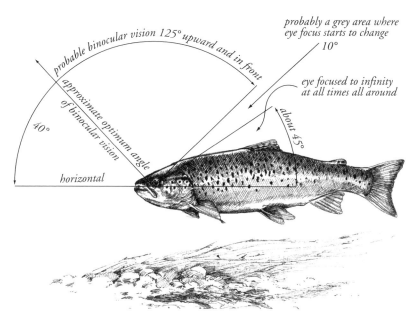

Figure 5. The width of water covered by a trout's binocular vision

rately on the water a few feet in front of the spot where he was rising. To start with I was drifting the fly down to him at a predetermined distance to each side, and each time it passed over he rose and took it very confidently, eventually rejecting it. By this method I established that my theory seemed reasonably accurate as, with the trout lying only about twelve inches below the surface, he completely ignored my fly if it was drifted down to him more than about eighteen inches to either side of his lie. I was about to retire and leave the trout in peace when to my astonishment he broke through the surface in the most perfect arc and took my fly in the air as it was hanging about fifteen inches above the surface and about twenty inches upstream of his lie. Now the only way he could have seen this fly in the air was over the edge and in front of his window, and as I was reasonably sure that he had not tilted upwards before jumping I realized that if I could persuade him to jump and accept the fly a few more times, I might also be able to prove, or disprove, my first theory that trout may have cones of binocular vision to some extent overhead as well as in front. Never had I met a more cooperative trout: During the next fifteen minutes or so I persuaded him to launch himself into the air an incredible seventeen times. His reactions were absolutely fascinating as each time I lowered the fly and swung it down towards him I was in no doubt at all as to whether he had seen it. When he did, all his fins—particularly his tail—would start vibrating, and these vibrations would increase in intensity as I swung the fly closer until it was in range of his lie when he would jump and try to take it in midair. I established that he would first see the fly in the air if I swung it to within three or four feet directly upstream of his lie. Now of course what I wished to establish was whether or not the trout was observing this fly over the edge of his window through his binocular vision. If my theory were to be confirmed, he would be unaware of the fly if I positioned it in the air between three and four feet upstream and more than eighteen inches off-centre, and so it proved to be. If I swung the fly down to him anywhere near that centre line he would see it every time, but I could swing it down to him repeatedly about two feet off-centre and not once did he seem to be aware of it.

Now what conclusions can we draw from the above—and how will this help the fly fisher improve his chances of success? 1. A trout lying and feeding within say eighteen inches or so of the surface will probably be concentrating through his binocular vision and therefore the approaching fly fisher would probably not register unless he made any sudden movements. 2. A trout lying very close to the surface will probably also be focused below infinity so any approaching objects, including the fly fisher, will be even less likely to be seen. In both cases, however, accurate casting will be necessary, as the fish is unlikely to be aware of any fly drifting down to him either on or below the surface either side of his narrow arc of binocular vision. In view of this I am now beginning to wonder whether this may explain the difficulty in tempting trout during those infuriating evening rises on stillwater when every trout in the lake seems to be rising and yet any pattern you offer is ignored. At this time the trout are usually cruising along almost on the surface so would be unlikely to see any fly less than about fourteen inches immediately in front or twelve inches on either side of them. Maybe during this evening rise we would increase our chances if we fished a team of three flies much closer together.

Finally, what about those trout that are lying and feeding at a much deeper level? All the angling books that contain a section on trout vision tell us that the deeper a trout is lying the farther off he can see the angler as, of course, the deeper he lies, the larger his window overhead. While this is certainly true, the additional distance he will be able to see is at best marginal, so I am now inclined to think that the more likely explanation for his increased awareness of our presence is due to the fact that at this depth he is unlikely to be concentrating through his binocular vision so everything on each side of his head within the whole 160° arc of his vision will be clearly seen at infinity. This also means that when presenting a fly or nymph to such a trout, even more care will have to be taken with your approach, but at the same time accurate presentation of your fly will not be so crucial as the fish will be aware of approaching food over a much wider area.

In conclusion, I would add that the detailed information provided by Professor Muntz on the structure of a trout's eye and exactly how he moves his lens to provide focusing ability has thrown up a most interesting new fact. The lentis muscle is apparently so positioned that when it contracts to provide the necessary focusing adjustment to the lens, it moves in at such an angle that it leaves the front section of the lens more or less equidistant at all times from the front section of the retina. This means that even when a trout is focusing at very short range immediately ahead of it, an arc of about 45° on each side and to the rear of the fish is still focused to infinity, while on each side somewhere between 85° and 95° he probably has a grey area where his vision changes from infinity to close range. (See figure 6.) This would indicate that a trout feeding close to the surface and focused at close range would be less likely to see you if you were either opposite him or even slightly upstream, rather than well downstream, where you would come within range of this 45° arc to the rear of him. In confirmation of this point I am sure most river fishers have experienced evenings when there has been a heavy fall of spinners and the trout are all lying so close to the surface feeding that their dorsal fins are protruding. During this period you can often approach a trout so closely that you are almost casting down on to him and more often than not he appears to be completely oblivious to your presence. Over the years I have also caught many, many trout that have either swum upriver and taken up a lie right opposite where I have been standing on the bank, or where I have approached the bank slowly from a 90° angle and found a trout feeding immediately below me. Providing you make no sudden movements and flick your fly to him, while keeping the rod below waist level, it is amazing how often they seem to be unaware of your presence despite the fact you are standing extremely close. In future when the opportunity arises, try positioning yourself opposite or even slightly upstream of any trout rising a fair distance across the river from you, and providing he is holding fairly close to the surface I am sure you will find he is less likely to see you, but do remember to cast sideways and not overhead.

Refraction

When light passes from the air and into the water, the difference in density between the two mediums slows the light waves and bends them. A trout lying in clear water and viewed from the bank above the surface is never actually where he appears to be due to this refraction, or bending of the rays, of light; he will always be lying much deeper than he seems to be. (See figure 7.) Likewise, refraction affects the trout's vision of the world above the surface. The angle at which the light rays enter the water surface is reduced from 180° to 97°, and the trout's view of the outside world through his window is thus somewhat restricted, as the maximum angle at which the light enters to the centre of his window is reduced to 48.5°. (See figure 8.) Outside of this circular window lies the undersurface or mirror, as it is called, which appears to the trout to be sloping down to the bed of the river all around him. (See figure 9.)

Imagine yourself sitting inside a bell-shaped tent with the top section cut off, forming a circle through which you can see the sky. This circle of light above you would be the equivalent of the window through which the trout can see some of the outside world, and the

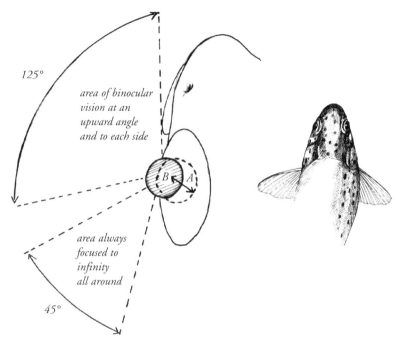

Figure 6. The trout's focusing distances with the eye seen from above. In A, with the lens retracted for all-around vision to infinity, the arc of binocular vision is probably far less than 125°. In B, with the lens extended for close focus in front of the trout, the distance from the lens to the part of the retina providing vision to the rear remains constant, thereby giving him an arc on each side of about 45° that still remains focused to infinity. However, this does leave a grey area of poor vision about 10° to 12° slightly to his rear, where his forward close-up focus changes to infinity behind him.

sloping sides of the tent all around you would become the mirror that reflects all below the surface.

The deeper the trout lies in the water, the larger is his window and the farther he can see towards the horizon of the outside world (see figure 10), and it is important to us fly fishers to know the effects of this on both us and the trout. From the trout's point of view, there is no distortion directly overhead, but the closer he looks towards the edges of his window the more the light rays become depressed, so the more the image becomes blurred and the squatter and wider both the angler and

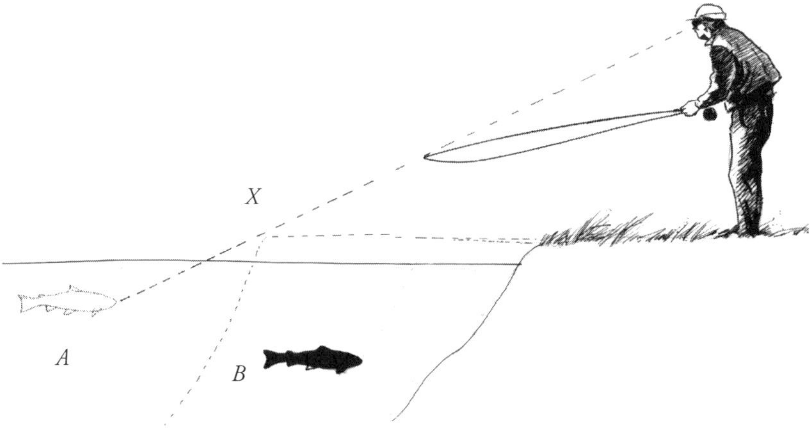

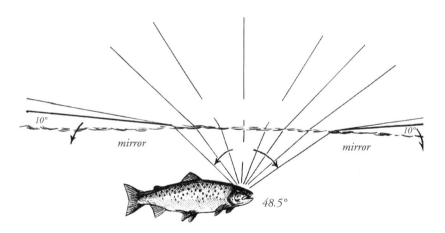

Figure 7. This is what refraction means to the fly fisher. He sees the trout at A, although the actual position of the trout is at B. This means that the trout is lying much deeper than he appears. If the bank were at X, the angler would still be able to see the fish, even though a straight line drawn between his eyes and the fish's actual position would mean his view of the trout would be cut off by the bank.

Figure 8. 180° of useful light is funnelled down by refraction into 97° below the surface. The lower 10° of rays close to the surface are so compressed that they allow no vision above the surface at all. The greatest crowding of rays occurs closest to the surface, resulting in distorted vision for the trout down below.

his equipment will appear. This applies particularly to the angler's rod. Held and cast vertically from overhead it will appear to the trout as thick as a telegraph pole, but cast sideways from a more horizontal position it will appear to him so thin it practically disappears. So where possible, particularly when fishing on rivers, if you are close enough to his window to be seen you should never cast to him from directly overhead.

Little can be seen by the trout in the lower 10° from the horizontal, where the rays are very compressed (see figure 8); if this is extended from the edge of his window it would mean that an angler six feet in height standing on the water's edge thirty feet or more away would be out of his

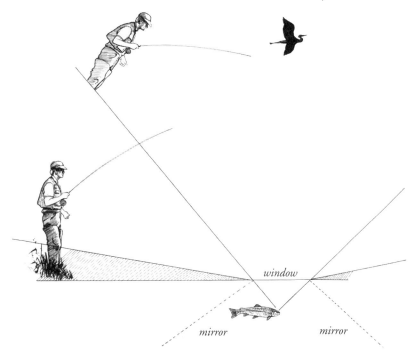

window

mirror   mirror

Figure 9. The trout viewing the angler through his window is unable to appreciate that ground level is much lower than it appears. The bird directly overhead, where the light rays are not compressed, will appear normal sized. However, the trout's view just outside his window will show a very distorted fly fisher where the rays of light entering the water are most compressed. The shaded zones are blind areas for the fish. The undersurface acts as a mirror reflecting everything below the surface.

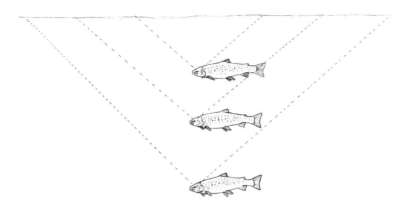

Figure 10. The trout's window increases as the fish swims deeper. His cone of vision through the window is approximately 97°, irrespective of how deep he is lying.

field of view. At a distance of twenty feet the trout would see nothing below four feet, so only the angler's head and shoulders would be visible. These calculations are made from the edge of the trout's window and not from the spot where he may be lying or rising, therefore the depth at which he is lying must be taken into account. As a rough rule of thumb, the diameter of his window is two and a half times the depth at which he is lying—a trout lying one foot below the surface would have a window two and a half feet in diameter; one lying five feet below would have a window twelve and a half feet in diameter. (See figure 10.) Therefore if, for example, you were to spot a trout in clear water lying in your estimation four feet below the surface, to keep out of his sight you would approach no closer than thirty-five feet, which would be thirty feet from the edge of his window. This of course only applies to trout that can be clearly seen; in fast, rippled, or roily water or in a surface rippled by strong winds where it is difficult to spot the trout, they will have even greater difficulty in seeing you, as under these conditions their view through the window will be very blurred and distorted.

The Window and the Mirror

In angling literature the mirror seems to have received less attention than the window, which is rather strange as, to the trout at least, it is of far more importance. The mirror appears to slope all around him and tends to look very dark, as it reflects anything below the surface—dark green weeds, the muddy or silty bottom, boulders or stones, or the relatively dark gravel or sandy bed of the river or lake.

The trout relies upon this mirror when seeking his food. To start with, anything that moves below the surface will be reflected in it, which in many instances will make it easier for him to locate food, such as shrimps, caddis larvae, or various species of nymphs, on or near the bottom. It will make it easier for him to spot nymphs or pupae drifting in midwater, as not only will these be directly visible to him but they will also be reflected in the mirror. In fact, he will be presented with an almost three-dimensional view, as he will see not only the front and underside but also the top and rear in the window. This is something that some of our more innovative fly dressers should take into account when devising wet flies, lures, and nymphs, and may well account for the present popularity and effectiveness of flashback nymphs.

The mirror signals the presence of food either in or on the surface, which can be clearly seen from as far away as the clarity of the water allows. Much of a trout's food, such as hatching nymphs, pupae, stillborn flies, the spinners of upwinged flies, and the many species of terrestrial flies that are blown onto the water surface, will either pierce the surface or drift along just beneath it where they show up very clearly indeed. The mirror will disclose the presence of insects, such as the freshly hatched duns of the many species of upwinged flies, as their feet will cause a slight depression in the surface film, which will show up very clearly in the undersurface as a bright sparkle of light. The six feet, sometimes a portion of the underbody, and at times even the tail of upwinged flies resting on the surface after they have hatched form an easily recognizable pattern to the trout, so he will often rise and intercept them before they reach his window. (See figure 11.)

Most experienced fly fishers are aware that at certain times, trout will become preoccupied with feeding upon one particular species of fly or insect to the exclusion of any others that may be available. A good example is the preference some trout show for small upwinged duns,

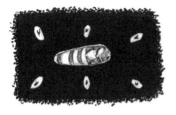

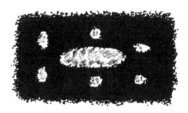

A: The image in the mirror made by the depressions of the feet and underbody of an upwinged fly on the surface, as seen by the human eye.

B: The same view as seen by a trout. Note that the pattern is the same but the resolution is much poorer.

C: The depressions made in the surface film by an upwinged fly.

D: A side view of how the foot of a fly makes a depression in the surface. This allows sparkles of light to pierce the mirror.

Figure 11

which they will often select with unerring accuracy from among larger species that are hatching at the same time. This would certainly seem to indicate not only that the trout is aware that these light patterns in the mirror indicate approaching food, but also that his eyesight is sufficiently good to differentiate between the sizes of the duns on the surface above. When trout are feeding exclusively on freshly hatched duns on the surface, the pinpricks of light made by their feet and body in the mirror most certainly act as the first trigger that results in the trout's rise to intercept one. Those trout that are a little more wary may wait until the tips of the wings appear over the edge of the window (see figure 12) before they intercept it; this is trigger number two. Those very educated trout that may have been caught and returned several times may wait for

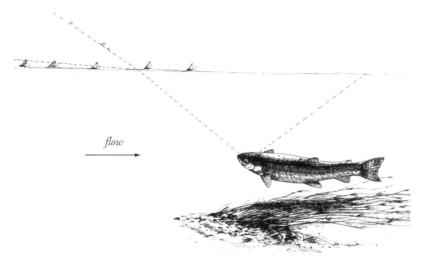

flow

Figure 12. How a trout views a dun approaching from the mirror into his window. The wings gradually flare over the edge, followed by the body of the dun.

trigger number three, which occurs when the fly appears fully in the window. These trout will often drift along with it while they thoroughly inspect it. On evenings when there is a nice sunset, flies such as spinners with their outstretched transparent wings show up in the dark mirror as orange-red blobs—which may account for the success of orange-bodied patterns on fine evenings, such as the Orange Quill so beloved of the great G. E. M. Skues.

Some facts have come to light recently in respect to a trout's acuity of vision, which go some way towards explaining the phenomenal success of many nondescript patterns such as a Grey Wulff or Hare's Ear. They may also explain the situation that so often occurs when the tattier the fly is the more effective it seems to be. This, it now transpires, could well be due to the trout's relatively poor acuity of vision. According to Gordon A. Byrnes, M.D., of the USA, who has undertaken exhaustive studies on this subject, the trout's acuity of vision is roughly 20/200 (6/60 European terminology), which means that those items you see clearly at two hundred feet (sixty metres) a trout would have to view at twenty feet (six metres) to gain the same resolution. It should be noted, however, that although this may sound like poor vision it is very good compared to most other fish. As a rough example, figure 11 shows that the pinpricks of light, caused by the feet and body depressions of a fly on the surface, which can clearly be captured on film and seen by the human eye, are seen by the trout as fuzzy blobs of light, although arranged in the same pattern as we see. Dare I suggest, therefore, that exact imitation in our fly patterns could well be a waste of effort.

Colour Vision

It has long been established through many practical scientific tests that trout can not only differentiate between different colours but also see or respond to some colours or patterns better than others. Colours correspond to various wavelengths of light emanating from an object, and underwater these wavelengths are again affected by the amount of light entering the water; therefore the greater the depth, the less visible certain colours become. Starting at one end of the spectrum, blues produce the shortest waves, followed by greens, yellows, and oranges, until red at the other end produces the longest waves, which are absorbed most quickly in the medium of water. The shorter waves, blues and greens, are absorbed more slowly, so the deeper the water, the more blue and green there is in the remaining light. Red loses its colour very rapidly and even in very clear water all but disappears at depths of about twenty feet. Therefore when dressing wet flies or lures for use in deep or coloured water, these facts should be borne in mind.

It is interesting to note that, despite the fact that red is less visible underwater than any of the other colours, to many species of freshwater fish inhabiting mainly shallow water, the colour most visible is red. Experiments have also shown that red is particularly attractive to trout. This seems to be confirmed by the colour's popularity in many traditional fly patterns where a red tag or tail is featured, such as the Butcher, Soldier Palmer, Zulu, and Red Tag. Red also features in the bodies of many old and famous patterns as well as in the wings of many salmon flies.

Colours, therefore, may provide a key factor in many artificials. We are all well aware that at certain times or under certain conditions trout can become very selective indeed, feeding upon one particular species of insect to the exclusion of all others. How a particular species of insect may be chosen by the trout from the many other species that may be available is a question for speculation. In some cases it may be due to size, in others it may be due to shape or some other key factor that the trout may be looking for, but in some cases it would certainly seem to be a particular colour that triggers the response. There are many examples one can think of to substantiate this. At times trout can be observed feeding upon spinners with a pale yellow body; at other times they may ignore these and only take the spinners of the blue-winged olive, which have a sherry red body. Trout are particularly fond of blue-winged olive duns, and on evenings when hatches are encountered the trout will assiduously pick these out from other similar duns hatching at the same time. How do they do this? Could it be due to the orange highlights that seem to be present in the bodies of this species? On stillwaters early in the year midges (chironomids) often predominate, and two of the most common species at this time have either black or silver/orange bodies. It is not at all uncommon on some days to find the trout feeding upon one species to the exclusion of the other. Likewise, later in the summer the same applies when either small brown or green midges are hatching. It is interesting to note that many of the older and very successful traditional patterns contain key colours in their dressing, such as the red body section in the centre of the Royal Wulff, or the yellow body centre in the Caperer; the touch of bright red at the rear of the body of the Iron Blue, and the bright green tail section of the Grannom. A touch of fluorescent colour in a pattern can also work wonders, such as the signal green tail on a Viva, or the small amount of fluorescent pink added to the body of my own successful Shrymph pattern.

Experiments have also shown that most fish, and in particular trout, are very good at picking out anything with stripes or, to a lesser extent, spots, which accounts for the popularity of certain feathers used in many fly patterns—teal, widgeon, partridge, and pheasant, among others. Many old and well-known patterns incorporate jungle cock feathers tied in at the shoulders, and in recent years the painting or addition of artificial eyes has proved to be very attractive to the trout. Whether the trout view these as eyes or just spots is a moot point.

However, when it comes to designing artificials, colour and pattern should be taken into account, as either or both of these may provide the focal point or trigger needed for a successful fly.

From this scientific approach to the investigation of the trout's vision and his other senses, we can deduce many facts of considerable importance to the fly fisherman. The trout, a fish that lives by hunting, requires and possesses extremely efficient senses, particularly vision. We must not imagine that the trout sees objects or even hears sounds in the same way that we do. He is limited by refraction and water conditions in his view of the world above as well as below the surface. We must always bear this in mind and not be too dogmatic when advancing theories, which should be based on sound scientific principles.

THE TROUT'S HABITAT

In rivers, trout, particularly brown trout, which are more territorial than rainbows, usually choose a lie where either the prevailing wind or the current will channel the maximum amount of food to them and where they can hold their position in the current with the minimum of effort. Once a brownie has taken up such a position, he is likely to be found there whenever feeding throughout the summer, unless water conditions change or he is chased from his lie by a larger fish. This will be his feeding lie, and in most cases he will also have a resting lie, which is usually close by on the bed of the river.

In rain-fed or freestone rivers the trout will be found in one of several places—holding close to the main current, below fast riffles, in front of large boulders or smaller stones, in pockets or depressions in the bed of the river, in the eye of any pools that may be present, in channels of deeper water where the current flows, or tight into undercut banks on inward bends. On these rivers the trout are seldom seen, so it is really a case of being able to read the river and spotting the likely places, which is something that will only come with experience.

In chalk or limestone streams, where the water is usually clear, once you have trained your eyes to look underwater the trout can usually be observed, although it helps to know where they are likely to be holding. This may be in pockets in the weeds, in the deeper channels or runs, or tight into the banks where tussocks have formed or where surface weed has collected; or it may be in fast and shallow runs, in depressions or pockets in the bed of the stream, or underneath trees or bushes that may overhang the water.

In those rivers where rainbow trout have been introduced they will often be found in similar lies to brown trout, but at times they seem to have a preference for a beat or particular stretch of the river, which they will patrol.

RISEFORMS AND FEEDING HABITS

The pattern of the rise is of immense importance to the fly fisherman, as the form the rise takes is usually indicative of the species of food upon which the trout are feeding. This is particularly the case on clear chalk or limestone streams where surface or subsurface food is likely to be present, and also on lakes and lochs where the water is of an acid nature and the trout have to look to the surface for the bulk of their food. On fast rain-fed or freestone rivers or in rich alkaline lakes or reservoirs where most of the food is likely to be found below the surface, other clues to their feeding habits will have to be sought. This is dealt with in chapter 8 on stillwater-fishing techniques. So how can riseforms help identify the food upon which the trout may be feeding? In fact, it is not possible to identify the actual species of fly by the riseform, but it is possible to identify the type of insect, which can be a tremendous help.

The Simple or Standard Rise (Figure 13)

This is certainly the most common riseform and is likely to be encountered on all types of rivers and, to a much lesser extent, on stillwater. The trout responsible for this rise are usually lying eighteen inches to three feet below the surface, where they will have the maximum view

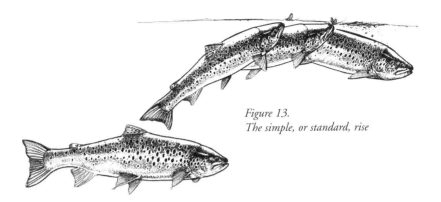

Figure 13.
The simple, or standard, rise

of any approaching surface food, such as hatching upwinged flies or some terrestrial species such as hawthorns or black gnats.

When a fly is spotted the trout will make a leisurely move upwards, assisted by the current, until his neb (or nose) just breaks the surface. He will open his mouth for an instant to suck the fly in and at the same time expel air in his mouth through his gills. This will sometimes but not always result in a bubble or two forming on the surface from the expelled air. Once again utilizing the current, he will sink back down to his lie, leaving a slight depression in the surface followed by a circle of concentric rings. Grayling as well as trout rising to a surface fly will form this particular pattern, but as grayling usually lie much deeper in the water than trout, they are far more likely to leave several bubbles on the surface.

During summer in the higher water temperatures, trout will often be found in the well-aerated, fast, and often rather shallow water running into the deeper pools on chalk or limestone streams and spring creeks, and also in the fast glides on freestone rivers. Despite the very fast water in these locations, trout will hold there quite happily in shallow depressions or in front of stones or small boulders on the bottom, watching the surface for approaching food. You may imagine that trout holding in such positions would use up a lot of energy, constantly rising and descending in such fast currents. Not so—they lower their pectoral fins like the ailerons on an aircraft wing and the current takes them up to the surface to intercept the fly; reversing their pectorals, the current takes them back down to their lie with very little effort. The riseform made by these trout is again the simple rise, but in this faster water it is often more difficult to spot. It is also worth remembering that trout in such lies will only rise to food passing immediately overhead, so your casting to these fish has to be very accurate. They will move from side to side to intercept a fly only very marginally, as, if they moved too far to one side of the current or the other, they would have to swim back to their lie, which would use up too much energy.

At times, particularly on heavily fished waters, you may come across a trout feeding heartily on duns upon the surface during a good hatch of these upwinged flies, yet he will studiously ignore any dry flies you present to him. This will be a trout that associates apparently innocuous floating flies with danger, so he will only be taking the emerging nymphs or stillborn duns floating in the surface film. The simple riseform will appear to be exactly the same as for those trout taking the duns upon the surface.

The Bulge (Figure 14)

This rise results from trout lying fairly close to the surface and just tilting up to take insects in the subsurface. With experience, this riseform is clearly visible in water with an even flow. There is a slight swirl in the centre of which the surface appears to hump up, followed by a vortex as the insect is sucked down. In faster or broken water it is

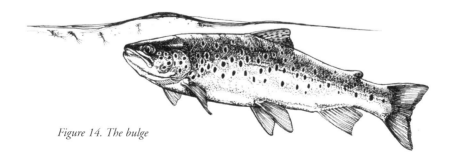

Figure 14. The bulge

much more difficult to spot. The trout making this type of rise are feeding upon small emerging aquatic insects such as the nymphs of small upwinged flies, caddis, or midge pupae, and are intercepting them just before they reach the surface.

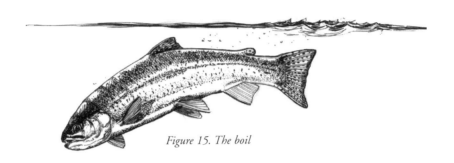

Figure 15. The boil

The Boil (Figure 15)

This rise is more easily seen in fairly calm water, although if you know what you are looking for and have good eyesight, it can be spotted in rougher water. It is caused by trout pursuing ascending insects and taking them below the surface. On large bodies of stillwater in windy conditions where waves have formed, this boil will appear more as a shimmer in the waves. Those fly fishers on the drift, fishing loch style, who know what to look for will have a big advantage, as a shimmer, if covered quickly enough with your team of flies, will often result in a trout.

This rise, as the name indicates, takes the form of a surge of water towards the surface, caused by the body of a trout, mainly the tail, as he turns to go back to his lie after intercepting larger aquatic insects, such as the nymphs of the larger upwinged flies or caddis pupae, swimming to the surface to hatch.

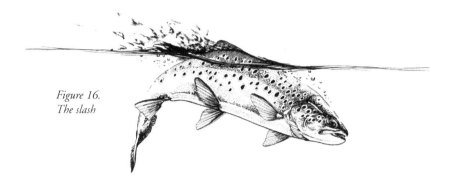

Figure 16.
The slash

The Slash (Figure 16)

This rise is very violent and is caused by trout surging up to intercept large active insects on the surface. These include green drakes, mayflies, hoppers, caddis, and large stoneflies, the latter two species particularly when they are fluttering on the surface laying eggs. These rises are often very splashy and can be seen from a long way off. At times the trout will arc right out of the water or even jump to intercept the insect on the way down. These violent, splashy rises may also be observed on those odd occasions when trout are taking adult damselflies just above the surface or when feeding upon damsel nymphs that are swimming along the surface close to the margins on stillwaters, looking for weeds or projections above the surface on which to hatch.

The Kiss, or Sip, Rise (Figure 17)

This riseform is likely to be encountered on slower streams rather than on fast or even stillwater and is looked upon as one of the classic riseforms on chalkstreams and spring creeks. The kiss is made by trout lying almost in the surface film, where they only have to open their mouth to inhale the approaching fly. This opening and closing of the mouth sounds like a subdued kiss, and at dusk on windless evenings these trout can often be located by the sound alone. The rise is so gentle it produces few, if any, of the concentric rings usually associated

Figure 17.
The kiss, or sip, rise

with a surface rise; the larger the trout, the less the surface is disturbed, so the more difficult the rise is to see. This type of rise only occurs during heavy hatches of small duns during the day or heavy falls of small spinners during the evening.

The sip rise is very similar, also occurring during heavy hatches of surface flies or falls of spinners. It is caused by trout lying an inch or so below the surface and just tilting up so their neb breaks the surface as they suck the fly in, but in this case a few concentric rings often accompany the rise. These rises are more likely to be encountered in the quieter, slower current close to the bank.

If quickly repeated sip rises are observed in open water during the day, the chances are that the trout are feeding upon tiny smuts or even very tiny chironomid pupae. Hatches of these tiny chironomids (midges) also occur during the summer on many large lakes and reservoirs in both the UK and America. During heavy hatches the trout will often travel up wind lanes sipping them down, but in calm conditions they will usually rise in circles.

The Head and Tail Rise (Figure 18)

Sometimes referred to as the porpoise rise, this is formed by trout arcing up to the surface from just below it to intercept an abundance of small flies, such as black gnats or midges, or on odd occasions even ants upon the surface. It is a very slow and deliberate rise; the neb of the trout appears first, followed by the dorsal fin and then the tip of

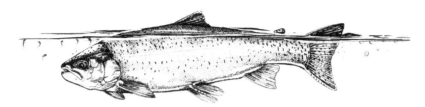

Figure 18.
The head and tail rise

his tail as he arcs back below the surface. Trout when head and tailing often appear to be much larger than they actually are, and in some light conditions look positively huge. On stillwaters, it is a very common riseform early in the morning or late in the evening, when trout are feeding on large hatches of midge pupae hanging in the surface film prior to and during hatching. It usually occurs when the trout are feeding upon heavy hatches of insects that cannot escape.

In rivers, this riseform is less common and is only to be observed in quiet backwaters or areas where there is little or no current. On rivers, particularly the chalkstreams, it is often accompanied by a distinct waggle of the tail as the trout sinks back below the surface. I have found these trout very difficult to catch and am still unsure on what they may be feeding. It could be on very tiny hatching midges or their pupae, or it could be on the spinners of small upwinged flies that drift with the current just below the surface. Some authorities have suggested that it may be a phenomenon connected with newly stocked trout that have been reared in trout farms on pellets.

When trout are observed head and tailing on large bodies of stillwater it is most likely that they are feeding upon midge pupae hanging in the surface film, but it is very easy to be misled as at times they will also rise in this same manner to sparse hatches of caenis or, in America, to hatches of tricos or callibaetis. It should also be noted that in the late summer, large quantities of small snails will often float to the surface and travel with their pad uppermost with the wind and currents. Trout are inordinately fond of them and nearly always sip them down with this distinctive head and tail rise. It is very easy to be fooled at this time, as it is impossible to see the snails on the surface. The only way to see them is to wade out into the water and look straight down onto the surface.

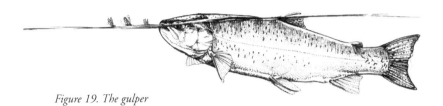

Figure 19. The gulper

The Gulper (Figure 19)

This can hardly be termed a rise at all as, when the trout are so engaged, they are actually swimming along in the surface film, opening and shutting their mouths, often taking in several flies at each gulp. I have observed trout feeding in this manner on very few occasions in the UK and only on large lakes and reservoirs. It only occurs during very heavy hatches of small surface flies such as caenis.

In large lakes in the USA and possibly parts of Canada, however, it is more likely to be seen, usually on windless mornings during large hatches of callibaetis or similar small upwinged duns. It is very common on some large lakes in Montana. On Hebden Lake, where the name gulper was originally coined, it is often a daily occurrence during the warmer late-summer months. These gulpers or gobblers, as some fly fishermen call them, are also to be seen during heavy hatches of tricos on some of the larger rivers in the USA, in slower runs out of the main current.

Tailing Trout (Figure 20)

At times on rivers, usually among the denser weed beds, the tip or even the complete tail of a trout will be seen waving in the air. The trout is

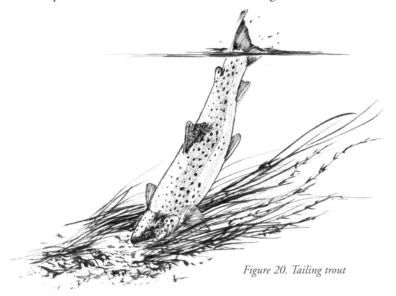

Figure 20. Tailing trout

rooting through the vegetation or along the bed of the river, trying to dislodge nymphs, shrimps (scuds), or other items of aquatic food. It also occurs, although less frequently, in the shallow weedy margins of some lakes. When the trout are so engaged, a heavily weighted shrimp pattern cast as close as possible to the fish, allowed to sink, and then retrieved slowly will often result in a take. However, casting to such trout can often prove to be very frustrating, as you are constantly snagging the fly on bunches of weed.

FEEDING HABITS

Most people are diurnal creatures, active throughout the day, becoming lethargic and often sleepy after sunset. We are therefore tempted to go fishing late in the morning after a leisurely breakfast and to return well before supper in the late afternoon—but trout and grayling seldom, if ever, feed solely at this time. Their feeding habits depend on many factors, first of all upon the availability of terrestrial and aquatic insects, which form the basis of their diet; also upon the condition or state of the water, weather, temperature, barometric pressure, and a host of other factors.

Of course, unless you live near a fishery it is not possible to take many of these factors into account, except for the weather and barometric pressure. If the forecast looks bad and you do not have boats or beats booked, it may be better to put off your visit for another day. However, if you are committed, upon arrival at the waterside look for signs of rising or feeding fish; when fishing rivers or streams, walk slowly along the riverbank for a short distance, looking for any signs of activity. If there are few fish to be seen, or few insects in evidence, go back to the car or fishing hut and have a leisurely coffee while keeping one eye open for any rises or hatches of flies. At times you may have a long wait, so learn to be patient; it will often pay dividends in the long run. The same advice applies on small, clear stillwaters or lakes, but on large lakes and reservoirs it is usually all but impossible to tell whether the fish are feeding or not. Under these circumstances, remember the old Scottish adage: "You won't catch any fish with your fly out of the water, laddie." While this may well apply on stillwaters, it certainly does not when fishing on rivers. If the trout are not feeding, do not hammer away at them. Walking up a river, indiscriminately casting into all the likely looking spots (often referred to as fishing the water), is a very unproductive method (except possibly on fast rain-fed rivers when fishing a wet fly), which does little but spook the trout for some considerable time.

Under certain circumstances the feeding habits of trout are predictable. For example, on chalkstreams or spring creeks where hatches of upwinged flies are prevalent, feeding usually takes place in the middle part of the day, between eleven and four, and again late in the evening as dusk approaches. During the height of the summer, particularly in periods of very hot weather, the trout are often disinclined to feed during the day, but will feed avidly for an hour or two shortly after dawn, usually on egg-laying spinners or, on some rivers, on big hatches of caenis, which are prevalent at this time of day. On big lakes and reservoirs during the height of the summer, the peak feeding periods usually take place shortly after sunrise and again as dusk approaches. On the other hand, during the early spring and again in late autumn when temperatures are lower, the peak feeding will take place during the middle part of the day, and usually in the deeper water where temperatures are more constant.

The feeding habits of trout on large bodies of stillwater are often unpredictable; at times the trout can be very selective, only feeding upon one particular species. Under these circumstances you can only persevere, trying different patterns until a trout is eventually caught. This can then be spooned and his stomach contents analyzed to establish the main species upon which they are feeding.

On those rivers holding a good head of wild brown trout, such as rain-fed, freestone, or spate rivers, the trout, after they have spawned, will often migrate downstream to rest up in the deeper, less turbulent water. This means that the headwaters of those rivers will hold few, if any, trout at all during the early part of the season. As spring unfolds and the trout regain their strength, the fish will begin to move back upstream. To fish this type of water early in the season will obviously be a waste of time.

Limestone rivers, chalkstreams, or spring creeks, where on a sunny day every stone on the bottom can be clearly seen, may also appear to hold no trout. In fact, this may be an illusion as, if no flies are hatching, they will have taken to their resting lies where they cannot be seen. These streams are often almost covered with dense beds of aquatic weed, and may also have undercut banks, both of which provide ideal cover. On this type of stream the trout nearly always have two lies: a resting lie, where they are safe from predators, and a feeding lie. The latter is always in open water, in pockets or runs between weed beds, or alongside obstructions in the water. Trout that have been stocked usually have one lie fairly close to the other, but wild trout will often have their resting lie quite a long way from their feeding lie. In some stretches of river, trout, particularly wild browns, will have a different feeding lie as dusk approaches. Where there are extensive gravel shallows you can often observe pale-coloured patches on the riverbed where there are slight depressions. These have been formed by the constant movement of the fins of trout lying in the depressions and dispersing the silt. During the hours of daylight these shallows will be completely devoid of any trout, but as the light begins to fade trout will move up from the deeper water and occupy the lies, often in close proximity to one another.

It amazes me how adept trout are at choosing their resting lies. Many times over the years, especially during the heat of midsummer, I have arrived by the gin-clear waters of a chalkstream or spring creek and looked in vain for any sign of fish. Yet eventually when flies start to hatch, the water surface will suddenly become dimpled with rising trout that have moved into their feeding lies. On some days when there are particularly poor hatches of flies the trout may not appear at all, but come the evening the river will be alive with feeding fish.

We still have a lot to learn about the feeding behaviour of trout. How often have you stood by a trout stream observing flies hatching in profusion but not a rise in sight, and yet within minutes the river is suddenly full of rising fish as if someone had fired a starting gun; or late in the afternoon, despite the fact that flies are still hatching, noticed rises suddenly cease? No-one seems to have an answer to this. Is it something to do with weather conditions or a rise or drop in temperature? Personally I feel it is probably due to a rise or fall in barometric pressure, but I can offer no proof for this theory.

Another quite common phenomenon occurs when there are big hatches of flies, but not a rising trout to be seen. I can understand this during the dense hatches of large mayflies such as the green drakes, when the trout quickly become sated on such large and juicy mouthfuls, but it often occurs during periods when for days hatches have been quite sparse. One possible explanation may be that the trout are just not hungry if they have been feeding heavily very early in the morning.

At times trout will become very selective in their feeding, especially in rivers, and the fly fisher, unless aware of it, can easily be misled.

A classic example occurs during hatches of very large upwinged flies, such as the various species of green drakes. In most rivers, hatches of these large ephemerids take place over a relatively short period (three to four weeks), and to start with the trout will often completely ignore them. However, once they realize what a juicy mouthful the green drakes provide, the trout will feed on them to the exclusion of all other flies that may be hatching at the same time. Eventually, though, the trout become gorged, and will cease feeding altogether or concentrate upon other, much smaller species.

Similar situations occur throughout the summer on most streams, particularly on the richer limestone or chalkstreams or spring creeks where multiple hatches of different species are often the order of the day. There may be three or even four different species of upwinged flies hatching, yet some trout will only be feeding upon one particular species. On the English chalkstreams during hatches of medium-sized upwinged flies, such as pale wateries or medium olives, a very small upwinged fly will start emerging called an iron blue. This very tiny, dark-coloured fly is a member of the *Baetis* genus; many trout seem inordinately fond of it and will pick it out from the other species with unerring accuracy. At other times the trout may be feeding exclusively on small black flies such as black gnats, ignoring hatches of larger upwinged flies. During the evening rise on many rivers the trout are often very selective, particularly later in the summer when there are many different species on offer, including various spinners, upwinged flies, caddisflies (both adults and pupae) and even various species of midges (chironomids).

Selectivity has been and always will be one of the major problems facing the fly fisherman. On rivers where much of the feeding and activity take place either on or close to the surface, observation is the main key, but on stillwater the problem is more complex, as much of the feeding takes place well below the surface. The problem can often only be solved by trial and error, using local knowledge and experimenting with different patterns.

2

THE TROUT'S FOOD

T HE TROUT'S DIET CAN HARDLY be described as limited, as up to a point they seem to accept anything that looks vaguely like food. When examining the stomach contents of trout, I have come across all manner of strange objects—sticks, stones, pieces of plastic, paper, and even cigarette butts. Where streams run past houses, some trout will live quite happily on bread and kitchen scraps that are thrown into the river. They will thrive on a diet of pellets when they are reared on trout farms. We can therefore see from this that they are opportunist feeders and will accept whatever is on offer.

To a large extent the trout's food, and therefore the fish's size and condition, will depend on their environment. In clear, unpolluted, alkaline waters, which are always very rich in aquatic life, the fish will thrive and grow fairly rapidly. These conditions are found in chalk and limestone streams, in small spring-fed ponds, in large lowland lakes and reservoirs in lush valleys or meadowland, and also in many freestone rivers at lower altitudes. Rivers, streams, and lakes at higher altitudes or in rocky or more sterile countryside, or those flowing from heavily wooded areas, are usually of an acid or even peaty nature, incapable of sustaining heavy populations of aquatic life. In these waters the trout have to rely to a large extent upon terrestrial insects being blown onto the water surface for much of their food and therefore tend to be rather lean and hungry, slow growing, and much smaller than their counterparts in the richer alkaline waters.

Apart from the waters that are too muddy, dirty, or polluted to sustain gamefish, there are other rivers and lakes in Europe and the Americas that come in between the above two categories; they are neither too alkaline nor too acid. Some of these seem incapable of supporting healthy populations of trout, while others, despite a shortage of normal aquatic insect life, sustain populations of very large fast-growing trout. The reason for this is always the introduction or natural establishment of some rich food source. Good examples are to be found in large lakes and reservoirs that harbour huge populations of various species of snails or large juicy damsel nymphs, which are very high in protein; or in American rivers where large stoneflies abound, such as the big salmon flies the larvae and adults of which often exceed three inches in length. Other rivers throughout the world, particularly in the Americas and New Zealand, hold big populations of various species of crayfish throughout the season, which are a wonderful and very rich food source. Another excellent example of the rich protein provided by a single food source is to be found in the world-famous Lake Taupo in New Zealand, which probably holds the fastest-growing trout in the world. This superfast growth is provided by millions of smelt, a tiny freshwater fish that breeds in this great lake; it was artificially introduced in the earlier half of this century.

AQUATIC AND TERRESTRIAL FLIES

Many fly fishers go through their fishing life with little or even no knowledge of the different species or even genera of flies upon which the fish may be feeding. These fly fishers may be successful, catching large numbers of trout, but let me assure you that this is due to their expertise in casting, water knowledge, approach, and correct presentation of the fly, all of which are essential to success. Some of them carry just three or four different patterns of flies, yet still catch their quota of trout. But it is an inescapable fact that no matter how good a fly fisher you are, without a knowledge of entomology and the ability to present the correct pattern to match the hatch when the fish are feeding selectively, you will not be able to match a competent fly fisher who has the necessary patterns and knowledge. Apart from this, a study of the subject will provide you with an added interest at the waterside during those blank periods that are so often encountered when no fish are feeding.

For the average fisherman, a basic knowledge of entomology will suffice; you only really need to be able to identify the various physical characteristics of the different insects to enable you to establish the family and genus. It is seldom necessary to identify the actual species, and it is certainly not necessary to know all the scientific names, which are so confusing.

There are four main orders of insects of interest to fishermen, and most of these are aquatic species. There are also many terrestrial species that at times are blown onto the water surface, where they are readily accepted by the trout. It is not my intention in this volume to delve too deeply into the entomology of all the various flies—there are plenty of books available that cover the subject in depth*—but the following information should enable you at least to recognize the various orders, families, and, in some cases, genera that are applicable to most trout waters throughout the world. It is amazing that in areas as far apart as Europe, America, and even New Zealand, a large percentage of the flies in all four orders are to be found at least down to the genera.

For the fly fisher intending to make a study of entomology, it is important to understand that all insects on this planet are divided into orders, which in turn are divided into families, and then genera, and finally into the actual species. The table opposite illustrates how two of the more common flies are classified under this system.

The four main orders in which most fly fishers are interested are Ephemeroptera, Diptera, Trichoptera, and Plecoptera.

* Including *Waterside Guide,* John Goddard (Collins, London, 1988).

MAYFLY		MIDGE	
CLASS:	Insecta	CLASS:	Insecta
ORDER:	Ephemeroptera	ORDER:	Diptera
FAMILY:	Ephemeridae	FAMILY:	Chironomidae
GENUS:	*Ephemera*	GENUS:	*Chironomus*
SPECIES:	*danica*	SPECIES:	*plumosus*

The flies in the Ephemeroptera order have semitransparent, veined, upright wings and long tails and are commonly referred to as upwinged flies (figure 21). All those in the Diptera order are tailless but have small-ish, semitransparent wings that lie flat on top of their bodies and are commonly referred to as flat-winged flies (figure 23). All those in the Trichoptera group have opaque or patterned tent-shaped wings but no tails and are usually called caddisflies (figure 22). All those in the final order, Plecoptera, have hard, patterned wings along the top of their bodies and two substantial tails that vary in length according to species. These are commonly referred to as hard-winged flies (figure 24).

The Upwinged Flies (Ephemeroptera)

The Ephemeroptera, commonly referred to in angling circles as mayflies or upwinged flies, develop through four stages. (See figure 25.)

The Egg

The females of most species in this order deposit their eggs on the water surface, although some species actually crawl beneath the surface. The egg stage of development lasts anywhere from a matter of days to many weeks, according to species and the time of year the eggs are laid.

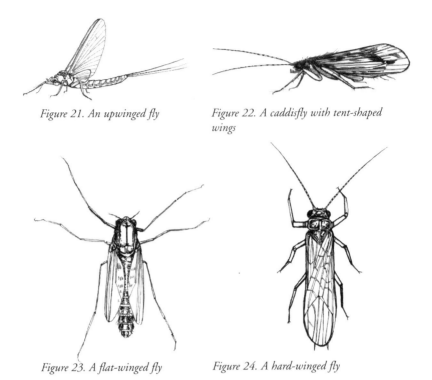

Figure 21. An upwinged fly

Figure 22. A caddisfly with tent-shaped wings

Figure 23. A flat-winged fly

Figure 24. A hard-winged fly

The Nymph

This stage may last from two to twelve months or even longer, depending on species and the time of year the egg was deposited. During this stage, the nymphs continually moult as they increase in size. The nymphs of upwinged flies vary in colour from pale watery olive to a dark sepia brown, and have six legs, a thorax with wing cases, a segmented body, and three short tails. Some have streamlined bodies and are active swimmers, while others are slow moving, and some species have flattened bodies to allow them to cling to stones in fast-moving currents.

The Subimago or Dun

The fully mature nymphs usually have very dark wing cases and, when they are ready to hatch, swim to the surface, where the nymphal case

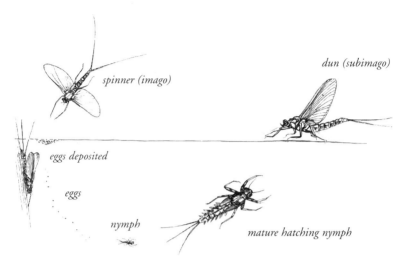

spinner (imago)

dun (subimago)

eggs deposited

eggs

nymph

mature hatching nymph

Figure 25. Life cycle of an upwinged fly

splits and transposition into the adult winged form takes place (see figure 25). A few select species crawl to the surface via emergent vegetation. The duns have large, upright, semitransparent or slightly opaque, veined wings, and most species have small hind wings; both sets of wings are lined with tiny hairs along their trailing edges. The duns have rather dull coloured bodies and either two or three long tails, according to species.

The Imago or Spinner

After the duns hatch they seek shelter on streamside vegetation and usually within about thirty-six hours transpose into fully mature adults capable of reproduction. These spinners are beautiful creatures with bright shiny bodies, sparkling, semitransparent wings, and very long tails. The males are usually a little smaller than the females, and form huge swarms along the banks or in the vicinity of bushes and trees or, in some cases, over the water. In many cases the location of these swarms can assist you in identifying the particular species. Swarming of the males takes place either very early in the morning or, more often, during the early evening. When conditions are right, the females join the swarms and mating takes place; the females eventually die after egg laying, providing a fine feast for the waiting trout.

All the flies in this relatively small order have either two or three long tails, a segmented body with a thorax, six legs, and large upright wings. Most species also have small hind wings, but in some species these are so small that they are difficult to see with the naked eye. There are many dozens of different species and, while most of these are found in running water, a few species are also found in stillwater.

The Flat-Winged Flies (Diptera)

This order of insects includes all the true flies, such as houseflies, bluebottles, hover flies, horseflies, drone flies, dung flies, mosquitoes, and so on, and is considerably larger than the other three orders put together. Despite this, relatively few of them are of importance to fly fishers.

The majority are of terrestrial origin. Under windy conditions, some may be blown onto the water surface. They include such genera as black gnats and Tipulidae (daddy longlegs, or harvestmen), of which there are many different species, hawthorn and heather flies, and also occasionally some of those species first mentioned.

Diptera also includes some aquatic families, of which two are of particular importance to fly fishers, reed smuts and midges, the former being found only in running water while the latter are of equal importance to both river and stillwater fly fishers.

The Reed Smuts (blackflies or buffalo gnats)

While the true reed smuts are nonbiting, the same does not apply to the closely allied blackflies, which are a curse to both animals and humans on many rivers throughout the world. The adult females lay their eggs in masses of jelly on any protruding vegetation, stones or posts, and so on. Some species lay their eggs actually underwater. The eggs hatch within a week or so, and the small wormlike larvae, which attach themselves to aquatic weed, moult at regular intervals as they grow in size. Finally, the larvae spin a cone-shaped case in which they pupate. When the pupa reaches maturity, the case splits and the fully winged adult rises to the surface in a bubble of air or gas, from which it emerges at the surface quite dry and immediately takes to the wing. This method of emergence, combined with the adults' very tiny size, means that the trout are notoriously difficult to catch when feeding upon these minute insects.

The Midges (Chironomids)

There are many hundreds of different species in this family, varying both in colour and in size, some being less than an eighth of an inch (a couple of millimetres) in length while others are close to three-quarters of an inch (two centimetres). Like the reed smuts, they pass through four stages of development. (See figure 26.) The larvae are wormlike creatures varying in colour from pale olive through to bright red, and are often freeroaming on the mud or silt. The pupae spend much of their life in tubes or tunnels formed in the silt and when they reach maturity, they swim up to the surface, where the case splits and the winged adult emerges and flies off.

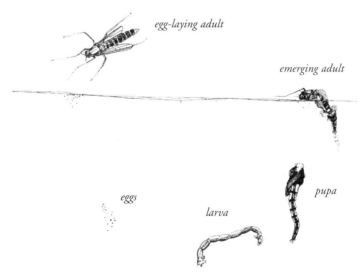

Figure 26. Life cycle of a flat-winged fly

While the trout will feed on both larvae and pupae on the bottom, it is when the pupae swim to the surface that they are most vulnerable. The trout feed avidly on both the ascending pupae and the pupae as they are hanging vertically beneath the surface film. They are vulnerable at this time especially under calm conditions when the film is relatively thick, as it may take them some time to break through, and they will often adopt a horizontal position, wriggling to find a weak area through which to emerge. This accounts for the very heavy surface rises of trout on lakes and reservoirs where hatches occur either early in the morning or late in the evening when there is little or no wind. In stillwater, the trout take the pupae hanging in the film with a distinctive head and tail rise, but on rivers when the trout are feeding upon midges and reed smuts, they lie almost on the surface, merely raising their neb to sip the flies down. There are many special patterns to represent both midges and reed smuts; when the trout are feeding upon them, my own Suspender Midge Pupa pattern is particularly effective. The species of midges found in rivers are usually much smaller than those found in the big lakes.

All Diptera flies are tailless and have only two transparent or opaque wings mounted on top of their rather dumpy bodies.

The Caddis or Sedge Flies (Trichoptera)

This is a fairly large order with several hundred different species. The majority are of little interest to the fly fisher, as they are either exceedingly small, very uncommon, or locally distributed.

Those few species that are common and widespread, however, are very important indeed both to the fly fisher and to his quarry. There are probably upwards of twenty or so species that must be taken into account. It is seldom necessary to use specific patterns to represent any of these, as there are so many good general caddis patterns available for the fly fisher to choose from, and in most situations you only need to match roughly the colour and size of those naturals that are hatching at the time. Unlike patterns representing the upwinged flies, it is seldom necessary to match the hatch to any extent.

The caddisflies go through four stages of development: egg, larva, pupa, and fully winged adult. (See figure 27.)

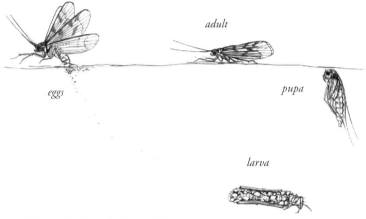

adult

eggs

pupa

larva

Figure 27. Life cycle of a caddisfly

The Egg

Most species lay their several hundred eggs in a gelatinous mass on the surface of the water, although there are a few species that actually crawl underwater to deposit them. They normally hatch within ten to twelve days.

The Larva

The body colours of these larvae vary from grey to greyish brown and from cream to pale green; most have a head and thorax of a different colour from the body, varying from chestnut brown to yellow. The majority of species live on or near the bottom, on or among stones or weed, and make cases from various local materials. In stillwater they tend to use light materials such as vegetable matter or sections of leaves, while in running water they use heavy materials such as sand, gravel, small stones, or sections of discarded shells. These cases are often works of art, although they do restrict movement. Some other species such as the *hydropsyche* and *rhyacophila* are free swimming, while a few select species live in cracks and crevices among the stones on the bottom, weaving nets that are strung across the entrance to trap food drifting in the current. There are various patterns to represent these larvae, but they are only fished in lakes and reservoirs.

The Pupa

The larvae usually pupate in their own cases, which they vacate when they are ready to transpose (even the free-swimming species, which make cases especially for the purpose). According to species, they either swim to the surface using their front legs (which are always free of the pupal envelope), where they hatch on the surface into the winged adult; or swim towards shore, where they emerge and hatch above the surface via stones or vegetation. The trout feed on the ascending pupae and also on the pupae as they hatch into the adult on the surface, and there are many excellent pupal imitations available to represent them. Most of the natural pupae tend to be either a greenish or cream colour.

The Winged Adult

The winged adults vary tremendously in size, from tiny microcaddis barely an eighth of an inch (two millimetres) in length, to the great red sedge, which has a wingspan of nearly two inches (five centimetres). They have four roof-shaped wings and in appearance can easily be confused with moths. However, a close examination will reveal that their wings are covered in very fine hairs, while those of the moth are covered in tiny scales. Apart from this they have a slimmer appearance, particularly across the thorax, which is very wide in moths. They have six legs, some of which display prominent spurs (the number and position of these can assist you in identifying the species), a tailless body composed of nine segments, a thorax, large compound eyes, and (on many species) two very long antennae. Most caddis are rather dull looking creatures with bodies and wings that vary from light chestnut brown through dark brown to black. In some species the wings may be mottled or spotted, and a few species have bodies that are a distinct green colour.

May Dun

Poly May Spinner

ddard Western Drake

Poly Caddis

ching Midge Pupa

Mating Shrimp

Super Grizzly Emerger

Black Gnat

Suspender Midge

Gerroff

PVC Nymph

Super Grizzly

rymph

Goddard Smut

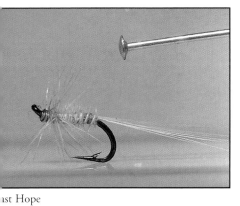

ist Hope

Persuader

dge Pupa

Goddard Caddis

A nice-sized snook

A super brown trout of 10 ½ pounds taken on a small dry fly

Two graylings

A big barracuda of 28 ½ pounds

A fine bonefish of 11 1/2 pounds

The author's first permit taken on a fly

Max King with a big tarpon taken on a fly from a small boat in rough seas

Author with sailfish taken on a fly. This was the first ever taken on a fly off the Kenya coast under IGFA regulations.

Nymph of *Baetis;* an agile darter

Nymph of *Leptophlebia;* a laboured swimmer

Nymph of *Heptagenia;* a sto[...] clinger

Nymph of *Ephemera;* a bottom burrower

A mayfly female dun *(Ephem[...]*

A mayfly male spinner *(Ephemera)*

A blue-winged olive female dun *(Ephemerella)*

A yellow may dun female *(Heptagenia)*

A pond olive male dun *(Clo[...]*

iron blue female dun *(Baetis)*

A sepia male spinner
(Leptophlebia)

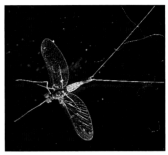

Small spurwing male spinner
(Centroptilum)

rge spurwing female spinner
entroptilum)

Caenis male spinner *(Caenis)*

sherry female spinner
ohemerella)

male spinner with egg ball
ohemerella)

Transposition of dun to spinner,
an upwinged fly

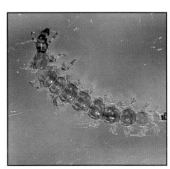

Free-swimming caddis larva
(Rhyacophila)

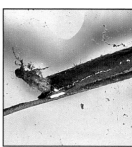

Typical caddis larva found stillwater

Typical caddis larva found in running water

Typical caddis pupa

Caddis pupa about to transpose into the winged adult

A large red sedge *(Phrygania)*

Typical caddis in flight

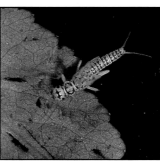

A medium-sized caddis *(Sericostoma)*

A medium-sized stonefly nymph *(Isoperla)*

A large stonefly nymph *(Perlodes)*

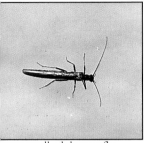

A very small adult stonefly
(Leuctra)

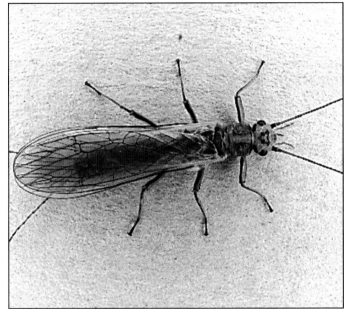

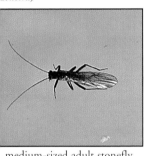

A medium-sized adult stonefly
(Protonemoura)

A medium-large stonefly adult (Isoperla)

Larva of midge (Chironomus)

Hatching midge pupa
(Chironomus)

Large red midge buzzer adult
female (Chironomus)

Large golden midge buzzer
adult male (Chironomus)

Small green midge buzzer
adult male (Endochironomus)

The hawthorn, a flat-winged
fly (Bibio)

Dragonfly nymph *(Sympetrum)*

Damselfly nymph *(Enellagama)*

Green damselfly adult feeding on a captured mayfly

Blue damselfly adult *(Enallagama)*

Freshwater shrimp, a scud *(Gammarus)*

Water hog louse *(Assellus)*

An alder fly *(Sialis)*

An alder larva *(Sialis)*

A crane fly, a daddy longlegs *(Tippula)*

ser water boatman *(Corixa)*

A common waterbug

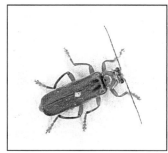

The sailor beetle *(Cantharis)*

e soldier beetle *(Cantharis)*

A green leaf beetle

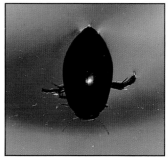

Whirligig beetle *(Gyrinus)*

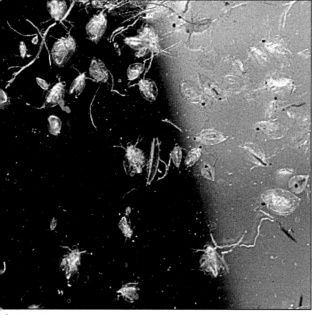

ohnia, a tiny crustacean

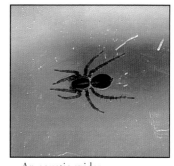

An aquatic spider

A common grasshopper

PLATE **12**: VARIOUS FLY PATTERNS MENTIONED IN TEXT

A Red Palmer

A Dunkeld

An Elk Hair Caddis

The Little Red Sedge

Gold Ribbed Hair's Ear Winged

An Iron Blue

A Partridge & Orange

Kite's Imperial

The Grey Wulff

A Sparkle Dun

A Gold Head Gold Ribbed
Hair's Ear

A Zeelon Caddis

Henry's Damsel Nymph

Roman Moser's Balloon Caddis

A Humpy

Adams

A Mallard & Claret

Terry's Terror

rging Pupa

Lunn's Particular

Sawyer's Grayling Bug

nvicta

A typical stillwater dry fly

The Booby

A Muddler Minnow

A nice, bushy caddis

A Marc Pettijean Cul Du Canard fly

The Deerstalker

A Pheasant Tail Spinner

A stonefly pattern

A Daddy Longlegs

Clouser Deep Minnow

The Caperer Caddis patter

Carnhill's Black Buzzer Pupa

The Viva

A Baby Doll

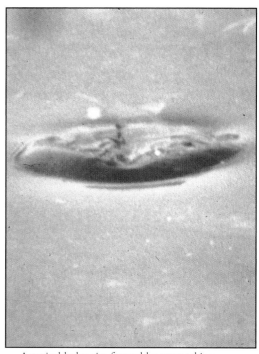

A typical bulge rise formed by trout taking
nymphs just below the surface

typical simple, or standard, rise

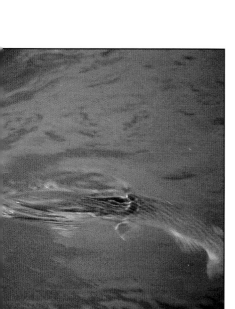

s trout is taking a nymph just below the surface,
ning a bulge rise

A typical boil rise formed by a trout's tail as he
returns to the bottom after chasing a nymph or
pupa towards the surface

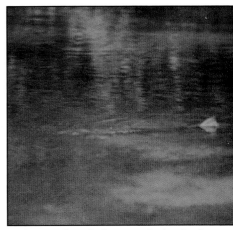

Showing the tail of a trout which is head and tailing

A typical sip, or kiss, rise formed by trout lying just below the surface and taking very small flies or spinners

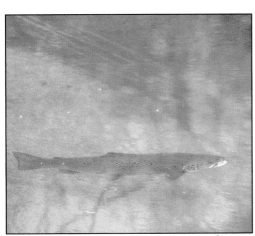

The little white blink as a trout below the surface inhales a nymph

An underwater photograph of a trout rising to intercept a floating artificial fly. The body and hackle of the fly can be seen in the mirror while its wings can be seen appearing over the edge of the trout's window.

The Hard-Winged Flies (Plecoptera)

Commonly referred to by most fly fishers as stoneflies, this is a rather small order, but nevertheless on those waters where they are to be found they can be of considerable importance. This is mainly in the faster rivers that have gravelly, stony, or boulder-strewn beds.

The flies in this order develop through only three stages: egg, nymph, and adult. (See figure 28.) The eggs may take many weeks to hatch and are deposited on the surface by the adult winged females, and it is only during this period that the adults are available to the fish.

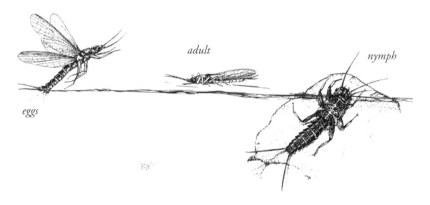

adult

nymph

eggs

Figure 28. Life cycle of a hard-winged fly

The nymphs are very robust creatures with strongly segmented bodies, a thorax, six legs, and two short tails—unlike the nymphs of the upwinged flies, which are much slimmer and have three longish tails. They are nearly always very dark brown in colour, and many species have distinct yellow markings on the body and head. They are very active creatures, and it is thought that some of the larger species spend two or even three years in the nymphal stage. When they are fully mature and ready to transpose into the winged adult, they crawl ashore or onto stones or boulders above the surface, where the transposition takes place.

The Adult Stonefly

The adults vary in size from the relatively small needle fly with a wingspan of less than three-quarters of an inch (two centimetres) to the large stonefly, which has a wingspan of over two inches (five centimetres). In many freestone streams in the United States there occurs a colossal species of stonefly that has a wingspan of nearly four inches (ten centimetres). These are commonly referred to as salmon flies and hatches, which usually occur over a two-week period each season in July, are eagerly awaited.

The life of the adult stonefly can vary from a few days to a few weeks, according to species; they never wander very far from the water and mate at rest. They are very poor fliers; the wings of some of the males of the larger species are little better than stumps and they are incapable of flight. The four wings are heavily veined, hard and shiny, and, in the larger species, lie flat on top of the body, while in many of the smaller species they are wrapped over the top and slightly down the sides of the body. They have the usual thorax, six legs, and a strongly segmented body usually of a greyish brown colour, although some species such as the yellow sally and the small yellow sally have bodies and wings that are distinctly yellow and two short tails. The adults are only available to the fish when the females either dip down onto the water surface to lay their eggs or actually alight onto the surface and flutter around laying all their eggs in one mass. At this time they make a very tempting target for any hungry trout. There are many special stonefly patterns to represent these adults, but it is only really necessary to match the colour and size of any particular species that may be hatching.

Sundry Insects and Other Fauna

Apart from the four main insect orders, there are several other items of food in the diet of the trout, listed here in order of importance.

- The alder fly is important in some areas, particularly the larvae on stillwater in the early part of the season when they are very active prior to hatching. There are several good patterns to represent these.

• The nymphs of dragonflies and particularly damselflies are very important on many stillwaters, as are the adult damselflies on many ponds and lakes in the USA. While there are many patterns to represent both the damsel nymph and the dry adult, two of the best in my opinion are those perfected and popularized by Gary Borger.

• In America various species of grasshoppers and cicadas are of great importance when these are blown onto the water surface under windy conditions. There are many excellent hopper patterns to represent these.

• Crustaceans such as the various species of freshwater louse and shrimps (scuds) also form a valuable source of food in all types of water, especially in winter when other forms of food may be in short supply. Of the two, the scuds are more important, and there are many patterns to represent these. Another crustacean important as a source of food on many rivers is the freshwater crayfish.

• Many stillwaters harbour fairly high concentrations of various water bugs, and the most important of these are the corixae. These are normally only found in the shallower margins of lakes less than three feet in depth, as these tiny, beetlelike creatures have constantly to surface to replenish their air supply. Late in the summer they take to the wing over short distances and at this time seem particularly attractive to trout as they enter and return to the water. There is a host of good corixa patterns to represent them.

• The beetles (Coleoptera) are a very large order and, although there are a few semi-aquatic species, few of them seem to be of much interest to the trout. On the other hand, some of the many terrestrial species are manna from heaven when they are blown onto the water surface or drop off trees or bushes onto the water, so it always pays to have a few green to dark-coloured or black, floating beetle patterns in various sizes in your fly box.

• Finally, there are two different items of fauna that at times can be of the utmost importance. These are various species of ants and snails. The former usually take to the wing during hot, muggy weather late in the summer, and on those somewhat rare occasions when this event takes place in the vicinity of water, many hundreds of ants may be blown onto the surface, providing a real feast for the trout. When this happens the trout become very selective indeed, so if you do not have an artificial ant pattern in your fly box, you will rue the day. Most species of ants are either brown or black, so patterns in these colours in size 14 or 12 will usually suffice.

At certain times of the year in lakes, ponds, and reservoirs, trout develop a taste for snails and often become preoccupied with feeding upon them. When this happens the stomachs of the trout often become distended and you can feel the snails crunch if you squeeze. If you suspect the trout are feeding upon snails below the surface, an excellent pattern to use is one developed by Gary Borger. In the latter half of the summer on many stillwaters, often during a spell of very hot weather, such species as the wandering snail will rise to the surface in the hundreds and float with their pad uppermost. Whether this phenomenon is due to lack of oxygen in the water or has something to do with mating behaviour no-one has yet established, but when it happens the trout feed upon the snails avidly, to the exclusion of any other floating food that may be available. They take the floating snails with a very deliberate head and tail rise, and as the snails are very difficult to see when looking across the surface it is very easy to be fooled and assume the trout are taking either midge pupae or caenis (tricos), which they also take with a typical head and tail rise. By far the best floating snail pattern that I know is a cork-bodied pattern developed by the late Cliff Henry many years ago.

ORDERS OF INSECTS OF
INTEREST TO FLY FISHERMEN

(Listed roughly in order of importance)

Ephemeroptera	upwinged flies
Trichoptera	caddis or sedge flies
Plecoptera	stoneflies
Diptera	midges, reed smuts, gnats, etc.
Crustacea	shrimps (scuds), louse, crayfish
Odonata	dragonflies, damselflies
Megaloptera	alder flies
Hemitpera	water bugs, corixae, etc.
Coleoptera	beetles
Arachnidae	spiders
Lepidoptera	moths

3

THE APPROACH

THE APPROACH TO TROUT, particularly on rivers, is extremely important; failure to appreciate this will always result in few trout being seen or caught. Probably the most important aspect to consider is movement, or rather lack of it. Over aeons of time fish that live in relatively shallow water, particularly trout, have developed the ability to spot sudden movement. Among the main predators of fish are birds, such as herons, cormorants, shags, and other birds of prey. These can appear like a bolt of lightning out of a clear sky, so the fish's lives depend upon their ability to spot the danger instantly. Trout in their feeding lies are constantly on the alert for any sign of movement from any quarter, and the first indication of danger will send them bow-waving for cover, possibly not to return for an hour or even longer. This not only applies to clearwater chalkstreams and spring creeks, but also to trout lying close to the surface in the more turbid rain-fed or freestone rivers. Therefore, when looking for rising or maybe nymphing trout, or even when fishing the water, walk very, very slowly and keep any arm and head movement to an absolute minimum. It is also important to tread lightly, as heavy or clumsy footsteps will reverberate along the banks and alert fish long before they can see you. How many times have you seen fellow fly fishers charging along the banks, looking for fish? In most cases they just cannot wait to see what is rising around the next bend. Sure, they catch the occasional trout, but more often than not when you meet them later in the day you will find that they have had a blank. I find that the slower I traverse the banks, the more activity I spot. In fact, I often pause for quite long periods and just observe; if I come across one of those lovely old angling seats made from the trunks of trees I will sit quietly for five or ten minutes. It is amazing how often this can pay dividends. Remember, the golden rule on the riverbank is to move slowly, smoothly, and softly, with as little head or arm movement as possible, and to carry your rod low to the ground, not waving in the air above you.

Along open banks, a bush or tree overhanging the water is manna from heaven. Circle round it as far away from the bank as possible, until it is directly between you and the river. You can then creep slowly up to it and use it as an observation post. Better still, if the foliage is particularly dense and overhanging the bank, you can sidle around to the front, where you will have an even better view of the water. Open banks are always a problem; normally it is all but impossible to see a fish before he sees you, no matter how slow your approach. This is particularly true of clearwater streams in open meadowland or spring creeks in open ranchland. The best approach in this instance, if the water is not too deep, is to wade slowly and carefully close to one bank or the other. This is often the only way you are going to get close enough to the fish either to see or to cast to them.

There is one other ploy that can be effective under these conditions: Walk along the bank well back from the stream, and then every twenty-five or thirty yards walk as slowly and as smoothly as possible towards the bank, stopping as soon as your head reaches a level where you can see the width of the river in front of you and also twenty or so yards upstream. This way, providing your approach is really smooth with no sudden movements, it is surprising how close you can get to rising or nymphing fish without spooking them. Many times over the years as I have raised my head above the level of the bank, I have found myself observing a trout busily feeding immediately in front of me within a rod length. It is surprising how often these fish can be caught. With a minimum of arm movement, remove your fly from the keeper ring and pull off just enough fly line to aerialize the leader; a yard or two will usually suffice. A gentle flick cast putting the fly out just in front of the trout will often result in an immediate take. This flick cast is not as easy as it may sound and may require a little practice, but correctly executed it is a lethal method. When making this cast it is important to realize that the trout can probably only see the top of your shoulders and your head, so, providing the cast is horizontal to the bank with the tip of the rod kept below shoulder level, he will be unaware of the movement. This flick cast is well worth practising as it is also very useful when fishing along lines of trees that may be over-hanging the banks.

When casting to a feeding fish, you must take account of the distance involved. The closer you are, the lower you will have to crouch; in some cases, particularly on open banks, it may even be necessary to lie down. On the other hand, it is always fairly safe to cast to a fish when you are standing—providing you are out of his sight, which is roughly any distance over thirty feet. Even at thirty feet, though, you should avoid casting directly overhead, as even at this distance the fish could spot the rapid movement of the top of the rod. On clearwater streams it pays to make sure that there are no fish lying between you and the one to which you are casting, as these will invariably rush off in panic the moment they see you and spook the quarry.

This all applies equally to small, clear stillwaters, but when it comes to the big lakes and reservoirs there is little advice I can give other than for bank fishing. Today bank fishing on these large waters seems to be far less popular than it used to be, so it is now possible to find long stretches of prime water without a single angler in sight. During the warmer summer months, trout will often move into the shallower stretches of banks to feed, so at this time it pays to stand well back from the water's edge and fish in an extended arc from where you are standing. Alternatively, it is a good ploy to fish slowly along these stretches of bank covering both the shallow water close in and the deeper water farther out.

CLOTHING AND EQUIPMENT

Clothing is, of course, a very personal matter, and I would not dream of suggesting any particular outfits. During the early days of game-fishing one was expected to dress with Saville Row elegance—a crisp shirt, well-knotted tie, plus fours, and tailored jacket. In today's society, casual dress for most sports is the order of the day, so my advice is to wear comfortable clothes and dress according to the weather. Remember that you are basically a hunter, so do wear clothing that will at least blend into the background. You may see fly fishers wearing camouflage shirts and hats, but this is not strictly necessary; on most occasions, soft browns and greens will suffice.

When fishing in open meadowland or ranchland, though, with little or no cover, dark clothing is less desirable. In these conditions I would suggest you consider a light grey or even pale blue shirt and hat, depending on whether there is a blue or dull grey sky.

You may still come across the odd fly fisher dressed in a white shirt or other gaily coloured apparel, topped off with a white or even red hat. These gentlemen seldom catch many fish, for obvious reasons. You will also do well to remember never to wear any bright metal objects on your upper body that will flash in a bright sun. I learnt my lesson in this respect several years ago when fishing in New Zealand. I was fishing with a guide on a gin-clear stream when we spotted a huge trout close to the surface in the middle of a deep pool. Knowing how spooky these large trout are, I decided upon a very long cast, so there would be no possibility of him seeing us or any movement we made. Despite this, as soon as I aerialized the line a large bow wave marked the rapid departure of the trout. The guide agreed that there was no chance of that fish having seen us or the fly line in the air. Looking me over carefully, he spotted a bright silver badge on my cap and suggested, I am sure quite correctly, that this must have flashed in the sun as I moved my head to cast.

While discussing clothing, we must also consider rainwear. In England, Barbour waterproofs made from waxed cotton are extremely popular with fly fishers. They are excellent in heavy rain and the colder weather of early spring or late autumn. During the summer months, though, they are far too hot to wear, so for this time of the year, I would suggest a dark-coloured jacket with a hood in one of the lightweight waterproof materials that have recently become available, such as Gore-Tex. These are expensive but worth every penny, as the materials can breathe so you do not get wet from perspiration inside them. Choose a hip-length one so that if you are wearing hip waders, unless the rain is torrential, you will not also need waterproof trousers. During inclement weather in the summer, with hot sunny periods and showers, it is a nuisance to have to carry a waterproof jacket around with you all day even if it is lightweight; when folded up, even these may be too bulky to carry in your small haversack, hip bag, or fishing-waistcoat pocket. I carry a superlight nylon jacket, which folds up to a very small size. These can be purchased at low cost from most tackle shops, but they are only showerproof, useless in heavy or prolonged rain.

Hats

Although hats are far less fashionable than they used to be, they are still synonymous with gamefishers, as they always have been. Before the last war few people would venture forth without a hat of some kind, and anglers were no exception, but gamefishers always wore hats for other reasons—to keep the head warm in cold weather (in cold weather, the greatest heat loss is through the head) and dry in wet weather. The brim at the back would protect their necks in hot weather, and in the front it would cut out the glare from the sky and allow them to better see into the water. All these points are just as valid today. In fact, the brim at the front is even more important. With the advent of polarized sunglasses, the brim should be as substantial and as long as possible to reduce the overhead glare to an absolute minimum. Choose dark colours not only to blend in with the background, but also to reduce reflection on the underside of the peak or brim. If your chosen headgear is not of a very dark colour, it is advisable to paint or dye the underside black.

There are now so many different types of hats available that the fly fisher has a tremendous choice. If you require a practical hat that offers most of the features mentioned, you might like to consider the old-fashioned trilby, which has a brim all around. It is very elegant and also very expensive. A better choice might be a bush hat similar to those worn by Allied soldiers in the Burma campaign during the last war, although this may appear a little eccentric in colder climes. Straw-type hats with very wide brims are ideal for saltwater fly fishing in the tropics, but much too light in colour for trout fishermen. Deerstalkers at one time were very popular with fishermen, but the brim around these is far too narrow to be practical. Personally, I prefer the American baseball cap. These are available in many different shapes and designs. They keep your head warm yet not hot, they are all but waterproof, and some makes can be purchased with very long peaks. The only minus is the lack of cover for the neck, so in hot weather anyone with a weakness for sunstroke should consider an alternative. A baseball-type hat is now available in the States with earflaps and a flap that covers the neck, rather like the kepi worn by Legionnaires, but it looks a little inelegant.

Fishing Waistcoats

These have become increasingly popular with many gamefishermen over the last fifty years, and there is now a huge variety to choose from. There are basically three types: the standard waist-length model for the bank fisherman; a much shortened model to be worn in conjunction with chest waders for deep-water wading; and a fairly recent innovation that incorporates flotation devices to save you if you fall or are swept into deep water. I have tried some of these and while the idea is excellent, particularly if you are wading in fast, boulder-strewn water, I found them very bulky and uncomfortable to wear. For the average stream or river they are not really necessary, unless you are a nonswimmer. If I am fishing dangerous water, I favour a suspender-type flotation device that is worn around the neck, where it is nonrestrictive.

They all have masses of pockets of different shapes and sizes, plus rings and clips and other gadgets for holding all sorts of different items, many of which are used so rarely that they are hardly worth carrying. In the early days, I wore the same waistcoat for several years, but as time went by the bits and bobs that I added weighed it down so that it became uncomfortable to wear. Unless you are very strong willed, I am sure that these waistcoats encourage you to carry far more than you really require; it is for this reason that I do not like them.

For the last few years I have been using a waist belt that I designed myself. The adjustable belt is attached at the front to a shaped leather section that has pockets to contain scissors or clippers, pliers, a tin of line grease, a disgorger, and a bottle of dry-fly flotant. On each side of the belt is a zip-top pouch for holding a fly box and spools of leader material, which can be slid along the belt around to the front for easy access. At the back of the belt is a zip-top bag large enough to hold a lightweight nylon jacket, a few odds and ends, and a packet of sandwiches. Normally worn around the waist, it can be slid up to just under the armpits and retained with a halter around the neck—useful when deep wading. Similar belt bags for fly fishers have recently been advertised in the fishing press. Another good alternative is the European-type chest pouch fitted with Velcro-ed pockets and a large pouch that hangs down the front of your chest. It is fitted with adjustable straps and, for deep wading, can be pulled up just under the chin. Both of the above items are much better than any fishing waistcoats or the old-fashioned haversack that many fly fishers still carry, as they restrict you to the necessities. After all, surely two fly boxes is enough for any fly fisher.

Chest Waders, Waders, and Boots

Steelhead and salmon fishers have used chest waders for years; in fact, I think they were originally designed for them. More recently, chest waders have become popular with trout fishers who travel a lot, and also with the increasing numbers who use float tubes.

Most manufacturers of chest waders are based in America, and there are several models available. They are made in neoprene for cold water and low temperatures, either with a stocking foot over which wading boots have to be worn, or with a built-in boot foot. There is a lightweight nylon version for summer, also available in either stocking foot or boot foot. Neoprene models are far too hot in warm weather, but while the lightweight models are fine while standing in cool water, as soon as you come out they start to sweat on the inside and you will finish up as wet as if you had waded without them. Within the last year or so Simm's has put a new lightweight stocking-foot model on the market, manufactured from Gore-Tex. This is a fabulous material, very light in weight yet immensely tough, completely waterproof and, wonder of wonders, it does not sweat on the inside, as this material actually breathes. Unfortunately, at the moment such waders are expensive, at least three to four times the price of standard lightweights.

If you want to save money the answer is to wet wade, which means wearing only wading boots. You wade in either shorts or long, cotton, lightweight pants that dry quickly. This has been very popular in New Zealand for some years, and is now becoming a favourite method in many of the western states of America, such as Idaho and Montana.

The only type of boots manufactured especially for fishermen are wading boots, as there is little or no demand for ordinary boots or shoes, unless of course you have a rod on a beat on the middle Test, England's premier chalkstream, where the grassy banks are mowed and manicured nearly every day. There is a large variety of wading boots available; most of them are supplied with either studded or felt soles.

The most popular footwear for the average trout fisherman in England is waders, available in either knee length or hip length with a choice of cleated, studded, or felt soles. Unless you intend to wade or cross the river you are fishing, the cleated soles—which are cheapest—will suffice. For freestone rivers where wading may be necessary, the felt soles are probably best, while in slippery, rocky rivers the studded variety should be favoured.

When fly fishing from a boat on the big lakes or reservoirs, I find the knee-length waders, or Wellington boots as they are often called in England, excellent. They are also very good for fishing rivers or small streams, ponds, and gravel pits where wading is not necessary. On those rivers where it is sometimes necessary to enter the water to reach a feeding fish, the thigh or hip waders are ideal. These are available in both heavy-duty and lightweight models, the former being ideal for bank fishing on the big lakes and reservoirs, while the lightweight ones are ideal for general river fishing. In warm weather they can be worn with the tops down to prevent sweating.

Nets

Personally, I abhor landing nets. They are a nuisance to carry, taking great delight in catching up on every barbed-wire fence you cross, while the mesh attracts branches of trees and bushes like instant glue! Providing you know what you are doing (see the relevant section of chapter 7 on landing fish, page 148–150), you really do not need a net, as even the biggest of fish can be either landed by hand or beached. Only recently, when fishing in New Zealand, I landed by hand three brown trout of over ten pounds and also one huge brown of over fourteen pounds, all of which I took on the dry fly. I can honestly say I had no problem landing any of these trout despite their large size. In fact, I think it is probably true to say that small trout—between one and two pounds—are often more of a problem than their bigger brethren.

It was in the summer of 1974 that I last carried a landing net. I was fishing the Littlecote Water on the upper river Kennet when one day, towards the end of the season, I arrived at the waterside and realized I had left my landing net at home. Could I manage without one, I asked myself. Knowing that from midsummer on, this water is regularly stocked with large rainbows, some in excess of seven pounds, I was very dubious. The only alternatives were to return home for a net, or to seek out the nearest tackle shop and buy a new one. Neither of these options appealed to me, so I decided to try to manage without. Since that day I have never even considered carrying a net again. I quickly learnt to use my hands in place of a net and managed to cope quite well, grassing several trout, including two rainbows weighing over six pounds apiece.

If you must carry a net, do choose one that is big enough to accommodate the largest trout you are likely to encounter in the water you are fishing. Many times I have seen fly fishers really struggle to get a trout into a net that is too small and eventually lose it. Another factor to consider is the length of the handle, which should be telescopic or long enough to cope with high banks if necessary. I would also strongly recommend that you purchase a net with a rigid frame; those that fold with cord or a chain across the front are not really suitable if you are fishing water that is heavily weeded, such as chalkstreams or spring creeks. Finally, I would suggest you consider those models that are designed to be carried down the back, as they are less likely to get tangled than those carried on the hip.

Polaroid Glasses

There are exceptions to every rule, and despite my oft-repeated principle never to be dogmatic about fishing, when it comes to glasses, no fishermen, particularly fly fishermen, should ever fish without wearing a pair. Your eyesight is one of the most precious things you possess, and a fly badly or carelessly cast by either yourself or a companion can suddenly rob you of sight in an eye. I can still vividly recall reading the reports in the national press during the last war of how the American ambassador in London, fly fishing on a very windy day on the river Test, hooked himself in the eye and consequently lost the sight in it. I therefore implore you, when fly fishing do at all times wear glasses. Plain or sunglasses will suffice, but I am sure if you are a keen trout fisherman you will opt for a pair of Polaroid glasses, as not only will these provide the necessary protection but they will also allow you to see into the water and spot many more trout than you would without them. In fact, they are indispensable on those waters where this is important. They are usually available with either greenish grey or amber lenses. For spotting fish in rivers, particularly on dull days, I find the amber colour is more effective, but when saltwater fly fishing on tropical sand flats where it is always sunny I find the greenish ones are marginally better. Polaroid sunglasses are more expensive than ordinary sunglasses, so make sure when buying them that you get genuine Polaroids. This is easy to check. Hold up two pairs and rotate one pair in front of the other. If they are genuine Polaroids, the lenses will go from dark to light to dark as you rotate them. The darkening should be uniform over most of the lens; if it is not, or if there are any dark or light spots visible, do not accept them. They are faulty.

Gadgets

Today there are so many gadgets available that the fly fisher could very easily fill every pocket in the average waistcoat twice over. I am a firm believer in travelling and fishing as light as possible, so I only take those items I consider necessities. These are, of course, my personal choice, but the list may offer a rough guide.

- One or at the most two fly boxes. I have several dozen boxes at home all labelled and filled with flies for specific rivers and even countries; so most of the time I can manage with one, which will have all the flies I am likely to need on the particular water I am fishing.
- Four or five spools of leader material from 2X to 6X.
- A couple of packets of tapered leaders for emergencies.
- A pair of clippers, plus a spare.
- A pair of pliers for flattening barbs on hooks.
- A pair of forceps for removing the fly from a deep-hooked fish.
- A tin of grease for floating the leader when required.
- A bottle of liquid fly flotant such as Permafloat or Cul De Canard oil, plus an alternative such as the semisolid Gherke's Gink. Or you might like to consider one of the new dry-fly powders such as Tiemco Dry Shake.

- For stillwater fishing, a bottle of Leader Sink or a container of glycerine and fuller's earth that you can make up yourself, is my favourite.

- When dry-fly fishing, I always carry a pad of amadou. This is an absolutely fabulous material for drying flies at the waterside. It is a very absorbent, dried, and prepared natural fungus. Popular with dry-fly fishers in the early part of the century, it all but disappeared after the last war, but it is now once again available from specialist tackle suppliers.

- Finally, I always carry for emergency use a spare top ring for my rod, a spool of whipping silk, a needle, and a tube of instant glue.

HOW TO SEE TROUT

A lot of fly fishers may ask why it is important to see fish when much of your time is spent either looking for rising trout on spring creeks or similar clearwater streams, or fishing the water with nymphs or wet flies on more turbulent spate or freestone rivers. The answer is very simple: It increases your chances of success during a day's fishing. For example, on clearwater streams where it is possible to see well below the surface, you may with careful observation spot a deep-feeding trout taking nymphs, which with a little luck you may eventually catch. On the other hand, you may spot a fish that has just taken up his feeding lie, so it may be worth waiting for him to commence feeding, or to mark the spot and come back later in the day. On dour days when for some reason the fish are not feeding, a trout in such a feeding lie may be tempted to rise to some unusual offering, such as an artificial bluebottle, beetle, or hopper. If you are lucky, you may spot a particularly large trout and, although he may show no interest in your offerings at the time, you may come back and catch him on another occasion.

In fast, turbulent spate rivers it is almost impossible to see trout, but when fishing the water the observant angler who really concentrates may for a fleeting moment spot the odd fish, which can make the difference between success and failure. The same, of course, applies to those coloured rivers where visibility may be confined to inches rather than feet below the surface. On relatively fast freestone rivers it is also difficult to spot trout, but on this type of water where they are less likely to be spooked, a trout spotted is often a trout caught.

The ability to see fish underwater is almost an art form, and it may take several years for the average fly fisher who fishes one day a week to become really competent. Over the years I have fished in many different countries with many excellent, and a few indifferent, professional guides, most of whom had the ability to spot fish in any type of water. I am sure that this was mainly due to the amount of time they spent on the water. Other factors essential to good fish spotting are, of course, good eyesight, patience, and concentration. While these capabilities are important on any type of water, they are undoubtedly far more important on clear waters, such as spring creeks, chalk or limestone streams, and small, clear ponds or lakes, as without them you will spook far too many fish. Let us therefore look at the different factors that will assist you in becoming more competent at spotting fish, mainly in these clear waters, under any conditions.

Contrary to popular belief, when fishing clear water the best conditions for seeing into the water and spotting fish occur on bright, sunny, windless days, particularly during the mornings when the sun is either behind your shoulders or directly overhead. Conversely, the worst conditions occur on wet, windy days, yet despite this how many times do we encounter nonanglers who think that these are the best fishing days? In my experience grey, cloudy, and windy days are often quite good for fishing the big lakes and reservoirs or even large turbulent rivers, but on clear waters grey skies make seeing into the water very difficult, while even a light breeze that ripples the surface makes it impossible to see into the water at all.

Upon arrival at the waterside, if it is sunny choose the bank with the sun behind you to give you the best chance of seeing into the water; but if this is not possible, or if there is little or no sun, there are other ploys that will assist you to see into the water. High banks or rocks, logs, and so on that you can stand on, providing you have cover behind, will allow you to see down and into the water. Concentrate on finding stretches where the far banks are lined with trees, as these will remove that silvery sheen that restricts your vision below the surface very severely and that occurs on many stretches of water along open banks. Even a single large tree on the far bank will assist you in this respect, as the trunk and branches will provide a narrow band along which you can see below the surface. If you move slowly, this band will move with you and allow you to scan the reflection-free area little by little. As already mentioned, wind causing a strong ripple makes it impossible to see below the surface so your only recourse is to seek out stretches of calm water around bends or where trees, bushes, or other obstructions provide some shelter.

When surveying the water, move very slowly with frequent pauses. Cover the water in an extended arc, and look *into* it, not onto it. This ability to look *into* the water is of the utmost importance, and is a feat that the tyro often finds most difficult to accomplish. If and when you spot a fish, make a mental note of where he is and continue surveying the whole area from where you are standing, as there may be other fish close by that should be taken into account before presenting your fly. When looking for trout in any given area, it is good practice to look first for spots where they are most likely to be lying, such as in front of rocks, boulders, or other obstructions, or in depressions, pockets, or runs on the bottom, or in pockets or runs between weed beds. In such locations the trout are often easily spotted, particularly if they are in a feeding lie and fairly high in the water. At other times when they are resting or on the fin but not actively feeding, they may be extremely difficult to spot.

Remember that all fish, particularly trout, are adept at the art of camouflage, so the last thing most experienced observers are looking for is a complete fish. They will be looking for shadows, odd shapes that seem out of place, maybe the head or tail only of a fish, or even the straight, shadowy edge of a tailfin.

On many clear rivers you will come across long, shallow stretches of bright gravel or sand that appear completely devoid of fish. Very often these shallows contain slight depressions that will hold the odd good trout, but in sunny conditions such a fish will be all but invisible. The reason for this is that the bright flanks of the trout act like a mirror and reflect the bottom on which they are lying so that they disappear against the background. Depending upon the angle of the sun, this will sometimes cause a shadow that is clearly visible; but it is extremely difficult to spot the actual fish. This phenomenon was illustrated to me some years ago when I first started saltwater fly fishing for bonefish. These are fished for in shallow, clear water on white or silver sand flats. When they are approaching you head on, they are highly visible, appearing as very dark— almost black—shapes against the silver sand, yet they sometimes seem to completely disappear. One minute they are there, the next minute there is no sign of them. It was some time before I realized that this only happened when the sun was behind me, so that, when the fish turned either to the right or to the left, their bright silver flanks reflected the bottom—which in effect made them invisible.

Apart from looking for visible signs of fish, you should also be acutely aware of any sign of movement, the greatest betrayer of prey to predator. This factor alone is of the utmost importance when looking for fish, and it is not only the movement of fish you should be looking for. Any sudden movement that is out of sync with its surroundings, such as a swirl of water on or below the surface, will often betray the presence of a fish, as will any unusual movement of weed—for example, against the prevailing current. In fact, anything at all that suggests movement against the current or even anything that appears to drop downstream with controlled movement should be investigated further. More obvious signs are a sudden flash of light from a fish turning his flank into or away from the sun, or the blink of his mouth as he opens it to feed.

There are many other signs of movement that will lead you to a fish, but the most common one that betrays a trout is the movement of his tail. No matter where a trout is lying, the pulse or fanning of his tail to allow him to retain his station against the current so often gives away his position. This pulsating tail can also be a great help in establishing whether or not that shadowy shape you have spotted on the bottom is indeed a fish.

Once you have mastered the art of looking into the water, you may find at times it is quite easy to spot fish in the clear, relatively slow waters of spring creeks, chalkstreams, and so on, but when fishing fast, turbulent spate rivers or fast freestone streams lined with large stones or even boulders and rocks of different colours, it can be very difficult to spot any fish at all. Under very windy conditions, it can be almost impossible. Even in this type of water, though, it is possible to spot the odd fish; although I must admit it is usually simpler to present your fly onto or into obvious fish-holding lies, in the fast runoffs at the necks of pools, or along the edge of the faster currents. As on spring creeks, you should use the minimum of movement with frequent pauses to survey every inch of water in front of you and really concentrate. It is worth stressing again that you are not necessarily looking for fish or even fishy shapes; it may be vague shadows, it may be odd light reflections, it may be local ripples where the wavelets move in different directions from the current, or it may be odd movements that are out of character with their surroundings. In fact, in these rivers, movement is again the key to success. If you think you have spotted some form of movement below the surface, even if it is only fleeting, concentrate on that area for a few minutes; move up- and downstream slightly, as by doing this you can often find breaks in the current that allow you momentary views beneath the surface. In this type of water you will also find small areas of upwelling currents that provide patches of calm in the ripple, which will give you a good but brief view into the water. The water in freestone rivers is usually pretty clear and there are often extensive areas out of the main current where you can see the bottom quite clearly. Look for fish in these areas, although it may be extremely difficult to spot them among the stones or boulders on the riverbed. Under these conditions a fish will show as a lighter or darker patch. If you do spot something that looks vaguely like a fish, be patient and concentrate on it for a minute or two. Movement will eventually establish whether it is a fish, or not as, in such fast water, it is all but impossible for a fish to hold his position for very long.

WEATHER

The weather plays a very important role in fly fishing. The ideal conditions for fishing on chalkstreams, spring creeks, or even small, clear ponds are sunny, windless days. Under these conditions, if hatches of flies are sparse or absent and no fish are rising, it does at least allow you to spot fish in the water. If on the fin, these may be tempted with a dry fly or nymph. Conversely, on large lakes the best fishing often occurs on warm, cloudy, grey days with a light breeze.

Several years ago before I retired, my fishing was largely restricted to weekends, so whatever the weather conditions I would go. Today I am fortunate to be able to choose, to a large extent, when I go fishing, so I do take the weather very much into account, particularly when fishing the large stillwaters. On these I avoid sunny, very windy days, days on which heavy rain is forecast, and days when it is wet with very strong gusty winds, which I think are the most unrewarding of all.

On rivers the weather plays a less important role. Under most conditions it is still possible to catch the odd trout, although I have found it is a waste of time during heavy, continuous rain, as this not only puts the trout down but also makes it impossible to see into the water. On the other hand, some wet days can prove to be very productive, particularly during the height of the summer. Some of the best fishing I have ever experienced on English chalkstreams has been on warm, windless days with a steady drizzle. These conditions seem to encourage heavy hatches of flies and consistently rising trout. My good friend the late Major Oliver Kite used to welcome such days with open arms, and if I shut my eyes I can still hear him enthusing on such conditions with great delight as we approached the water.

Other vagaries of the weather can upset fishing or make it more difficult. Thundery weather can have odd effects; sometimes the trout will stop rising at the approach of a thunderstorm, yet rise avidly after it has passed over, while at other times the reverse will apply. On rivers strong winds are always a nuisance and can make casting and good presentation very difficult, particularly if the wind is upstream. At such times, with the wind fully extending the leader and fly, it is virtually impossible to get a drag-free drift when fishing the dry fly. It is better to move to a section of river where the wind is blowing in a different direction. The average fly fisher understandably hates a very strong downstream wind; unless you have mastered the art of presenting a fly into a strong wind, it is next to impossible to extend the leader at all, and the fly invariably finishes up downstream of the fly line itself. If you can master casting into the wind it will pay dividends, as it usually means you will have a stretch of river all to yourself. As you become more proficient at it, you will find it better to reduce the length of your leader to around eight or nine feet; in fact, you will probably not be able to turn a longer leader than this into the wind.

The temperature is another aspect of the weather that affects fishing. Fluctuating temperatures can put the fish off the feed, sometimes for quite long periods. In the spring and also in the fall there is often a sudden drop in temperature during the day; when this occurs on large bodies of stillwater, the trout immediately cease feeding. When it happens late in the evening, on both rivers and stillwaters, it nearly always results in a heavy mist caused by the rapidly cooling surface water. Most fly fishers are only too familiar with this phenomenon on rivers. You will often hear one say to another, "The old White Lady has arrived—time to go home." During the spring and sometimes in the late autumn there may be several days of hot, sunny weather, when the water literally comes to life with the trout feeding well all day, but if the weather quickly deteriorates with a subsequent drop in temperature, the fish will sometimes cease to feed altogether for several days. This is particularly noticeable during winter grayling fishing. With the first heavy frosts or snowfalls, the grayling go off the feed and are all but impossible to catch. However, after a few days of these lower temperatures they stabilize, and often come back on the feed with a vengeance.

Cloud or lack of it affects fishing in several different ways. On some summer days, the sun will shine from a blue sky interspersed with heavy banks of cloud. On rivers this will make little difference, but on large lakes and reservoirs, when it clouds over you may expect to see signs of activity or even rising fish, so it pays to be extra alert when this happens. Low-lying, uniform, grey cloud with little wind provides excellent conditions for fishing on the big stillwaters, but on chalkstreams or spring creeks the reverse applies as, in these conditions of poor light, the overall vision of the trout is much enhanced and they will nearly always see you before you see them. During high summer, days may be sunny despite the fact that the sky is full of large, white cumulus clouds. While this does not affect the fishing, it does affect your ability to see into the water on stretches of open bank. These very white clouds reflect on the surface of the water and make it impossible to see into it. For this reason they are particularly unwelcome to saltwater fly fishers working shallow-water flats, as these conditions are almost as bad as a strong wind that ripples the surface to such an extent that you cannot see below it.

While the sun or lack of it plays a big part in fishing, the moon also plays a part—but to a much lesser degree. For example, we know that seatrout fishermen fly fishing rivers at night avoid the full moon like the plague. We know that big-game anglers fishing for marlin also avoid the period of the full moon, as they reckon that the marlin feed at night under these conditions and not during the day. I understand that anglers fishing for broadbill swordfish at night do not like the full moon, as at this time the fish often feed close to the surface where the light sticks the anglers use are far less effective. In some areas where bonefishing is popular the local guides will tell you to avoid the periods of the full or new moon, as these coincide with high spring tides. Bonefish love to feed in the shallow water among the mangroves where food is most plentiful, but they can only get into these mangroves and out of reach of the fly fisher when the water is high enough. Therefore, during high spring tides they can remain in the mangroves much longer and spend much less time on the sand flats where they are accessible to the fly fisher. During the last century much was written about how the different phases of the moon may affect fishing, with dates and times when fishing varied from excellent to very poor given. Whether this is an old wives' tale or not, I am not sure. Over the years I have tried out some of these theories and fished on the recommended dates but frankly, I have not noticed any marked difference in my catches.

One final aspect of the weather that must be taken into account is the effect of barometric pressure. Unfortunately, little research has been carried out on this, which is a great pity as the more I fish the more important I think it is. Although I have no hard evidence to back it up, I feel sure that barometric pressure affects or maybe even governs the feeding behaviour of fish as well as the hatches of aquatic insects upon which they feed. I am now inclined to think that both hatches and feeding behaviour are governed by a combination of weather, temperature, and barometric pressure. So far as insect hatches are concerned, I feel that weather and temperature alone cannot account for these. I am sure that, like myself, you have all experienced days in the early spring or late autumn or even in winter when grayling fishing, when the weather has been absolutely awful with near-freezing temperatures, and you have decided you must be mad even to consider fishing under these circumstances. Yet upon arrival at the waterside there has been a splendid hatch of flies. Conversely, how often has the opposite been the case: Conditions have been ideal, but few or no flies have been in evidence throughout the day. The same situation of course occurs throughout the season, so it is impossible to forecast hatches relying upon the weather alone. I believe that barometric pressure in some way or another is probably responsible. Whether it is rising or dropping pressure that effects these hatches I am not sure, although I would hazard a guess that either probably has less effect than an unstable barometre. So far as hatches of insects are concerned, I have found that those periods when we experience good hatches day after day usually occur during periods of stable weather with little or no change in barometric pressure. I am now inclined to think that it is either big changes in pressure or fluctuating pressure that influence hatches, but the feeding behaviour of fish and trout in particular is to a large extent governed by much more subtle changes in pressure. How else do we account for the following situations that so often occur during apparently stable weather conditions.

- There is a steady hatch of flies but no rising trout, as they are not even in their feeding lies.

- There is a steady hatch of flies, and the trout are in their feeding lies.

- There is a good hatch but little activity when suddenly, as if someone has rung a starting bell, there will be fish rising up and down the river.

- The same situation occurs later in the day when the trout all stop feeding at the same time even though flies are still hatching.

The above situations are not uncommon. Are they due to a slight rise or fall in barometric pressure? I do not know.

We also get days when the fish will be seen feeding avidly below the surface yet not rising, and days when they are in their feeding lies but will not even look at a nymph or in fact at anything you care to present to them. So far as the latter is concerned, it could be due to the trout not being hungry, as this often happens during the large mayfly (green drake) hatches. It also happens later in the summer during days of extended hatches; maybe, although they are not hungry, the trout still move into their feeding lies out of habit.

4

Tackle for Trout

RODS

When it comes to tackle, rods are the most important as well as the most expensive item. They are very personal and what suits one person may not suit another, so it is up to you to choose a rod that you are happy with. Some of my friends still use old split-cane rods and cast and fish very well with them. I must admit that during the era of the glass rods I preferred split-cane, and indeed it was several years after the introduction of carbon rods before I changed over to them.

So far as trout fishing is concerned, three rods should suffice. For fishing small to medium-sized rivers such as chalkstreams, spring creeks, or slower freestone rivers, an eight-and-a-half-foot 5-weight rod that will take a No 5 double-tapered line or, as I now prefer, a No 6 forward-tapered line, is ideal. This outfit is good for drift fishing from a boat or even for fishing large rivers where distance is not of paramount importance. For fishing larger rivers or from the banks of stillwaters where longer casts are often necessary, a nine-foot 8-weight rod to take a No 8 forward-tapered line should be adequate. Finally, a long rod, around ten feet, to take a No 7 line is very useful to give you more control when fishing loch style from a boat on stillwater, or when fishing nymphs from the bank. The only other rod that may be necessary is a small one, around seven feet to take a light line such as a No 3 or 4 when fishing small brooks or rivers lined with trees or bushes, where a longer rod would put you at a serious disadvantage.

REELS

As with rods, the number of fly reels on the market is legion. Not only do all the large tackle manufacturers throughout the world offer a selection, but there are also many smaller companies and individuals who manufacture and sell specialized models. Some of these are real works of art, beautiful to look at and to handle, but also in many cases fabulously expensive. These never tempt me as, when it comes to any form of trout fishing, I look upon a reel merely as a container for my fly line when I am not using it. I rarely play a trout from the reel (see page 146–148). The usual advice on reels is to choose one of the correct weight to balance the rod. This is nonsense, as the weight of the reel has little or no bearing on the casting qualities of any rod. In fact, all rods cast better without a reel. My advice is to choose the smallest and lightest reel you can buy that will accommodate the weight of fly line and the amount of backing you will be using. Also, when choosing a rod, ensure that the forward seating for the reel is positioned underneath the cork grip, as the closer the reel is to the casting hand, the less fatiguing casting will be over long periods. For many years now I have been using geared-retrieve fly reels for all my trout fishing. I find they offer tremendous advantages when river fishing where you are constantly on the move, casting and retrieving line. They not only save a lot of time, but they also allow you to move quickly from one rising fish to another some distance away. Unfortunately, geared fly reels tend to be a little heavier, but in view of the advantages they offer I am prepared to live with this.

FLY LINES

When it comes to fly lines, fly fishermen today are really spoiled for choice. In the last two decades there have been bigger advances in fly lines than in any other item of tackle. They are available in all colours and in weights from size No 3 up to around No 15. There is a vast range of different types from floating lines to intermediate, sink tip, slow sink, fast sink, Hi-D, or even lead cored. Most of these are also available in double taper, forward taper, bass taper, or saltwater taper, so we now have lines suitable for any type of fishing from small brooks to deep reservoirs and even salt water.

For distance casting, shooting heads are available. These can be made up at home by cutting ten to twelve yards off an old fly line of the weight required. I well remember when they were first introduced into Britain from America, where they had been developed by steelhead fishermen to fish the big rivers on the West Coast. It was the midfifties and not for many years were they available commercially, so you had to make them yourself. At that time most of us were still using the old oiled silk lines, where twenty-five yards was a very long cast, so a line such as a shooting head that would allow you to cast effortlessly well over thirty yards was a great boon, even if you did have to carry a line tray to take the loose line. I was a great advocater of shooting heads, particularly for reservoir or lake fishing from the bank, and I also started to use them for saltwater fishing when I first became addicted to fishing the flats for bonefish. However, I rarely use them now. I find the backing prone to tangling, particularly under windy conditions, and modern plastic lines are so efficient that it is possible to cast almost as far with these as it is with a shooting head—and with far less aggravation.

The choice of a fly line to suit the rod you are using is of the utmost importance. As a qualified casting instructor, it is amazing how often I come across fly fishers using fly lines that are too light in weight for the rod they are using, which makes casting much more difficult. Most modern carbon or boron fly rods are very forgiving and, if you are a competent caster, will cope with lines a size to either side of the designated weight on the rod, but having said that I personally suggest that you err on the heavy side. My favourite rod is a Sage eight-and-a half-foot graphite III 5-weight, and with this I use a weight-forward No 6 line. Going back a few years most dry-fly fishers, myself included, preferred double-tapered lines, but today forward-tapered lines have almost as fine a tip, and if you are a reasonably competent caster you can present them just as lightly on the surface. The big advantage of a forward taper over a double taper is that when necessary, you are able to cast much farther with far less effort. Recently some manufacturers have produced a line with what they call a long belly; some dry-fly fishers now prefer these lines, as they offer an excellent compromise between a double taper and a forward taper.

Another important factor when choosing a fly line is colour, particularly when it comes to dry-fly fishing. During the late seventies when Brian Clarke and I were engaged in writing *The Trout and the Fly*, we carried out many experiments using underwater cameras on fly lines and leaders to determine the advantages and disadvantages of various colours. This proved, at least to us, that dull colours such as green or brown were far less fish scaring, both on the surface of the water and in the air, than bright colours. Fluorescent lines were poor in this respect; white lines were particularly bad in the air in bright sunlight, due to their more reflective surface. Under dull or windy conditions where the surface is heavily rippled, or in broken or coloured water, the colour of the fly line is of little consequence; and when, for instance, nymphing, bright colours can be a distinct advantage, as it is much easier to see the end of the fly line and observe any movement when the nymph is taken by a trout. However, bright lines, especially white ones, put you at a disadvantage under bright, sunny conditions, particularly when fishing rivers lined with high, dark trees or when fishing any very clear water. Over the past few years I have fished a lot in New Zealand where most rivers are gin clear and consequently the fish very spooky. During one of my early visits I was fishing with a companion who was using a white line, while I was using a dull brown. During the morning's fishing, nearly every trout he cast to took off upriver in panic even before the line landed on the water surface. After lunch he changed to a green line and caught several very nice trout. Unfortunately, today many of the leading fly-line manufacturers seem to favour bright colours, so green or brown lines are not always available. My answer to this is to dye the first few yards of line dark brown.

LEADERS

There are three types of leaders generally available for dry-fly fishing: made-up, knotted leaders, commercially manufactured tapered leaders, and manufactured braided tapered leaders. There is also another type, but more on that later (page 79–81). Before the introduction of the relatively modern tapered leaders, fly fishers had to make up their own by knotting together lengths of mono in different breaking strains to achieve the desired tapers. Much nonsense was suggested in relation to these, with the most complicated formulae and even the suggestion of various reversed tapers. All quite unnecessary as, if you are a reasonable caster, you can turn over even a level leader fairly well, although some forms of taper will allow you to roll it over better. If you wish to make up your own leaders, which of course will be far less costly than purchasing made-up ones, I suggest you keep the various lengths to a minimum, as every blood knot used, particularly if trimmed improperly, is potentially fish scaring. The more knots you use, the more you increase the risk of picking up pieces of grass, weed, or algae from the water, which they seem to attract like a magnet. In the past I always made up my leaders with four or five feet of fifteen- to twenty-pound mono, followed with four feet of eight-pound to which I attached my tippet, thereby keeping the number of knots down to two. With the introduction of custom-made tapered leaders, with a wide choice of lengths and tippet sizes, knots are eliminated altogether, which is even better. So far as the relatively new braided tapered leaders are concerned, I do not like them, as they soak up water like a sponge and give every trout you are casting to a free shower before presenting the fly. You can, of course, eliminate this to some extent by greasing the braid, but then when you come across a situation where you may require the leader to sink you are stymied. However, the braided mono from which these tapered leaders are made does have another very useful role to perform in the makeup of a leader. Long before these braided leaders, which are hollow, were put on the market, I used (and still do) at times a two-foot length of hollow braided backing material to join the end of the fly line to the butt end of the leader. This is quickly and simply achieved by pushing the fly line into one end of the hollow braid and the leader into the other and then treating with a light application of waterproof glue. This provides a wonderfully smooth connection between fly line and leader with no bulky or ugly knots. Today you can purchase small-diameter plastic sleeves to slide over and lock these connections, or you can purchase custom-made lengths of hollow braided line complete with sleeve to connect to your fly line. These are supplied with a loop on the other end to which you can connect your leader. Personally I have little faith in these as, with several different makes that I have tried out, the loops have opened, resulting in losing not only a fish but the whole leader.

For dry-fly fishing the length of the leader can be very important. For general use a leader of eleven to thirteen feet is fine, but you may have to reduce this length under very windy conditions. If you are fishing open water, particularly if it is very clear with little or no background cover, it may be necessary to use a much longer leader—ideally, in excess of fifteen feet. Conversely, when fishing rivers with trees and bushes overhanging the water, as on some chalkstreams and spring creeks, it often pays to use a leader less than nine feet in length in order to cast a tight loop to get your fly to trout lying in apparent safety underneath low overhanging branches. The above lengths of leader also apply when fishing nymphs on rivers, but on lakes or other bodies of still-water I prefer to use a leader as long as possible, often well in excess of twenty feet, with floating lines, as in this case the farther away your flies are from your fly line, the better.

When fishing with sinking lines, particularly when fishing lures or attractor patterns, the shorter the leader, the better. You require your fly to fish at the same level as the fly line, and the longer the leader, the higher—at least initially—it will ride behind the line. My good friend Lefty Kreh, one of Americas top fly fishermen, once carried out some experiments in this respect. First of all he used a leader less than five feet in length, then four, three, two, and he eventually came down to a leader less than twelve inches in length. Over a period of time he found that the length made little or no apparent difference to his catch rate.

There is now another style of leader that is becoming popular, incorporating a material called Power Gum, which is a clear elasticated product that stretches by about 70 percent. You can purchase this material on spools in three different breaking strains: seven pound, eleven pound, and twenty pound. For trout fishing on those waters that may hold fairly large fish I favour the eleven-pound test, and have been making up leaders incorporating this material for the past eight years or so. I think they are absolutely fantastic for two reasons.

First of all, not only do they cushion the strike, they also give you much greater flexibility when playing a fish. This allows you to use much finer tippets than would normally be possible, which is a big plus when midge fishing with very tiny patterns. Secondly, to a very large extent this solves a problem that has bedevilled fly fishers since the very first fly was cast on the water, namely the loss of your fly on your backcast when it catches on trees, on bushes, or in long grass. I can confirm from bitter experience over many years that even expert casters snag and lose their fly quite often on their backcast. I just hate to think how many flies are lost in a day's fishing by inexperienced casters. While Power Gum in the leader does not prevent you from snagging your fly on your backcast, it does mean you can nearly always recover it. Due to the stretch in the Power Gum you will rarely pop the tippet and leave the fly in the undergrowth. To achieve a good presentation of the fly and turnover of the leader, the position of the Gum in the leader is critical, so if you wish to tie up some of these, read on.

I was first introduced to this material several years ago when fishing a spring creek in Montana for large brown trout. My host, Herbert G. Wellington, a very experienced dry-fly fisherman, insisted I use one of the leaders that he had tied up incorporating Power Gum. He said it was the only way he had been successful landing the bigger browns from the very weedy water. In this gin-clear water where hatches of small flies were predominant, the only way to deceive the larger trout was to fish very tiny size 20 to 24 dry flies on very fine tippets, and on these it was all but impossible to land any of the bigger trout. He had found that the extra stretch in the leader provided by the Power Gum was sufficient to overcome breakages on the strike, and also gave you much more latitude while playing the trout. The position of the Gum in the leader was critical, as in the wrong position it badly affected the turnover and presentation. He eventually perfected a formula that to a large extent overcame this problem. He favours the use of a tapered braided leader six to seven feet long, onto the end of which he knots eight inches of 1X nylon. This is followed with eight to ten inches of Power Gum, followed by another eight inches of 1X. He then tapers the leader further by tying eight inches of 3X and then eight inches of 5X, onto which he knots his tippet, giving an overall leader length of around twelve feet. He also showed me how to offset the hook on these tiny dry flies with a pair of pliers; without offsetting the hook it is very difficult to hook a trout on a small fly.

Subsequently, I decided to try this Power Gum leader on the chalkstreams back in England, but found that the leader was too long. On these streams, where it is often necessary to cast beneath trees and bushes, a leader needs to be less than ten feet in total length. I therefore developed a new formula omitting the tapered braided leader, which I do not like very much, and this has proved to be very successful indeed. The turnover and presentation are excellent; in fact, I have let several well-known fly fishers fish with my rod with this leader and they were completely unaware of the Power Gum. My formula is as follows: For the butt of the leader I use four feet of twenty- or twenty-five-pound nylon, followed by twelve inches of fifteen-pound nylon, to which I knot ten to twelve inches of eleven-pound Power Gum, followed by another twelve inches of fifteen-pound. Onto this I knot about eighteen inches of ten- or eight-pound test, to which I attach my tippet. I was originally advised to use surgeon's knots treated with a touch of superglue to tie in the Power Gum, but this is rather a bulky knot and I found that a double blood knot was just as strong and much neater. Should you decide to use the blood knot, it is essential to use a matte-finish nylon; shiny nylon is useless, as it slips and the knots will not hold. Even with matte-finish nylon, when tying this blood knot leave plenty of overlap, as it will slip quite a lot before pulling tight.

Unfortunately, to make up one of these leaders with Power Gum requires several knots, which of course is undesirable; but personally I am happy to live with it, as the advantages of this leader far outweigh the disadvantages of the knots.

TIPPETS

This is the final length of monofilament at the end of your leader to which the fly is attached. This can be cut from a standard spool and knotted onto the end of your leader, or you can buy special spools of tippet material, containing approximately twenty-five yards per spool, in a huge range of sizes and types. For as long as I can remember, the breaking strain of the tippet has been given an X number, from 0X to 7X, which can be most confusing unless you know the formula. Subtract the number of the X factor from eight to give you the breaking strain of the line in pounds. When purchasing custom-made tapered leaders, you will see on the packet the length of the leader followed by the X factor, so that "12ft/5X" denotes a leader twelve feet in overall length with three-pound tippet or point. However, when applying this X factor to the double-strength nylons now available, add approximately 50 percent to the breaking strain—thus 5X denotes a breaking strain of around four and a half pounds.

The next point to consider with tippets is whether to use one of the premium brands of standard monofilament or whether to use one of the many different makes of double-strength monofilament now available. All the standard makes of nylon have a certain degree of stretch, which gives them a fairly high impact strength. The double-strength nylons have little or no stretch and therefore have a very low impact strength. Therefore, when using this tippet material you have to be much more skillful and gentle when striking or playing a fish than with the standard makes, or you are sure to be broken on the strike or when trying to stop the initial run, particularly if he is a larger-than-average fish. Furthermore, you will invariably lose your fly if you catch it on any obstruction on the backcast. As mentioned earlier, the use of Power Gum in the leader will to some extent eliminate this problem, but even so you have to face the fact that you are going to lose the odd fish or fly. For this reason I always prefer, where I can get away with it, to use a standard nylon such as Racine Tortue, which is my favourite. I am a firm believer that trout can see the tippet no matter how thin the diameter, although in most cases it probably does not register with them. I only use double-strength material when fishing very clear, shallow water when there is no wind—on the chalkstreams of southern England, for example—as under these conditions the thicker the tippet, the larger the shadow it will transmit through the surface or against any light-coloured bottom. In New Zealand, the double-strength nylons are virtually unsaleable despite the fact that most of the rivers are crystal clear. However, most of them are also fairly deep or fast with a broken surface, and windless days are the exception, so the diameter of the tippet probably makes no difference, and there is little sense in using tippets finer than necessary. These days I use standard monofilament size in 4X or 5X for much of my fishing, even when using very tiny dry flies, and only change to a finer tippet when I find it impossible to get the nylon through the eye of the hook.

Finally, a word or two of warning when using double-strength nylon. Knots in standard nylon may be tied in many ways—not so with double-strength. Only use recommended knots, such as a double grinner or four-turn water knot, for leaders and droppers, and a single grinner or tucked blood knot for attaching the fly. Whichever knots are used, they must be prepared extra carefully, moistening them and snugging them down. Normally with standard nylon, you only replace the tippet or dropper if there is a wind knot or obvious damage to the monofilament, but with double-strength I strongly recommend that you replace it after every second fish.

5

THE DRY FLY ON RIVERS

WHEN WAS THE FIRST RISING trout caught with a fly presented on the surface? An interesting question. According to most angling historians the art of dry-fly fishing was first practiced about the middle of the last century, which coincides with the introduction of heavily dressed fly lines and shorter rods. These made it possible to fish more accurately and at longer distances than was previously possible. Prior to this there are no records of trout being consistently caught on a dry fly that was actually presented dry and intended to be fished on the surface. Trout have been rising to surface flies for far longer than man has been angling for them and, even though no records exist, I am sure that for centuries trout have succumbed to a fly presented on the surface either by dapping, which is a very old method, or merely by dangling a fly from the end of a rod.

Dry-fly fishing reached its peak at the end of the last century under the auspices of F. M. Halford, who is looked upon as the father of the dry fly. At the turn of the century the dry-fly purist reigned supreme, and even today there is a small minority of fly fishers who consider themselves purists and who will fish nothing but the floating fly. Unless you are fortunate enough to live on or very close to the river you are fishing, this seems to me to be a very shortsighted policy. On those dour days or periods when no fish are rising, you will have little to do other than to admire the scenery. One of my greatest loves is fishing with the dry fly to a rising trout, especially in clear water where very often you can actually see the trout. That magic moment when you know he has seen your fly, and his fins start quivering in anticipation as he slowly tilts and rises to intercept it, is followed by that heart-stopping second when you do not know whether he is going to accept it. Then, if your pattern is acceptable, the mouth slowly opens and the fly disappears, and with a little bit of luck the fish will eventually be yours. While I am not a purist I really love my dry-fly fishing, and will always try to take fish on the dry fly if at all possible, whatever the conditions. However, I am not averse to taking trout on the nymph, or by any other methods that may be acceptable on the waters I am fishing at the time, when there seems little chance of them accepting a dry fly.

Before proceeding to the various methods and techniques connected with dry-fly fishing, let us look at one aspect that has probably led to more controversy than any other—whether to fish upstream or downstream. In the UK and also in many European countries, most fly fishers seem to favour the upstream approach. On all the chalk-streams in England it is *de rigueur* to fish the downstream dry fly, although you are allowed to fish downstream to a rising trout if there is no other way to reach him. In America the majority of fly fishers have always favoured the downstream dry fly, although in recent years a small but growing body of fly fishers seem prepared to fish whichever method is most productive on the particular river they are fishing.

There are of course advantages and disadvantages in both methods. Personally, I strongly favour fishing upstream to a rising trout for the following reasons. The trout is less likely to see you, so you can approach much closer and therefore cast more accurately, and when you strike you are pulling the hook into the trout's mouth so it is far less likely to come unhooked. In addition, casting upstream is less demanding and certainly less tiring. The main disadvantage is that when casting directly upstream to a rising trout, one under your own bank, for example, you are constantly covering the trout with your leader, which will often spook a wary trout.

When fishing downstream, there are several disadvantages: The fish is more difficult to hook, as you tend to pull the hook out of his mouth when you strike, and you always have the problem of retrieving the fly line from below the trout without spooking him, often very difficult if you are forced to fish directly downstream to a trout. Also, casting is more difficult, as you have to cast so much slack and work the rod to pay out more line to avoid drag. The main advantage is that the trout is never covered by the leader, so is less likely to be spooked. Most if not all of the following techniques applicable to dry-fly fishing can be utilized with either upstream or downstream fishing, so it is up to you to use whichever method you favour.

PREPARATION

This is overlooked by so many fly fishers. How often do I see other anglers arriving at the waterside for the day's fishing, absolutely overloaded—fishing waistcoats have every pocket bulging with a multitude of fly boxes and other odds and ends of tackle; large and weighty haversacks and landing nets are much in evidence. When dry-fly fishing you often walk long distances over difficult terrain, so it makes sense to travel as light as possible, which will enable you to enjoy your fishing without undue exertion, and also give you full mobility for any creeping or crawling that may be necessary. For river fishing I take two small fly boxes, one filled with a selection of dry flies in different sizes, plus a few terrestrial patterns and a selection of nymphs for daytime use. The other, for fishing in the evening, will have a selection of spinner and caddis patterns, as well as a few dry flies in case there are any late hatches of upwinged flies. When you are fishing rivers regularly you soon get to know what flies you are likely to require, so what is the point in burdening yourself with extra boxes of flies that you are never likely to use?

PRESENTATION

While the choice of fly can be very important, especially when the trout are feeding selectively, the art of presentation can often make the difference between success and failure. The ability to present the fly not only lightly but also accurately is absolutely essential to success. Other important details to be taken into account include your casting position in relation to the rising trout, the presentation of your fly, depending on where the trout is rising, and also the type of water on which you are fishing and the length of your leader.

First of all, let us look at casting positions. Probably the most important factor is distance. Many fly fishers tend to stand too far away from the trout they are casting to, while others approach too close and eventually spook the fish. The farther away you are, the more difficult it is to see your fly, particularly when using very tiny patterns; it is also more difficult to set the hook. To be consistently successful, always try to take up a position as close as possible, taking advantage of any streamside cover. Remember that at any distance over about fifteen yards it is impossible for the fish to see you, so at this distance it is quite safe to stand up to cast. If you are not on a completely open section of bank, it is usually possible to approach to within ten yards or so, as at this distance only the top of your shoulders and head will be visible and, providing no sudden movements are made, it is unlikely the fish will see you. Don't forget that at both these distances the trout will probably see the movement of your rod if you cast directly overhead; so where possible, cast sideways. Naturally, if you are prepared to crawl and kneel down you can approach much closer, often to within seven or eight yards. If you find a trout rising directly under your own bank you can, of course, approach even closer, providing you are casting upstream to him. It is also worth noting that you can approach much closer if you are directly opposite a rising trout; in this position it is suspected that they have a small arc of restricted visibility (this is fully explained in the section on trout's vision, page 4–22).

While I only wade a river when absolutely necessary, there are times when this is the only sensible approach. You may find stretches of river, particularly on chalkstreams or spring creeks, that run through open meadows or ranchland with no cover at all along the banks.

Under these conditions the only way you will get within casting of a rising trout is to wade up the river, if the water is shallow enough. When wading to fish upstream, remember that sound and water movement are the two most important factors. Wade too quickly and you will send a bow wave ahead of you that will spook the trout; if you wade without placing each foot very gently, the sound of shifting gravel or stones will have the same effect. You will find it is possible to approach to within a couple of rod lengths from directly downstream of a rising fish without spooking him.

The placing of your fly may also be important. On slowish, clear water, a trout will often move up to three or four feet to either side of his lie to intercept a fly, depending upon the depth at which he is holding. The deeper he lies, the farther he may move to intercept your offering, so accuracy is less important. Trout lying very close to the surface require very accurate casting—if the fly is more than a few inches to either side of them, they will not see it. Trout lying in riffles and runs in very fast water also require accurate casting—even if they are lying quite deep or in pockets on the bed of the river, they will only rise to flies that pass directly overhead; to move sideways to any extent would use up too much energy. At times we all come across those very educated trout that, while rising regularly and intercepting nearly every natural fly that passes overhead, steadfastly refuse any pattern you offer them. With such a trout, as a last resort, try casting your fly so that it lands on top of his head. This may spook the fish, but very often he will take it automatically before realizing his error. Very occasionally you will come across a trout rising consistently that rejects all your offerings for a different reason. Either due to light conditions or because he has defective eyesight in one eye or the other, he is unable to see flies that drift directly overhead or down one side. Before giving up on such a trout, try a few casts down the other side.

LEADERS

The choice of leader when fishing the dry fly is a personal matter. Some people prefer manufactured tapered leaders, or tapered braided leaders, while others prefer to make up their own knotted tapered leaders.

In dry-fly fishing, the most important factor is the length of the leader. For most rivers under average conditions a leader of between ten and thirteen feet in length is fine. Under very windy conditions, particularly with strong winds downstream, you will be well advised to reduce the length to eight feet or less. If you are fishing a river with bushy or tree-lined banks, where it is necessary to cast underneath such obstructions to reach rising trout, you will certainly need to keep the length to under ten feet—with a leader much longer than this, it is too difficult to keep a tight enough loop to cast under low overhanging branches.

On the other hand, there are times when a long leader is a distinct advantage. On fine days with light winds, when fishing rivers with open banks and few if any trees or bushes, I always fish as long a leader as possible. The longer the leader, the less the chance of the trout seeing your fly line. So far as the breaking strain of the point or tippet is concerned, I am a firm believer in using as strong a tippet as you can get away with. Up until comparatively recently I rarely used anything above 5X, as I find very fine tippets such as 6 or 7X are necessary only under very exceptional circumstances. Today, with Power Gum in the leader, I often use 4 or even 3X extra-strength nylons, as these are so much finer in diameter than the old-type monofilament.

Over the years much controversy has raged about whether to grease or not. Many eminent fly fishers are against applying any form of flotant. A greased leader lying on the surface tries to dispel the water from it; the globules of air that form along its length are visible from below, and could alert any wary trout to your approaching fly. This is a logical argument against the use of grease, but there is a problem in not using it. An ungreased leader rapidly sinks below the surface, so that when you retrieve your dry fly to re-cast, the sunken part of the leader pulls your dry fly below the surface and wets it. This means that you will have constantly to apply flotant to keep the fly floating. The answer to this problem is a compromise. I keep the leader well greased during a day's dry-fly fishing, but only to within about fifteen inches of the fly. This last fifteen inches I treat with detergent to keep it grease free, so that it sinks just below the surface where it is less visible to the trout.

SELECTING AND FISHING THE DRY FLY

Although there are times when the selection of the dry fly can be very important, on most occasions on the average river a few good general patterns in different sizes will suffice. It is impossible to list all the excellent patterns available, but my personal selection is as follows:

To represent upwinged flies:	Adams
	Royal Wulff
	Iron Blue Dun
	Gold-Ribbed Hare's Ear
	Olive Dun
	Ginger Quill
	Kite's Imperial
	Super Grizzly Emerger
	Poly May Dun
Excellent general patterns for fast, rough water:	Humpy
	Irresistible
	Small Grey Wulff
To represent spinners:	Pheasant Tail
	Red Spinner
	Lunn's Particular
	Pale Watery
To represent caddisflies:	Little Red Sedge
	Goddard Caddis
	Delta Wing Caddis
	Elk Hair Caddis

Before selecting a fly, watch the water and look for any flies that may be hatching, particularly a succession of similar flies. Try to gauge the size, shape, and colour, and then look through your fly box to match them. With practice and some basic angling entomology, you should have little difficulty in identifying the hatch, and selecting a matching artificial.

DRAG

This is one of the greatest enemies of the dry-fly fisherman. There is nothing that will spook a trout and send him running for cover quicker than a poorly cast fly that drags as it approaches him. Trout that are feeding upon literally hundreds of flies each day do not expect to see an approaching fly suddenly accelerate towards them moving faster than the current or maybe even against it. The trout must regard such a phenomenon with the same startled surprise that we would experience if we observed an elephant charging towards us in the middle of a busy town. At times flies may struggle to release themselves from the surface film and move an inch or two; in very windy conditions they may be blown across the surface for short distances; and of course there are some species of caddis that hatch in open water and skitter across the surface often for quite a distance in order to become airborne, but none of these will appear unnatural to a trout and scare him like a dragging fly.

It is disparities in surface currents that cause drag, which are much worse on some rivers than others. Those rivers with an even flow and not too many bends are seldom a problem, nor are freestone rivers flowing over small boulders, stones, or a fairly even bedrock. The worst are those rivers with many tight bends, big boulders, weed, or other obstructions that divert the current. Strange to relate, chalkstreams and spring creeks are often the most difficult to fish in this respect, because the heavy aquatic weed growths disperse the current in all directions. Before casting to any rising trout, the surface water should be carefully studied for any signs of drag; in some situations it is possible to cast from a position that will nullify it. For example, you may find trout rising in fast runs, with slack water between you and the fish, but by wading into the river and casting directly up to the trout you can overcome this. If it is too deep to wade you may, by using a longer cast, position yourself sufficiently far downstream to overcome the worst of the drag, or it may be better to approach the fish from the farther bank. When drag cannot be overcome by an advantageous position, the only other recourse is to present your fly with sufficient slack to overcome it. This is achieved by various methods of casting, which are fully described in chapter 7 on special casting techniques (beginning on page 133).

I can still remember very vividly a trout I was fortunate enough to catch a few years ago when fishing with the famed Al Troth. We were float fishing the Beaverkill and discussing drag when Al mentioned we were shortly coming to a small, shallow, very clear feeder stream entering the main river, where two big rainbows were resident that no-one had been able to catch, mainly due to fierce drag. We beached the boat on a sandbar where the feeder entered, and crept over to where he pointed out these two big fish, still in position and fortunately rising to surface flies. There was no cover whatever, so they could only be fished for from directly downstream. They were lying in slack water, but two or three yards above a gravel bar over which very fast water poured. My first cast, presented with very slack line, alighted above one of the fish and to one side—which was a bit of luck, because within twelve inches it accelerated towards me at a tremendous pace. Pausing to consider the problem, I realized that the only chance of taking either of these big trout lay in presenting the fly without drag. The only way to do this was with a wildly exaggerated puddle cast. Positioning myself at an angle of about 45° to the nearer trout so that I would not line him, I presented the fly upwards towards the sky, with a huge open loop, so that the leader fell in coils directly above him. Before the drag of the very fast current could straighten out the leader, the fly, drag-free, passed directly over him and he rose and took it most confidently. With such an exaggerated cast it is all but impossible to present the fly with much accuracy, so I guess the gods were smiling upon me on this occasion.

LACK OF RISING TROUT

On those dour days when few if any trout are rising, what can you do on a fine, pleasant, summer's day when you are perhaps a little reluctant to resort to the nymph? When this happens it is usually due to a shortage of hatching flies, but if there are some flies hatching, even in small numbers, you may find the odd trout rising by walking the river and diligently searching. At other times you may spot a "oncer." This is a trout that may rise once every ten or fifteen minutes, and, providing you marked the spot where you saw the rise fairly accurately, this fish is often catchable if you are prepared to spend a little time continually presenting your fly to where you think he may be lying.

When you come across a day, as you surely will, when no flies are hatching and there is not a rise to be seen, take heart, as even under these conditions it is still possible to take a few fish, providing you have reasonable visibility into the water. From midmorning onwards most trout will be anticipating a hatch, and even if not rising will be on their feeding stations, so the trick here is to walk the water very slowly and carefully looking for any trout on the fin. When one is spotted, present something unusual, such as a large Bluebottle, Beetle, Hopper, or even a Bushy or Goddard Caddis. You will be surprised how often trout can be tempted to rise to such a fly, even when lying at a considerable depth. On freestone or fast rivers with a broken surface, where it is very difficult to spot trout below the surface, try the same patterns and cast your fly into areas where from past experience you know trout are usually lying or, on unfamiliar water, into likely holding spots.

SELECTIVE OR EDUCATED TROUT

I am sure all fly fishers have experience of those frustrating trout that appear to be taking every fly that passes over them yet steadfastly refuse any pattern you may offer. These fish may be feeding selectively on a particular insect or stage, such as the emerging nymph, or hatching or stillborn fly; while the educated trout that has been pricked or caught and returned several times has learnt from past bitter experience to recognize certain concoctions of fur and feather that may pass overhead.

With selective trout a basic knowledge of entomology is a great help, as by close observation of the water surface it is usually possible to identify the fly or stage of fly that the fish may be feeding upon. When feeding in this manner, it is amazing how unerringly they will take just the fly of their choice when several different species are hatching. If you are uncertain what the trout may be feeding upon, it is a good ploy to approach the problem by elimination. First of all, try one or two different colours and sizes of Skues-type nymphs fished just below the surface. If these are not accepted, try one or two emerger patterns fished in the surface film, and if these are also refused try fishing some stillborn patterns on the surface. Finally, try some standard dry flies in different sizes, and if these also bring no joy—go and look for another fish.

There is one other technique that often proves successful. It involves accurate casting and good rod handling and is a method I employ with a difficult trout before going through the process of elimination. Cast your fly a yard or so directly above the rising trout, and just before it reaches him give a quick but short lift with the rod tip. This in effect activates the fly on the surface and moves it an inch or so, fooling the trout into thinking it is a fly struggling to escape. This has to be carried out very delicately—move the fly more than an inch or so and you are likely to spook him. Two of my fishing buddies on the river Kennet, Neil Patterson and Ron Clark, are absolute masters of this technique, and I have seen them take many all-but-impossible trout by this method.

If you are fishing on hard-fished waters, it is worth noting that a large proportion of the trout will steadfastly refuse to take the freshly hatched duns on the surface, as they will be feeding exclusively on the emerging duns in the surface film. This is a form of selectivity but one brought about by necessity rather than by preference. On such waters they have learnt the hard way to associate the floating fly with danger. The problem with these trout is that to all intents and purposes they are feeding upon the surface, as it is almost impossible to differentiate between the rise to a dun on the surface and the rise to the emerging dun. Therefore, when you find a trout that completely ignores your floating fly time after time, before taking other action sit back and closely watch the freshly hatching flies on the surface passing over the trout. If he ignores these, it is a fair bet he is taking either emergers or possibly stillborn flies.

Educated trout are a completely different proposition, particularly on slow sections of clear water as found on many chalkstreams or spring creeks, where they have all the time in the world to examine your offering at their leisure. Such trout, referred to as "Aunt Sallies," may be found close to areas of easy access or in the vicinity of fishing huts, and so on, where a lot of fly fishers congregate and the trout are subject to heavy fishing pressure. Alternatively, they may be very large trout that have only reached this size after several seasons, during which time they have learnt to distinguish natural flies from apparently innocuous imitations. These fish are extremely difficult to deceive; they rarely take the fly either on the first trigger point, when the leg indentations of the dun are observed in the mirror, or on the second trigger, when the wings appear over the edge of the window. They wait until the whole fly actually appears in their window, where they examine it minutely before acceptance. Sometimes these trout can be taken by offering them an unusual or very tiny pattern, but usually it will require a good imitation that looks, and floats on the surface, just like the natural. Several years ago Brian Clarke and I developed a series of patterns called USD Duns to cover such a situation. These were dressed upside down on hooks (hence the name we bestowed upon them) with wings and a parachute hackle beneath, which floated the fly with the body clear of the surface so that only the hackle indented the film. This closely represented the legs of the natural, which show in the mirror in the same manner. These proved to be very successful for difficult trout, but never became popular, as they were difficult and time consuming to tie.

Regarding the triggers that may influence a trout to accept or reject your fly, generally speaking the slower and clearer the water, the more triggers a wary trout is likely to use. In fast water the trout have little time to scrutinize the approaching fly and must make up their mind literally in a split second whether to accept it or not, using the basic trigger points. Also, in broken or coloured water the conditions make it difficult to use more than a few triggers. The three basic triggers are:

- The indentation of duns' legs in the mirror, or the piercing of the mirror by the bodies and legs of other flies.

- The appearance of the duns' wings or appendages of other flies over the edge of the mirror.
- The appearance of the whole fly in the window.

Other points that may induce a trout to accept or reject a fly are shape or silhouette, size, colour, and possibly behaviour.

SMUTS AND MIDGES

In the UK and Europe, smuts are commonly referred to by anglers as reed smuts, while in the States they are often called riffle smuts. They are all members of the Simulidae family, which includes such common flies as the buffalo and turkey gnats and the infamous blackflies or biting gnats that are such a plague on most waters in the Northern Hemisphere. They are all aquatic species of the very large Diptera order of flat-winged flies. They have stout cylindrical black bodies and two wings, and are exceedingly small. These and other tiny aquatic and terrestrial species are an important source of food for trout on many rivers, yet have been largely ignored by fly fishers until comparatively recently.

In England during the latter half of the last century and the early half of this, trout feeding upon these tiny flies (referred to as the black curse) were considered uncatchable. This was a problem that even defeated the father of the dry fly, the great F. M. Halford, but to be fair to him it was then impossible to produce patterns small enough, because very tiny hooks were not available in those days. With the advent of monofilament after the last war, tippet material became available in finer and finer diameters, which in turn led to the production of smaller hooks. Within a few years hooks in sizes from 20 up to as small as 28 became easily available, and midge fishing, as it is termed today, became a reality.

This form of dry-fly fishing really took off in the early sixties, and quickly became established on the West Coast of America, where much of the early research was carried out. One of the earliest midge patterns to become popular was called a Jassid. This simple pattern was dressed on size 22 and 24 hooks and proved to be very effective, accounting for some very large trout. A proliferation of tiny patterns quickly became available and today there are not only patterns to represent reed smuts and other tiny Diptera but also patterns to represent the hundreds of different species of midges (chironomids) and even microcaddis.

It is only fairly recently that midge fishing has become popular in the UK and Europe, as it took a long time for the secrets of its success to filter across the Atlantic. For years I, like many other fly fishers in the UK, tried with singular lack of success to catch trout using these very tiny patterns tied onto 6 or 7X tippets. First of all, I found it all but impossible to set the hook, and then on those odd occasions when I did actually hook a trout, if it was a big one we would quickly part company due to the very fine tippet material breaking. The solution to both these problems is really very simple, and was revealed to me a little over ten years ago by one of America's top midge fishermen. Before you start fishing, make up a special leader incorporating ten or twelve inches of Power Gum (see the section on leaders, page 79–81); this virtually overcomes the problem of popping your tippet. After you have tied one of these tiny patterns onto your tippet, use a pair of sharp-nosed, model-maker's pliers to offset the hook at the bend, and you will find that this very simple operation will result in a high proportion of hookups.

Smutting trout or trout feeding upon midges or other very tiny flies are normally only to be found in the slower-flowing sections of rivers, backwaters, or eddies. Trout so engaged always lie within a few inches of the surface and, due to their very restricted vision at this shallow depth, rarely rise to intercept a fly more than an inch or so to either side. For this reason, when midge fishing you have to present the artificial very accurately in front of the trout so that it drifts down directly over him. To provide the best chance of setting the tiny hooks being used, it is best to fish upstream to such a trout, preferably at a slight angle so that the leader does not land over his head. This demands accurate casting, as one bad cast will invariably put the trout down. If you are uncertain of your ability in this respect, it is better to take up a casting position to one side of him, between 45° and 90°, and cast your fly upstream and slightly beyond him. Then lifting your rod tip you can skid the fly until it reaches a position where it will pass directly over him. When trout are sipping down such tiny flies, they usually rise every few seconds and, providing your pattern is small enough, they are not too difficult to catch. At times they may be selectively feeding on one particular species, so it may take a little time to discover the correct pattern to use. This may vary from a small dry or emerger to a pupa pattern fished just below the surface.

When I started serious midge fishing using size 22 and 24 hooks, initially I found that, despite Power Gum and offset bends, I was still losing a percentage of fish. The hooks were either tearing out of the trout or opening, due to the very fine wire from which they are man-ufactured. Consequently, I decided to experiment with using larger, stronger hooks. I eventually came up with a pattern that has since proved to be very successful. It is dressed on a size 18 hook—which would normally be far too large for smutting trout, but I overcame this problem by using only half the length of the hook shank on which to dress the fly. This provided a very small silhouette and appeared little larger than if it were tied on a size 22 hook. (This pattern, the Goddard Smut, is included in chapter 9, on page 217–219.)

Several years ago I perfected a pattern called a Suspender Midge Pupa designed to hang in the surface film to represent the hatching pupae of chironomids in stillwater. Many of these pupae in stillwater are quite large and I dressed the imitations on hooks in sizes from 10 to 14. Having carried out many autopsies on the stomach contents of smutting trout, I discovered that, apart from smuts and other small blackflies, there was nearly always a large proportion of very small midge pupae. As a result I dressed some Suspender Midge Pupae on size 18 hooks and tried them out on the river. The results were quite startling. Most of the smutting trout that I offered them to took them with gusto, and this has now proved to be one of my most killing pat-terns for trout taking these tiny midges. The pattern was designed to hang vertically in the surface film on lakes and reservoirs to represent the natural prior to hatching. However, on rivers, due to drag, it would often be drawn into a horizontal position; yet despite this, smutting trout would often turn and chase it as it was dragging and to my astonishment, suck it in with gay abandon. This happened so often that I eventually realized that the fly probably appeared quite natural to a trout. When rising to the surface to hatch these midge pupae initially hang vertically for a period, but as soon as they are ready to hatch into the adult winged form they adopt a horizontal posture and wriggle along beneath the surface film looking for a weak area through which they can emerge onto the surface.

I dress both these Smut and Suspender patterns on size 18 Partridge CS20 arrow-point barbless hooks. Apart from having a nice wide gape, which facilitates hooking, they are also a very strong hook and I have yet to have one break or open out, even on some of the larger double-figure trout that I have caught. When you come across smutting or midging trout, I suggest you try out these two patterns. If they prove unsuccessful you can revert to some of the more traditional patterns on smaller hooks.

EVENING FISHING

Most fly fishers look forward to the evening rise on rivers with keen anticipation, hoping for a glorious two hours or so of intense excitement. For some completely illogical reason, you expect the next fish hooked will turn out to be that legendary monster trout of your dreams. However, in practice, the evening rise seldom lasts this long. It is very often confined to half an hour or so just before dusk, or if you are unlucky and run into bad weather it may even be a nonevent.

If you intend to walk the river looking for rising trout as the sun begins to set, you should be extra cautious at this period. As the light starts to fade, many trout will take up their positions in their feeding lies in anticipation of the feast to come, but until they move close to the surface and commence feeding, they can see very well in this failing light and are alert to danger. Once they start feeding in earnest, and particularly during the half-light of dusk, you can often walk right up to trout without spooking them. From half-light onwards I try to get as close as possible to the trout I am fishing for, often less than a couple of rod lengths, as in this poor light the closer you can get, the more chance you have of seeing your fly on the surface.

During the early part of the season the choice of pattern for evening fishing is not too much of a problem, as it is usually a choice between various spinner patterns, or some of the smaller upwinged duns. As the season progresses the choice will become much more difficult, and by the latter half of the season it can become downright frustrating. It is not so difficult during a prolonged rise that starts early in the evening, as all the time the light is reasonable you can observe what the trout are feeding on and change your pattern accordingly. The problem is greatest when the rise is of short duration and late, when the light is quickly fading. From midsummer onwards the trout have a much wider choice of food—late-hatching upwinged duns, various spinners, various species of caddis both pupae and adults, midges, and smuts, as well as stoneflies, hoppers, and so on. The list is endless. As the rise starts, even if it is late you can usually identify what the trout are rising to and mount an appropriate pattern. Unfortunately, this is seldom effective for very long, as most trout are adept at the art of switching without warning to another form of food. After early success, you find the pattern being consistently refused. It is then a race against time to discover what they have switched to, a battle you more often than not lose. Even if you do discover the answer, by the time you have located the appropriate pattern and tied it on, the rise is often all but over.

Another factor that has to be taken into account is your eyesight. This gradually deteriorates with age and it therefore takes longer and longer to tie on another pattern. These days I am quite happy to change flies and try to keep up with the whims of the trout when the rise starts early and the light is still good, but on those evenings when it does not start until dusk I give myself two choices, neither of which involves changing flies. I try to anticipate upon which natural the trout are most likely to be feeding and mount a corresponding pattern, which I stick with for the rest of the evening; or I tie on a general pattern that I consider most appropriate for the river I am fishing and the time of the year, and stick with this for the rest of the evening. Sometimes, of course, it gets too frustrating and I have to change, with the aid of a torch. My favourite general patterns are a Small Red Sedge, a Black Gnat, or a comparatively new pattern called the Zelon Caddis. This is dressed with a trailing shuck of amber Zelon, a body of olive Antron, and wings of deer hair tied sloping back over the body. It can be tied in various sizes but I prefer it on a long-shank size 14 hook. This is my current favourite general pattern. It can be treated with flotant and fished dry, or it can be degreased and fished in the surface film where, given an occasional tweak, it often results in a savage take.

Quite often these late-starting rises will continue until it is too dark to see your fly on the surface. This is usually very frustrating as, although in the half-light you can see many trout still rising regularly, you have only the vaguest idea where your fly has landed in relation to the rise you are covering. You have no option but to strike when the fish rises and hope it is your fly that he has taken. Very often it is not, and the act of striking puts the fish down. Fortunately, I have fairly recently discovered at least a reasonable answer to this problem. When I can no longer see my fly on the surface, with the aid of a torch I tie on one of my size 18 Suspender Midge Pupae, which float in the surface film, and cast this hard onto the water surface ahead of the rising fish. This makes a distinct plop as it alights that can be seen even when it is almost dark, so you can then judge roughly where your fly is in relation to the rising trout. Most trout are used to feeding on midge pupae very late in the evening, so they seem to take this Suspender with confidence. After I have made the cast, usually upstream, I try to lift the rod tip at the same speed as the current, which keeps me in touch with the fly. If you judge this correctly you can often feel the take, which takes the guesswork out of striking.

Some of the most rewarding evening rises occur when there is a good fall of upwinged spinners. They vary in size and body colour according to species, so on those evenings when clouds of these egg-laying spinners are observed dipping over the water it is a good plan to spend a few minutes locating a spot where the current flows close to the bank, so you can establish the size and colour of the dead and dying spinners as they drift along the surface towards you. You can then mount a corresponding pattern on your tippet, well greased to float in a similar manner. It is, however, easy to be fooled during one of these spinner falls. The spinners of most of the *Baetis* genus of flies, which accounts for quite a large number of species, lay their eggs underwater. They accomplish this by crawling down anything that protrudes above the surface, such as rushes, aquatic weed, posts, or even bridge supports. After they have laid their eggs, they die and drift downstream with the current. A large proportion eventually float up to the surface, where they drift along just below the surface film. When the trout are sipping them down, the form of rise is the same as if they were feeding upon spinners floating on the surface, so it is very easy to be misled. When the trout feed upon these they are often very selective, and will completely ignore any other species of spinners floating along on top of the film. So if you come across a trout that rises avidly to spinners but continually ignores your pattern, tie on a small red spinner, sparsely dressed and degreased so that it will fish just below the surface.

On those evenings, which unfortunately seem to occur far too often, when there is little insect activity and few trout rising, if all normal methods fail try an emerger pattern. There are now many good emerger patterns that can be tried; some imitate hatching upwinged flies while others imitate hatching caddisflies, or you can even try some of the many Caddis Pupa artificials. Whichever type you decide to offer the trout, it should be well degreased and fished just below the surface and given an occasional tweak to animate it. This method will provide a few trout where otherwise you may have had a blank. As an alternative to special emerger patterns, I have in the past had considerable success using some of the old traditional, very sparsely dressed Yorkshire Spider patterns. These are normally fished as wet flies, but I find they can be very effective fished just below the surface.

DRY-FLY TIPS

Occasionally, close into the bank, you may come across a trout that is rising immediately above some herbage or twigs extending out into the river between you and the fish, so that it is impossible to cover him with a normal cast. In some cases it may be possible to move upstream and cast down to him, but in such a situation more often than not there will be trees or obstructions preventing this. Over the years this has happened to me many times, but quite often I have been able to extract the odd fish. Cast over the obstruction and then, by pulling very gently on the line, dangle the fly so that it skims the surface and is given movement by the current. If you can get the fly close enough, trout often find this movement irresistible and will take confidently. If you do not get the fly close enough on the first cast, by lifting the rod tip very slowly you can often retrieve the fly without it snagging on the obstruction and make a fresh cast.

On some rivers trout seem to be inordinately fond of taking up lies close to the banks where tussocks or other obstructions provide small areas of slack water on the edge of the faster current. When this occurs on the bank you are fishing, it is no problem. When it occurs on the far bank, which may not be accessible, you will have no alternative other than to make a long cast, and it may be impossible to obtain a float free of drag with your fly over the fish. In such a situation, an effective ploy is to cast your fly deliberately onto the far bank just above the rising trout, and then, with a flick of the rod tip, lift it off so that it falls lightly on the water. This is particularly effective when fishing with beetle or hopper patterns, but you will have to accept that you are going to lose the odd fly if it gets badly snagged.

Trout are also very fond of taking up lies beneath overhanging trees or bushes where it is quite impossible to cast a fly. In such situations, it is often possible to present a fly from the bank beneath the tree by engaging in the ancient art of dibbling. To do this correctly, your leader, including your tippet, should be no longer than seven feet. In fact, the shorter it is, the more control you will have over your fly. Pull all of your leader and about two feet of your fly line through the top ring, and then slowly inch your rod tip out over the water in front of the rising trout through the branches of the tree, swing your fly out onto the surface, and drift or dance it down over the fish. This can be a very effective way of hooking a trout, but it is exceedingly difficult to play the fish through and around the branches. If you land one in three of such fish, you are doing well. Of course, great stealth and very slow movement are required to get into position without the trout seeing you, but these are easier to accomplish than you would imagine, as the tree behind and over you provides excellent cover even from the most wary of trout.

Small rivers, chalk and limestone streams, and spring creeks are often littered with small bridges, and you can rest assured that wherever there is a bridge, one or more large trout will be holding beneath it. Furthermore, the lower the bridge, the bigger the trout, and the more difficult it will be to cast a fly up under far enough to cover them. Apart from this, for some strange reason whenever you try to cast a fly up under a bridge the wind is sure to be blowing into your face, which makes a difficult task almost impossible. It is often necessary to wade out into the stream to cast up under a bridge, and on the small rivers on which these are found, it is extremely difficult to manoeuver a standard fly rod of eight or nine feet in length. The answer to this is to remove your fly reel and place it in an open pocket where the fly line will be free to pull off it, and, presuming you have a two-piece rod, remove the butt section and use the tip section only to cast your fly. With a little practice, you will find you can comfortably aerialize fifteen yards of fly line, which is enough to cover any trout under most bridges. When you do hook a trout, though, I can promise you some fun.

On most rivers, large or small, you will nearly always find shallower sections with long runs of fast and broken water. These well-aerated sections often hold many trout, but in the fast water they will only rise to a fly that passes directly overhead. Rises are very difficult to spot in such rapid and broken currents, and random casting is time consuming. In these conditions, I find it both rewarding and very exciting to dance down a big Bushy Caddis. Well grease both your fly and leader and cast directly across the river. When your fly drifts downstream and the line straightens, lift your rod tip and skate the fly over the surface towards you. Takes are usually explosive and savage, but you will have to learn to hesitate for half a second or so before setting the hook. Strike too quickly and you will pull the fly out of the trout's mouth; hesitate too long and he will have dropped it. I usually start off with a large, well-hackled fly, as this creates the maximum disturbance to attract the trout. However, occasionally you may find, even when you are certain you are timing your strike correctly, that you are just not hooking any fish. If this happens, try presenting a sparsely hackled fly. If this does not work, change to a much smaller pattern.

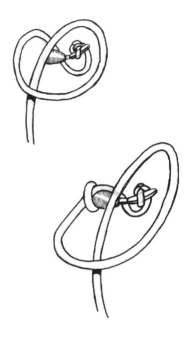

To dance a fly successfully across a fast run or riffle requires a certain expertise. In rough water it is desirable to create a considerable wake, while on flatter water too much wake will scare the trout. To a certain degree the amount of wake your fly creates can be governed by the knot used to tie the pattern onto your tippet. There are several knots

Figure 29. Move the riffle hitch away from the eye to increase the amount of wake the fly makes.

that will achieve the desired effect, but in my opinion the best way of doing this is to use a couple of half hitches behind the eye of the hook after you have tied it on. (See figure 29.) I believe this was first suggested by a well-known American angler named Brackett, who pointed out that the amount of wake could be controlled by the position of these half hitches. In practice, I have found this very valuable.

Over the years, fly fishers have posed the question: "If you were restricted to only one pattern for a whole season's fishing, which artificial would you choose?" This is a very difficult question to answer, as it depends on so many different factors. By no stretch of the imagination can a single pattern be acceptable all the time or cope with the many different flies and other fauna upon which trout feed. During this century many eminent fly fishers have experimented and written about how they have restricted themselves to using maybe half a dozen different patterns during a season, and in most cases have reported little difference in their catches. My late friend Major Oliver Kite used only three different patterns during the last three or four years of his life: his own famous Imperial pattern, a Pheasant Tail Nymph, and a Pheasant Tail Spinner, which he assured me covered most situations. Certainly his normally high catch rate did not diminish during this period; if anything it increased. As he would often say with a wry smile when asked, "I now waste less time changing flies." Today if I were asked this question I think I would be prepared to take a gamble on a new pattern that I have recently developed, which I dress on hook sizes from 14 up to 20. This is my Black Gnat and is broadly based on one of the oldest traditional dry flies ever invented. Trout often seem to be particularly attracted to dark-coloured flies, and I have noticed on many occasions that, even when they have been feeding selectively on one par-ticular species, they will invariably deviate and pick up the odd blackfly that passes by. Over the past two seasons this new pattern has accounted for many large trout. I tend to use it on those odd days when hatches of flies are sparse, as it seems to have the ability to pull trout up from the depths even when very few fish are rising.

GRAYLING

No chapter on dry-fly fishing would be complete without mentioning the grayling, often referred to as "our lady of the stream." It is one of the very few species of truly wild fish that is still available to the fly fisher in considerable numbers. Sad to relate, though, ever since the last century and even to this day in England on many of the premier fly-only streams, grayling are looked upon as vermin to be removed every season by any means possible. This in my opinion is a great shame, as I consider them to be a more worthy opponent than trout; on the dry fly, the larger specimens are much more difficult to catch.

Grayling are synonymous with clear, swift, unpolluted rivers and are widely distributed throughout the Northern Hemisphere, although recently numbers have decreased in many rivers in the States.

In Europe, particularly in some of the Austrian and Slovenian streams, specimens of over six pounds are not uncommon, while in many arctic regions a closely related species referred to as the arctic grayling grows even larger. In England they rarely reach this size, and any grayling of over two pounds is looked upon as a specimen. There are now a rapidly growing number of fly fishers who specialize in grayling fishing, particularly during the winter months, the closed season for trout.

I love my grayling fishing and in recent years have spent an increasing amount of time pursuing these delightful fish. I am privileged to fish a beat on the upper river Test, and, although this is well stocked with large brown trout, I must admit that during the latter half of the summer I spend more time fishing for the grayling than the trout. We are most fortunate to have many large grayling in this stretch of the river Test, largely thanks to our river keeper, Terry, who for the last twenty years has nurtured the grayling, unlike most of the river keepers up and down the valley, who still net them out of the river every season. As a result of Terry's policy, I enjoy superb fishing and every season catch and return many grayling well over the magic two-pound figure. I vividly recall a fantastic morning's grayling fishing on this stretch a couple of seasons ago. At the time I was fishing with one of my regular fishing buddies, Bernard Cribbins, and during a three-hour session when we fished side by side and took it in turns to cast, we caught and released from a deep run around a large bend in the river thirty-six grayling. The smallest of these was well over a pound, while five were well over two pounds; the largest was a superb specimen of two pounds, fourteen ounces. Most of them were taken on the dry fly.

Grayling may be fished for using the same tactics as used for trout; they are very susceptible to a deeply fished nymph. Many years ago Frank Sawyer, river keeper on the Upper Avon, perfected a nymph especially for grayling fishing that he called his Killer Bug. A very simple pattern— a few twists of greyish wool on a weighted hook—it proved an instant success, and has, at least in England, accounted for more grayling than any other fly. At times grayling will rise readily to a dry fly—particularly the smaller specimens, which is probably why they were so heartily disliked by so many dry-fly purists. Unlike trout, grayling tend to hug the bottom of the river so have to be tempted to rise, which is why many of the traditional grayling flies are rather large and gaudy compared to most trout flies. Over the last century or so, while most fly fishers fishing the chalkstreams abhorred these fish, grayling on many of the north-country streams were a much-sought-after species. Consequently, in these areas many excellent patterns were produced that are still just as effective as they used to be. Here is a selection in case you should like to try some of them: Red Tag, Terry's Terror, Sturdy's Fancy, Bradshaw's Fancy, Sage, and the White Witch. One thing they all have in common is a brightly coloured tag on the tail. Other well-known patterns are Steel Blue Bumble, Furnace Bumble, Treacle Parkin, Waterhen Bloa, and Partridge & Orange. Grayling often seem to prefer patterns that ride high on the surface, like the White Witch, but they are also susceptible to patterns fished in the surface or even well below it. A well-known pattern called Rolt's Witch was developed specifically to deal with these large deep-lying grayling that often refuse to rise. This is dressed with a weighted body so that it will sink, and can be offered to them at the same level at which they are lying. I still use some of these old traditional patterns and find that Terry's Terror is particularly effective on some of the chalk-streams. Dressed on a size 12 or 14 hook, this pattern will often entice some of the larger deep-lying grayling to rise. However, when the grayling are free rising I prefer quite small flies, and the three patterns that I find most killing are a small grey-bodied Sparkle Dun, Terry's Terror, and my own Super Grizzly Emerger, dressed on size 18 hooks.

BIG TROUT

The lure of the big trout is one facet of fly fishing that will remain with all of us until we have made that last cast. Talking with many very experienced fly fishers, it seems that all of us go through a similar sequence from the time we catch our first trout. As soon as we have become proficient, our main desire is to catch as many trout as possible in a day's fishing. This may last for several years but sooner or later we will lose the urge to catch every trout we see, and start hunting specifically for big trout. Then a time will arrive when your ego demands that you concentrate mainly on catching the more difficult or educated trout. This is a period when, if another fly fisher mentions an uncatchable trout, you will be like a greyhound straining at the leash waiting to be shown where he is so that you can spend the rest of the day trying to catch him. I went through this period several years ago when I had a rod on the famous Abbot's Barton stretch of the river Itchen, the same stretch that the great G. E. M. Skues fished for most of his life. The water is gin clear and relatively slow flowing, and the trout there have all the time in the world to inspect your fly before rejecting or accepting it. This provided the most demanding fly fishing I ever experienced and is one stretch of water where close imitation with your pattern really applies. Many times over the fifteen or so years that I fished it, I would be informed of the location of a difficult fish—then often it would still be rising as I left when it was too dark to fish any more. I would return the next Saturday and the next to do battle, until I eventually caught it or admitted defeat. Today I find that I am just content to be at the waterside and often spend more time walking the water and chatting to other fly fishers than actually fishing. However, I must admit that the sight of a really big trout feeding still starts the adrenaline pumping, the legs shaking, and the hands trembling to such an extent that I have difficulty in tying on a fly to present to him.

Over the years I have been fortunate enough to catch many large trout. A percentage of these were caught by perseverance, while others were caught by observation and careful planning, but many were taken more by luck than judgement, by being in the right place at the right time. I can clearly recall one such incident from five or six years ago. At the time I was fishing as a guest on my friend Alan Mann's stretch of the Test. Crossing a bridge early in the evening, I slipped and badly lacerated my leg. As it was quite a long walk back to his house and I was in some pain, about halfway there I decided to take a long rest on a convenient riverside seat. Within half an hour the evening rise had started. Just as I was about to go on I noticed a rise under the far bank and, by the displacement of water, I knew it must be a really big trout.

All pain forgotten, I commenced casting. To cut a long story short, an hour and a half later, after trying over a dozen different patterns of flies, I eventually succeeded in taking him almost at dusk on a size 18 Suspender Midge Pupa. He turned out to be one of the fattest brown trout I have ever caught; he weighed eight and a half pounds but was only twenty-two inches in length.

6

NYMPH FISHING IN RIVERS

S INCE I STARTED FLY FISHING in the early fifties, I have
been privileged to fish with many of the top nymph fishermen
both in Europe and in the USA. Most of them have impressed me
greatly with their skill, dedication, and powers of observation but none
more so than my mentor, the late Major Oliver Kite. Ollie, as he was
known to his friends, can only be described as a phenomenal nymph
fisherman; not only did he have all the normal skills honed to a very
fine degree, but he also had that sixth sense that is the hallmark of all
really top nymph fishermen. Through the sixties and early seventies we
were great friends and fished together on countless occasions.
Although I considered myself a pretty competent nymph fisher, it was
a real eye-opener to watch Ollie—a great character and a very gener-
ous person—at work. I was indeed fortunate to be taught the finer
points and skills by a veritable master. He had exceptional eyesight and
never wore Polaroids. He considered these newfangled devices to be
quite unnecessary. Despite this, at least in the early days, he almost
always spotted a feeding fish before me. Many times I have seen him

cast his tiny Pheasant Tail Nymph to a feeding fish and then for no apparent reason successfully set the hook, despite the fact that I had not seen any indication at all that the trout had taken his offering. When questioned, he would say, "Oh I just knew he had taken it." This, of course, was his amazing sixth sense in operation. In later years I was to experience this myself. Pupils to whom I have been demonstrating the hooking of a trout on a nymph have asked me the same question, to which I have been unable to give a logical answer.

For many years I became a dedicated nymph fisherman and much preferred it to dry-fly fishing, until it got to the point where if I spotted a fish nymphing I knew there was more than a good chance I would catch it, so the challenge departed. Now the wheel has completed its full circle and I only fish a nymph when there is little or no possibility of taking fish on the dry. I have finally realized that dry-fly fishing is in fact a greater challenge, as, although when trout are rising regularly to hatching flies they are usually extremely easy to catch, when they are feeding selectively they can be very difficult. In addition to this, during a normal day's fishing you are likely to come across the odd big trout that has only survived to reach this size by his ability to recognize the difference between an artificial and a natural fly. Such a trout is often a tremendous challenge.

Now what of the equipment required for nymph fishing? The most important item is the rod. The length will depend to a large extent upon the size of river you are fishing. For large, fast, freestone rivers you may require a nine-foot rod, but then if most of your fishing is confined to small streams or brooks you may have to consider a rod as short as seven feet. Personally I favour a rod eight-and-a-half feet in length, as this is a good compromise and will cover most situations. A good nymph-fishing rod should have a certain amount of tip action because to fish a nymph, particularly a weighted one, correctly, it should be delivered to pierce the surface rather than land upon it like a dry fly. Many years ago, before the advent of glass or carbon rods, most of us used split-cane. I used two rods, one with a soft action for dry flies and another with a modicum of tip action for nymph fishing. During the transition from split-cane through glass to carbon, and even with the introduction of graphite, I still stuck with my split-cane nymph rod, as I found that with most of the other types the tip action was too severe, which often resulted in the nymph springing back at the extremity of the cast. However, I must admit that most of the modern graphite or boron rods are a joy to use and it is now several years since I retired my split-cane rod. My current favourite is a Sage graphite 111 eight-and-a-half-foot 5-weight rod, which I use exclusively for all my river fishing. If you have a modicum of casting ability, it is capable of casting and presenting both nymph and dry fly perfectly.

Traditionally, the double-tapered fly line has been favoured on rivers both for dry-fly and nymph fishing, and I think to a large extent it still is favoured by the average fly fisher. Modern fly lines are so sophisticated that I find I can now present a forward-tapered line just as lightly as the old double-tapered lines, and not only does the forward taper allow me to cast that extra distance when required, but it also cuts into the wind much better. I therefore use a 6-weight forward taper, which is perfect on my 5-weight rod whatever the conditions. So far as the leader is concerned, I favour one between ten and twelve feet, as I find this is the optimum length for casting a nymph correctly and will cover most situations. It is sometimes necessary to use a much longer leader, such as on bright days when fishing very clear, shallow water in open meadows or ranchland with little bankside cover, but I try to avoid this as it is much more difficult to present the nymph correctly.

THE TRADITIONAL NYMPH

Nymph fishing was first introduced amid considerable controversy by that great fly fisher G. E. M. Skues, who is now looked upon as the father of nymph fishing. His nymphs were unweighted and were designed to fish in or just below the surface film. They represented nymphs of the upwinged flies rising to the surface where they hatched into the winged adults, a method still popular under certain circumstances to this day. It was not until well into the middle of this century, though, that the most popular form of nymph fishing as we know it today was introduced by that most knowledgeable of all river keepers,

Frank Sawyer. So far as I am aware, he was the first person to perfect a weighted nymph, formed from copper wire, and to develop a method of fishing it to deep-lying trout. His now famous Pheasant Tail Nymph created quite a sensation when it first appeared and quickly became established as *the* standard pattern. Over the intervening years a whole host of weighted patterns has appeared, many of them aimed at exact imitation of the many varieties of natural upwinged nymphs, prime examples of the fly tier's art. So far as I am concerned, unlike some dry flies, exact or even close imitation, except in exceptional circumstances, is completely unnecessary. When it comes to weighted nymphs, presentation and the action of the artificial underwater is of far more importance than the actual pattern being used. On rivers, unlike stillwater, I use just a few patterns (except when it comes to nymphs representing the various species of stoneflies and caddisflies, which is discussed on page 44–48). Most species of upwinged nymphs are either darkish brown or pale to watery olive, so I carry three patterns in various sizes: a Pheasant Tail Nymph to represent the darker species, a flat, dark pattern to represent the stone clingers, and my own PVC Nymph to represent the lighter-coloured species. My nymph is weighted with copper wire like Sawyer's pattern, upon which it is based. It is probably a closer representation of the natural than his, but it does take a little longer to dress. The only other nymphs I carry for river fishing are Sawyer's Killer Bug for grayling and my own Mating Shrimp pattern for trout browsing shrimps (cress bugs) off the weed, or a heavily weighted version to get way down into deep pools or runs.

I also carry a relatively new pattern that I call a Shrymph, which represents neither a nymph nor a shrimp but is somewhere between the two. I originally developed this for deep-lying grayling but I have since found it is an exceptionally killing pattern for trout as well.

Now how should you fish these nymphs? This will depend to a large extent on the type of water you are fishing. While weighted nymph patterns representing natural nymphs of the various species of upwinged flies may be fished in any rivers where these predominate, they are undoubtedly most effective on clearwater streams where the trout can be seen beneath the surface. In such clear streams where nymphing trout may be observed from a considerable distance, you can fish either upstream or down. Personally, I always prefer to cast my nymph upstream to a trout as, from this position, when you strike you are pulling the hook into the fish's mouth, which in most cases ensures a good hookup. When fishing downstream to a trout the percentage of hookups is considerably less, as you are tending to pull the hook out of the fish's mouth when you strike. Apart from this you are more likely to be seen by the trout when fishing downstream to him.

Over the years I have met fly fishers who never fish with weighted nymphs, and, while a small percentage of these have never tried and look upon themselves as dry-fly purists, the majority only fish the dry fly because they have never been able to master the techniques necessary to become successful nymph fishermen. With dry-fly fishing only two dimensions have to be taken into account: the distance to be cast to cover the rising trout, and the accuracy to cast above or nearby him. With nymph fishing you have to take into account an extra dimension: the depth at which to present the nymph. Apart from this, good eyesight is necessary, not only to spot trout feeding below the surface, but also to interpret correctly the signs or movement indicating that they have taken your offering.

THE DEAD DRIFT

When fishing weighted nymphs, many fly fishers consider it necessary to apply movement to the nymph to attract the fish. While this may eventually be required, I always start by offering the artificial without movement at the same level at which the fish is feeding. This is termed the dead-drift method, and for it to succeed it is essential to present the nymph at the right level. This can be achieved in two ways: either by the size and weight of nymph used, or by the distance the nymph is presented above or in front of the fish. The smaller and lighter the nymph, the farther upstream it will have to be cast in order to reach the level at which the fish is feeding. When fishing with tiny nymphs, say size 16 and upwards, it is difficult if not impossible to see them once they have sunk more than a few inches below the surface. It does therefore require some expertise, not only to judge the casting distance upstream but also to know when the nymph is close to the fish. Unless a fish is feeding on the bottom, very deep, or deep in fast water where you have to fish large, heavily weighted patterns, I prefer to fish as small a nymph as possible; in my experience the smaller the nymph, the more effective it seems to be. I normally try three or four passes with the darkish-coloured Pheasant Tail Nymph, and if this is not accepted I try my own lighter-coloured PVC Nymph; if this is also refused I resort to an induced take (see page 116).

The most difficult aspect of nymph fishing is knowing when to strike. In its simplest form, this will be obvious, as you will see the fish open and close his mouth as he accepts the nymph. Many years ago the great Skues coined the phrase the "little white blink" to describe the mouth opening, and it can be easily seen if the water is clear enough. If you are not in a position actually to see the head of the fish and the mouth opening, other, more subtle indications must be looked for. Unless the nymph approaches exactly on line and at the same level as the fish is lying, he will have to move to intercept it, and this will be indicated by a lift upwards or from side to side. Wait until he starts to return to his lie and then strike. At other times there may only be a barely perceptible movement, or even no movement at all, and yet, after much experience, for some inexplicable reason you will know that he has taken your nymph. This is your sixth sense coming into operation. At other times, especially if you are using the induced-take method and moving the nymph, he will turn and follow it towards you. When this happens it is difficult to time the strike. Ideally, you should hesitate briefly after he has opened his mouth, wait for him to turn, and then set the hook. Unfortunately, many trout will turn and follow the nymph but not take it, and in my experience if this happens several times, it is best to leave him and look for another fish, as your chances of tempting him are pretty slim.

THE INDUCED TAKE

To the best of my knowledge this method was first used in England and is applied when fishing upstream to a feeding fish. It is certainly a very killing method, and is accomplished by lifting the tip of the rod as the nymph drifts down to the feeding fish. While many natural nymphs drift or swim downstream with the current and can be simulated with the dead-drift method, others swim up to the surface to hatch, and it is these that the induced take simulates. When the tip of the rod is lifted upwards, it moves the artificial nymph in a very natural manner towards the surface, which the fish find irresistible. The fish should still be watched for indications of a take, but they will very often hook themselves as the rod is lifted. On most American waters, where many fly fishers fish downstream, the same method is employed but is called the Leisenring lift. The method was perfected by the great American wet-fly fisherman James Leisenring.

FISHING THE WATER

On many sections of the English chalkstreams where nymph fishing is not allowed until after 1 July, you are restricted to unweighted or small weighted nymphs fished upstream to trout that you can see. Fishing the water is frowned upon. On the many streams and rivers where this attitude does not prevail, fishing the water is a good alternative, and in fact in fast, turbid, or coloured water it is the only practical method. When fishing the water with a nymph, you have to read the water, endeavour to pick out the likely lies, and present your nymph at the level at which you think the fish may be feeding. This is governed to a large extent by the depth of the water. Your required depth can be achieved either by the weight of the nymph or by heavily greasing your leader, or by a combination of both. The only indication you will have that a fish has taken your nymph will be a slight check on your line as it drifts down with the current. It is therefore necessary to watch the end of your fly line like a hawk, or, better still, the end of your greased leader lying on the surface where it enters the water, and, at the slightest sign of any check or movement, to strike. In some cases the movement may be caused by weed or other obstructions beneath the surface, but in most cases it will be by a fish. The induced take or Leisenring lift may also be employed, as both methods can be very effective at this time, particularly on slow-flowing water where very often your nymph may be taken without showing any draw or movement on the leader at all.

STRIKE INDICATORS

This is another method of fishing a nymph that is becoming increasingly popular. I am not sure where it originated, probably in the States at least two decades ago. The first indicators were strips of bright-coloured wool, which were secured onto the leader with a clinch loop. The position of the indicator on the leader was established according to the depth of the water or the depth at which it was desired to swim the nymph. The indicator should be secured twice the length up the leader as is desired to fish the nymph. In recent years, however, custom-made indicators have become available in a wide range of sizes and shapes, made of various buoyant materials from cork to hollow plastic. Most of these have a tapered hole through the centre, so that they can be slid up the leader onto the end of the fly line, and then the length of the leader can be reduced or extended according to the depth desired. Available in bright fluorescent colours, they can be seen clearly at considerable distances and allow you to fish fast, turbulent, or broken water where it would be all but impossible to see the end of your fly line or greased leader. Personally I do not like indicators—certainly they have no place on clear or even slow and placid waters, where they are more likely to spook the fish than increase your chances of catching them. On rough or fast, broken water, where it is often necessary to use them, I much prefer a small piece of fluorescent wool soaked in flotant and secured to the leader. This can be trimmed to as small a size as possible to support the size of nymph being used. Buoyant indicators in any shape or form have been banned on all New Zealand waters, a rule of which I heartily approve. You are now only allowed to use wool or yarn indicators—maybe this rule has been introduced in view of the number of sheep inhabiting the Islands. Indicators do have one other very distinct advantage in that they allow you to fish a much larger area of water than would otherwise be possible. Due to the considerable distances at which they can be seen, they can be delivered upstream as far as you can cast, and then fished downstream for as long as you can pay out line without getting drag.

THE DROPPER NYMPH

This is a method brought to my attention over twelve years ago when I first visited New Zealand. Where it originated I do not know, but it had already been established for several years on the famous Tongariro River for catching steelhead. This is a very powerful, turbulent, and fast-flowing river where it is absolutely essential to swim your nymph as close to the bottom as possible. The only way to get a nymph anywhere near the bottom in this river is to wrap lead around your leader, a far-from-satisfactory method. The ever resourceful Kiwis solved the problem in an ingenious way. On the end of the tippet they tied a large, heavily weighted nymph, to the bend of which, using an eight- to twelve-inch length of nylon monofilament, they attached a tiny Hare & Copper Nymph on which to catch the fish. (See figure 30.) They have found in practice that most of the time the trout accept the tiny nymph, but occasionally a trout will be hooked on the large one. This dropper-nymph combination is always fished by the Tongariro fly fishers in conjunction with an indicator and is fished as far up- and downstream as possible.

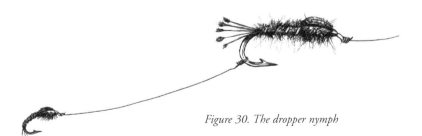

Figure 30. The dropper nymph

Within the last two or three years, some European fly fishers have refined this dropper nymph for fishing for grayling without the indicator, and this has proved to be very killing. I have recently adopted the method myself for large deep-lying grayling in the winter and have found it extremely effective. I have found that the most efficient method of fishing this combination is by casting a relatively short distance upstream; by holding the fly rod very high with no slack between the rod tip and the nymph, even the gentlest of takes can be felt. This method can be used wading in fast, freestone rivers, and is particularly effective in either fast or deep runs close to the bank where you have cover from trees or bushes behind you, which will allow you to get close to the fish without being seen too clearly.

Another method of getting down to trout or grayling in deep, fast water is to use one of the fast-sink, braided, tapered leaders, which can be used with or without an indicator. When casting with these or, indeed, with large weighted nymphs, it is essential to wait longer on your backcast for the line to extend fully behind you before commencing the forward cast to deliver the fly. Failure to do this will result in the leader and fly landing in an untidy heap on the water in front of you.

On fast, wide rivers that are not too deep and have few rocks or large boulders or other obstructions, a medium- or even fast-sink fly line in conjunction with a very short leader may be utilized to get your nymph close to the bottom. With this you should cast upstream diagonally across the river, mending the line as it comes downstream to stop any drag that will lift the nymph off the bottom. With this method you can fish as far downstream as you can cast up, and fish are often tempted to take as the nymph is pulled to the surface at the end of the drift.

SKUES' NYMPHS

Having dealt fairly extensively with the deep-fished nymph, let us now look briefly at the subsurface- or surface-type nymph as perfected by the great Skues so many years ago. His nymphs were unweighted and could therefore only be fished either in the surface film or a little way below, which on most trout rivers with a fairly good flow of water meant that, in practice, it was impossible to fish them at a much greater depth than about six inches. Now, while I think that Skues was probably the most innovative and observant fly fisher ever to put pen to paper, and that his new method was at the time a revelation, I do not think the result would have been the same today. At the time he introduced his nymphs, fishing on the chalkstreams in England was confined to the dry fly. If you could not tempt a trout to take a dry there was no alternative, so there is little doubt that his new method opened up new horizons for fly fishers of his era. Trout, in order to conserve energy, will usually seek out the food that is available to them with the minimum of effort, which means that during a hatch of surface flies, particularly when it is rather sparse, the trout will often take the nymph lying inert in the surface or the emerging dun as it struggles to leave its shuck, ignoring the freshly hatched dun on the surface, which may take to flight before they can intercept it. Today we are not so dependent on Skues' nymphs to solve this problem as we also have a wide variety of both emerger dry-fly and hatching-nymph patterns available to us that the trout will often accept more readily than the Skues-type nymph.

The only other time that the unweighted nymph is useful is when the bulge rise is observed. This is caused by trout feeding just below the surface on the ascending nymphs, which is a phenomenon usually confined to stretches of fairly shallow water (see page 25–26).

FISHING THE CADDIS LARVA AND PUPA

In most rivers during the latter half of the summer, hatches of caddis-flies often predominate, particularly in the late afternoons and evenings. Unfortunately, by this time of the day with the sun getting lower and lower, visibility into the water is very restricted, until it is all but impossible to see into the water at all. It is therefore not a practical proposition to fish imitations of the underwater stages of the caddis (apart from larval patterns in slow-flowing water) in the same manner that we fish with artificial nymphs representing the early stages of the upwinged flies.

The caddisflies have two separate underwater stages of interest to the fly fisher. The bulk of their lives is spent in the larval stage on the bed of the river; most species are case making, although some are free swimming, while a few others live in the crevices between rocks and stones on the riverbed, where they form nets to trap their food. The only way the trout can feed upon any of these species is to grub them off the bottom. At times, though, the free-swimming and also the net-making species, and even some of the case makers, vacate their cases and are swept along with the current, where the trout will feed upon them quite happily often well off the bottom. The other stage of interest to fly fishers occurs when the mature pupae are ready to hatch into adults, and leave the bed of the river to swim either to the surface or towards the shore to transpose. These caddis pupae are slow swimmers and are at the mercy of the trout as soon as they leave the bed of the river. Some trout feed upon them in midwater or follow them to the surface, while in dense hatches many trout feed upon those species that hatch in open water just below or in the surface film as they transpose into the adult. It therefore follows that, at least on some rivers, it should be possible to present patterns to imitate the different stages.

During the past decade or so many patterns have been designed, but whichever pattern you choose the most important factor is to match the colour of the larvae on which the trout are feeding at the time. I tend to favour the Gold Head, as the metal bead secured at the head of this very popular European artificial provides the necessary weight to fish it close to the bottom.

There is only one practical way of fishing these larval patterns in fast rivers and that is by adopting the outrigger technique that was first perfected in the States by Chuck Fothergill (described in *The Masters of the Nymph,* published by Nick Lyons in 1979). The name given to this method is, I think, very appropriate. The basic principle is to hold as long a rod as is feasible, as far in front of and above you as possible, at a 45° angle so that the larval pattern is fished a short distance in front of you. The cast should be made upstream at an angle using either a modified roll cast or a tuck cast (recently publicised by the well-known Austrian fly fisher Roman Moser). Both of these are fully described in chapter 7 on special casting techniques. Long casts are seldom necessary, as the outrigger technique is normally only practiced in fast, broken water where you can get quite close to the fish without being seen. It can be used for fishing from the bank, but is a particularly useful technique when wading. The larval pattern of your choice should be mounted on a ten- or twelve-foot leader incorporating a fast-sink tapered braided lead-cored leader, with a strike indicator secured at the end of the fly line. The fly is fished downstream on the dead drift, mending the line as necessary, to keep your artificial as close to the bottom as possible while searching the water and fishing any runs or other likely fish-holding areas. It is seldom necessary to strike when fishing this method, as in such fast water the fish all but hook themselves. However, any dip or even slight check of the indicator should be matched with a sharp tightening of the line, which is normally sufficient to set the hook. This is also a very useful technique for fishing deep channels or fast white water and even torrents, but to get your larva down to the bed of the river in such fast water you will need a very fast sink, lead-cored, braided leader. Finally, this method can only be practiced on freestone or similar rivers that have a relatively clean bed. It is not feasible on weedy waters such as spring creeks, or on rocky rivers with big boulders.

The outrigger technique is also very useful for fishing various artificials to represent the natural mature caddis pupae as they ascend to the surface to hatch during the late afternoons or early evenings. At this time you will want to fish your artificial fairly close to the bottom or even in midwater, where most of the trout, at least in the early stages of the hatch, will be looking for them. Contrary to popular belief, the mature pupae rarely, if ever, ascend directly to the surface. They will often drift with the current for considerable distances after emerging from their shucks before commencing their often slow ascent to the surface or swim towards the shore. As you will now be fishing off the bottom, providing your artificial pupa is well weighted, you can dispense with the lead-cored, braided leader, and use either a standard-sink braided leader or, if the water you are fishing is not too deep, a standard-tapered nylon leader. During heavy hatches of caddis, boils and splashes will be observed in the surface where the trout are chasing the ascending pupae and taking them just below the surface; or you may see subsurface rises where the trout are taking the pupae as they hatch in the surface film. When this occurs, an unweighted artificial pupa pattern fished just below the surface on a lightly greased leader (the last two feet of the tippet should be degreased) will often prove successful. The natural pupae just prior to emergence often struggle and thrash their swimming legs, producing minor movement across the current, so that, when fishing a pupa pattern in the meniscus or just below the surface, a very slight lifting of the rod tip, giving minimum movement to the artificial as it drifts, causing a slight drag across the current, will often result in a positive take. If you are fishing a fairly long line, this movement can be achieved better by mending the line in an upstream arc. When fishing with deep-sunk larva or midwater pupa patterns, the indicator should be secured onto the leader a little longer than the depth you wish to fish the artificial. Most of the time, however, unless the depth you are fishing is critical, you can get by with the wool or yarn indicator secured to the top of the leader where it joins the fly line. Where the depth is critical, the indicator should be looped onto the leader in the required position. For even greater accuracy, the indicator can be secured onto the leader using the hinge method developed by two American anglers, Hickson and Schubert. (See figure 31.)

There is one other relatively new method of taking trout feeding on caddis below the surface. There are certain species of female caddis that either crawl or swim below the surface to deposit their eggs. This has been known to entomologists for many years, but it is only fairly recently that a noted fly fisher in America, George Odier, developed a technique for fishing artificial patterns to represent the females either diving beneath the surface or exhausted, drifting and struggling in midwater, after egg laying. This has proved to be a very killing method, but only on those waters where such species are to be found in considerable numbers. In his book *Swimming Flies,* published in 1984, Odier claims

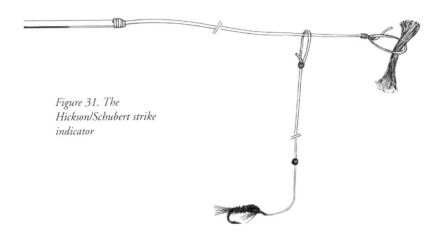

*Figure 31. The
Hickson/Schubert strike
indicator*

that an experienced fly fisher using a Coachman, Rio Grande King, or similar pattern and his line-swimming technique can take twenty or thirty trout in a relatively short period of time, when they are feeding on these adult egg layers. (See figure 32.)

Using the fly line to swim a fly is a very ancient technique dating back to the beginning of fly fishing, so why should Odier's method be so successful under the right circumstances? The reason seems to be a combination of the method he uses to present the artificial plus the way he fishes the chosen pattern. This technique is most successful on fairly fast, freestone streams where you are able to wade, and hot spots are to be found in strong riffles made by large boulders, rocks, or other obstructions on the riverbed. It can even be successful in the faster runs at the heads of pools and in fast pocket water. Long, deep channels alongside the riffles are also good for the larger trout. For presenting the fly, use a standard-tapered leader ten to twelve feet long, in conjunction with a floating weight-forward No 5 or 6 line. To swim the fly correctly at the desired depth, which is the most important thing, lead-free split shot or twist-ons should be attached to the leader about eighteen inches above the fly. The amount of weight required

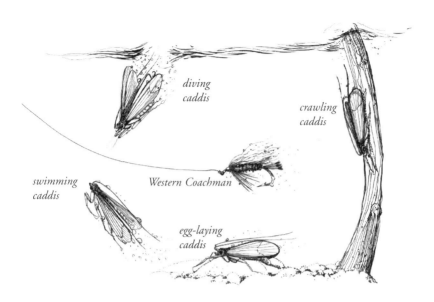

diving caddis

crawling caddis

swimming caddis

Western Coachman

egg-laying caddis

Figure 32. George Odier's line-swimming technique

will depend upon the depth of the water being fished as well as the speed of the current. You will want your artificial to fish fairly close to the bottom and, with experience, you will soon be able to judge the amount required to achieve this. When fishing long riffles it may be necessary to adjust the amount of weight as you work down them.

To present the fly correctly, a water-haul cast should be used. Strip forty or fifty feet of fly line off your reel and allow the current to float this downstream immediately below you (see figure 33). When it is fully extended, cast upstream at a slight angle out into the current towards the head of the riffle, and make one or, if the water is very fast, even two hard mends (see figure 34). As the weight on the leader sinks the fly and the line drifts downstream towards you, strip hard with the hand controlling the line, sufficiently fast to keep pace with the current and thus in touch with the artificial. Providing you strip hard enough to keep in touch with your fly, it is seldom necessary to strike

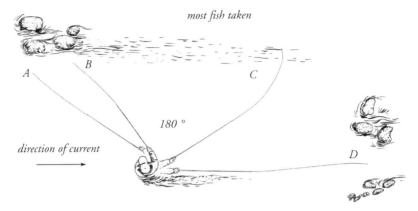

Figure 33. A to D is the zone in which George Odier's swimming fly can be fished effectively. B to C is the zone within which you should expect most takes.

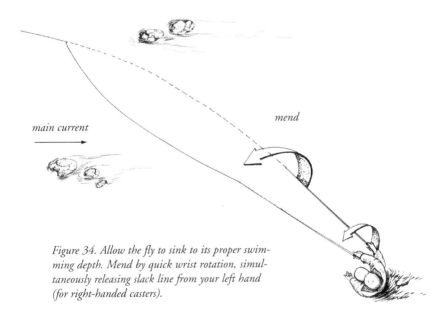

Figure 34. Allow the fly to sink to its proper swimming depth. Mend by quick wrist rotation, simultaneously releasing slack line from your left hand (for right-handed casters).

hard, as takes are usually quite savage when fishing in this manner. Most of your strikes will take place in the zones from two to four o'clock but if this does not happen, continue to fish the fly until the line is fully extended below you, as during a heavy feeding period strikes are likely to occur in any of the zones (see figure 33). With the Odier method, mending and stripping control are the key elements if you expect to recreate the image that the trout anticipate seeing in the midwater section of the stream.

THE WRY FLY

There is one other method of fishing nymphs, caddis larvae, or pupae beneath the surface on rough, turbulent, freestone streams. This is by fishing a buoyant dry fly well dressed with flotant on the surface, with a nymph on a long dropper beneath it. Nicholas Fitton coined the name wry fly for this method when he described it in his book *In Search of Wild Trout,* published in 1992 by Ward Lock, London. Although the method is certainly not new, it has never received very much publicity. I was introduced to it in New Zealand over twelve years ago, by a guide on the Mangles River on the South Island. This is an extremely fast, turbulent river that I had fished on my own the previous day. The guide showed me how to mount a large, bushy Caddis with a Hair & Copper Nymph on a long dropper below it, with which we proceeded to take several nice trout, most of them on the nymph, although we did take two splendid fish on the dry Caddis. I have little doubt that this method first led to the introduction of the relatively modern indicators, as the two methods are very similar indeed. Many experienced fly fishers are averse to the use of indicators as they consider them akin to float fishing. The wry fly in my opinion not only offers an excellent alternative, but also provides the opportunity for taking trout both on and below the surface.

Figure 35 shows how the method is set up and fished. The size of the dry fly and the nymph below will depend upon the river being fished; as a general rule, the faster and the more turbulent the water, the larger the dry fly and the heavier the nymph. On slow-flowing rivers or streams you can use very tiny dries and nymphs.

I have used this method with much success on rivers in both England and the States and have found it particularly useful on those

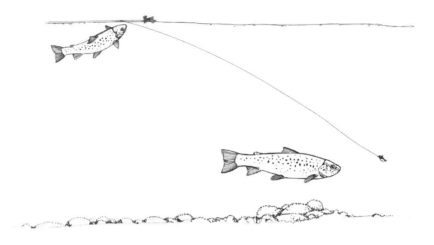

Figure 35. Wry-fly setup with nymph on the point. The nymph swims deeply here, attracting the deep-lying trout, while the dry fly tempts the surface feeder. This gives the angler a double chance.

dour days with few surface flies when few trout are rising. It is not recommended, and indeed not very effective, on clearwater streams such as spring creeks or limestone or chalkstreams, and certainly it is not a method you would even think of using on the English chalkstreams, where if you were found fishing with more than one fly you would probably finish up hanging from the nearest tree.

When setting up the rig, take into account the depth of the water being fished, as the deeper you wish to fish the nymph, the longer the dropper you will require. The most popular method for making droppers is to use a blood knot, but in practice this is rather difficult if the length of the dropper is over six inches. I use a clinch knot for attaching the dropper to the tippet, similar to the system developed by Hickson and Schubert for indicator fishing (see figure 31 on page 124). I tighten the clinch knot onto the tippet about six to eight inches from the dry fly, which can be secured to the end of the tippet with whatever knot you favour. I grease the leader heavily as far as the clinch knot securing the dropper, and then degrease the remaining six or eight inches of tippet to the dry fly. When fishing the wry fly, any movement at all of the dry fly on the surface should result in an instant strike, as failure to strike quickly will result in a lot of fish being missed. On the other hand, if the dry fly on the surface is taken by a trout in slow water, it will be necessary to delay your strike.

STONEFLY NYMPHS

Stoneflies are important on American rivers where large hatches are often experienced, and on rivers in the northern parts of Britain when the winged adults return to lay their eggs.

Many of the dry-fly patterns available were designed more than a century ago. In the earlier half of this century, stonefly nymphs, or creepers, as they were called, were a very popular bait with float fishers in the northern parts of Britain. Despite this, until fairly recently they have not received much attention from British fly fishers, probably due to the inability of most to fish a nymph successfully close to the bottom in the faster stony streams where the naturals are likely to be found in some numbers. The only practical ways to fish artificial patterns at least fairly close to the bed of the river are by attaching lead-substitute split shot or twist-ons to the leader to get the fly down, or by using fast-sink braided tapered leaders, both to be used in conjunction with a strike indicator. These may then be fished in a manner similar to that used for fishing caddis larva patterns.

In the not-too-distant future I think that fishing with deep-sunk stonefly nymphal patterns may become popular in the north of England, where at the moment indicator fishing is in its infancy. American fly fishers have been using indicators now for very many years, which probably accounts for the popularity of fishing artificials to represent stonefly nymphs, and which also accounts for the number of different patterns available to fly fishers in the States.

NYMPH FISHING FOR GRAYLING

Big grayling tend to hug the bottom in the deeper pots or channels in the stream, and even during a good hatch of surface flies are often very reluctant to rise. For this reason, your best chance of coming to grips with these larger fish is to use a very heavily weighted nymph to get down to them. Over the years I have had considerable success with Sawyer's Grayling Bug, particularly a variation dressed with a crimson tag at the bend that was first suggested by my friend Bernard Cribbins, but this is by no means infallible. Fairly recently I developed a new pattern that allowed me to add a lot more weight to the rather slim dressing of Sawyer's Bug. It looks rather like a cross between a shrimp and a nymph and during the past two years this "Shrymph" has proved to be even more effective than the Bug, particularly for those grayling lying in relatively deep water. It has also proved to be effective for deep-lying trout.

Another recent addition to the armoury is one of the new Gold Head patterns that have become increasingly popular over the past two seasons on stillwater. It is very simple and quick pattern to dress. You first of all cement a gold-coloured metal ball immediately behind the eye of the hook. The body is then dressed on the shank behind this. I have found that the grayling seem to love this pattern dressed with a dubbed gold-ribbed Hare's Ear body. I dress it on size 18 and 16 hooks with a very tiny gold ball for fishing in shallow water, or size 14 or 12 with a much larger gold ball, which will take it down even in the deepest of channels. For very clear water I prefer a copper-coloured metal ball with a partridge hackle wound palmer style over the body.

Grayling are an odd fish and take a nymph differently from trout. I heavily grease the top section of the leader and watch this for any sign of a take, which is often very fast. If you do not react quickly enough, you will take very few grayling. Although I normally fish my nymph upstream, I do find at times it is more effective fished downstream. Grayling, much more than trout, seem to have periods when they feed avidly and are relatively easy to catch, while at other times even when conditions seem absolutely perfect they will ignore every offering you present to them. I have still not figured out the reason for this and it can be most frustrating. However, when they are not feeding or when they appear to be feeding rather reluctantly, I have found that you can often tempt them to take by lifting your rod and giving a long, slow draw to your nymph. This seems equally effective when fishing both upstream and down. Another method that has proved to be successful is a technique used by many European grayling fishers. They mount a very heavily leaded nymph on the tippet, and to the bend of the hook of this nymph they secure with an eight- to twelve-inch length of monofilament a very tiny unweighted nymph. (See figure 30.) This is cast a short distance upstream, and, as soon as they estimate it has reached the bottom, they draw it back to the surface by lifting the rod. While any of these methods proves killing at times, my favourite by far and certainly in my opinion the most effective is, once you have located some big grayling or a substantial shoal, to position yourself slightly upstream of them where you can see them clearly. This is difficult to achieve without spooking them, but it can be done if you crouch down and move into position extremely slowly. If you are fortunate, there will be some streamside cover, which usually allows you to cast your nymph without disturbing them. By presenting your nymph on a very short line with a sideways cast, it is usually possible to pick out individual fish and drift your nymph down to them with the current. When the grayling are actively feeding they may move a considerable distance to intercept it or even chase it, but when they are not feeding and hugging the bottom it is necessary to drift your nymph very accurately towards the fish. Unlike a trout, a grayling has a small mouth and you are seldom able to see him open it to take a nymph; therefore, when I am fishing this method and judge the nymph is very close, I strike if there is any indication of movement at all. Sometimes the take is indicated by a slight lift or more often a slight movement to one side or the other, while at other times the movement is so slight that unless you are really concentrating you will miss it.

There is still a lot to learn about the feeding behaviour and movements of grayling. In the south of England the best time for catching them is during October and November. As January approaches and the temperature drops, the grayling leave the shallower areas and move into the deeper holes and channels and become difficult to locate. By

February they seem to have disappeared completely from many rivers and no-one to my knowledge has yet found out where they go. In the northern areas of Britain, where these fish are much sought after, the situation is very different. As the cold weather approaches the grayling fishing improves. In fact, in many areas of the Midlands, Yorkshire, and Lancashire I understand the best period is often during January and February when there is a thick snow on the ground and along the banks of the rivers.

7

SPECIAL CASTING TECHNIQUES

*Hooking, Playing, Landing,
and Releasing Fish*

O VER THE YEARS there has been much argument about whether the approach, the presentation, or the choice of fly is the most important aspect of fly fishing. While all of these are important, they pale into insignificance unless you are a competent caster. Apart from when fishing on stillwater, where distance and not accuracy is at a premium, 70 percent of casting is carried out at distances of less than twelve yards. At these distances many fly fishers can present a fly both delicately and fairly accurately, but I am still constantly surprised at the high proportion who use an overhead cast and, furthermore, make six or more casts to lengthen the line before presenting the fly. Accuracy and delicacy are of little consequence if you have spooked the fish before your fly has landed. At such a relatively short distance, with an overhead cast the fish can clearly see the top half of your rod and, while he may not be alerted by one or two false casts, with more than this your chances are reduced. I would therefore suggest that, if you come within this category, you spend a little time improving your technique.

First of all, train yourself to cast sideways, keeping the tip of the rod within about eight feet of the ground, or less when you become proficient. Never make more false casts than necessary. It may be essential at times when dry-fly fishing to disperse water that has collected on the fly, but you can usually present a fly half a dozen or more times before it needs drying. This can then be carried out by false casting away from the fish. If you watch a really competent caster working on a fish at a relatively short distance you will rarely see him or her casting overhead or making more than one false cast. With practice you will find that by utilizing the surface tension of the fly line on the water, it is perfectly feasible to re-present the fly to the fish with one backcast, even at distances well in excess of fifteen yards. When you have mastered the technique and can present your fly accurately and consistently within a circle about two feet in diametre, you can start practicing specialized casting techniques. Some of these you may already know, but I would recommend that you study them carefully, as, in many cases, the ability to deliver a particular cast can make the difference between success and failure.

While many specialized casting techniques have become well established, there are others that have received little or no publicity. Fly fishers who have been fishing over a long period of time often subconsciously develop casting techniques to overcome certain problems that may occur on a regular basis on the waters they fish. I know I have, and over the years I have been astonished on at least two or three occasions to read of a "new" casting technique that I have been using for some considerable time. Therefore, please forgive me if any of the following specialized casts, a few of which are put forward as new, may not be new at all or are known under a completely different name. The first three may come into this category. These are all casts that have been developed by my good friend Roman Moser to fish particular fly patterns in specific situations. They are reproduced here by kind permission from *Trout & Salmon* magazine. Roman, one of the top European practical casters, lives in Austria close to the famous Traun River.

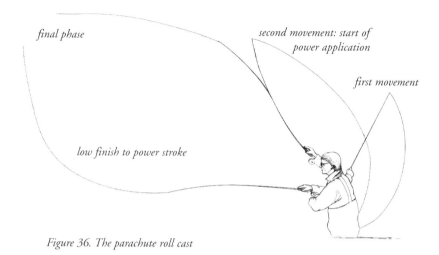

final phase

*second movement: start of
power application*

first movement

low finish to power stroke

Figure 36. The parachute roll cast

THE PARACHUTE ROLL CAST (Figure 36)

This is designed to get a free-swimming caddis or nymph pattern to the bed of the river very quickly, even in fairly fast water.

The nymph or caddis pattern should be well weighted and is fished with a lead- or copper-cored braided fast-sink leader in conjunction with a wool indicator attached to the end of the fly line. When the roll cast is made at a 45° angle upstream, do not stop the rod in the usual ten o'clock position, but continue until it is almost parallel to the water, creating a very large loop that causes the fly to drop almost vertically into the water close to the end of the fly line itself. This allows the fly to reach the bottom very quickly, even in quite fast currents. The fly should be fished downstream on the dead drift with the fly line being mended upstream, more than once if necessary, in order to keep the artificial as close to the bed of the river as possible. With this method, fish the water, searching any runs or likely looking fish-holding areas during the day. In the early evening, if using caddis pupa patterns, the naturals are more likely to be found travelling to the surface than on the bottom, so change your fast-sink braided leader for one of monofilament, which will allow your artificial to fish in midwater rather than on the bottom.

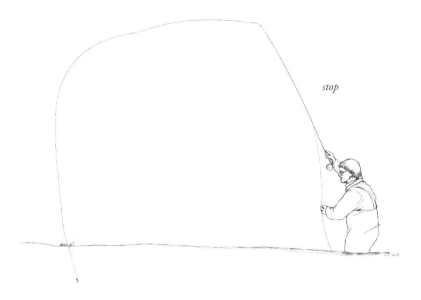

stop

Figure 37. The deep-water tuck cast

THE DEEP-WATER TUCK CAST (Figure 37)

Roman uses this for fishing fairly deep white water or fast-flowing tor-rents where caddis larvae, particularly the free-swimming variety, and also stone-clinging nymphs are constantly being dislodged from the rocks or stones on the bottom and swept downstream. Weighted nymph caddis larva or even pupa patterns may be fished successfully in this type of water providing that an extra fast sink braided leader is used, but even with this it is seldom possible to get the flies deep enough in this extremely rapid water so Roman developed his deep-water tuck cast, which more or less solves the problem. The fish have limited vision in fast water so, providing you wade slowly and carefully, it is possible to stand alongside the head of a fast run and catch fish within a few feet of you. The tuck cast is accomplished by aerializing about ten yards of line or less. The rod and arm should be held as high as possible and the for-ward cast stopped prematurely at eleven o'clock. If stopped quickly enough, the weighted fly will be flipped back under the end of the fly line and will drop vertically into the water, followed by the weighted leader, where it should sink reasonably close to the bottom.

Still holding the rod as high as possible, fish the artificial as far downstream as the relatively short length of fly line will allow. It is surprising how savage the takes can be in this fast water, and, with such a short length of line being fished, it is all too easy to break, so use a heavier leader than normal. The fish appear to be unaware of it in such rapid water, as they only have a split second to make up their mind whether to take the fly. This is one method where a ten- or twelve-inch length of Power Gum tied into the leader immediately below the braided section will be of immense value in avoiding breaking the fish off on the strike. For this method of fishing where the water surface is rough, a wool strike indicator fastened to the end of the fly line is strongly recommended, or better still, where it is allowed, a cork indicator, which is more buoyant.

THE WET-FLY SWING CAST (Figure 38)

Roman uses this technique to fish one of his unweighted caddis pupa patterns. It is best practiced later in the summer during the early evening, when big hatches of caddis start appearing and the trout swirl

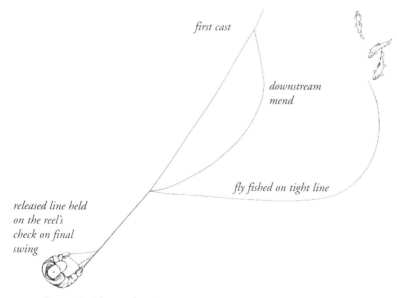

first cast

*downstream
mend*

fly fished on tight line

*released line held
on the reel's
check on final
swing*

Figure 38. The wet-fly swing cast

just below the surface as they take the ascending pupae. Mounting an unweighted and degreased pupa of the appropriate colour, cast as far as possible across the river, and give the line a downstream mend. Immediately this has been achieved, take your hand away from both line and reel and allow the line to swing downstream and straighten naturally. The majority of the takes will come as the end of the line starts to straighten and often they will be very savage indeed, certainly enough to break the trout off if you are either holding the line or checking the reel. In practice, providing you have a fairly strong ratchet on your reel, this will be sufficient to set the hook.

THE BOUNCE CAST

This is a well-known cast that allows you to present your fly on the surface fairly accurately with plenty of slack. It is used where a fly presented on a normal, fairly straight cast would immediately drag. Most rivers have swirling currents, boulders, or weed beds, with either slack or fast water between you and the fish to which you are casting, so that proficiency in either this or the following cast is essential to success. To make this cast the rod is stopped sharply at the eleven o'clock position on the forward cast, which will result in the fly on the end of the leader snapping back towards you, so that when it falls on the water there will be plenty of slack. To generate even more slack, should it be necessary, just before the line straightens pull back hard on the hand holding the line; although this often makes it more difficult to achieve very much accuracy. Under very windy conditions or where accuracy is important, stop the cast at about ten o'clock or even a little lower so that the line, leader, and fly are only about two feet above the water surface when the rod is stopped.

THE PUDDLE, PILE, OR PARACHUTE CAST

This is an alternative to the previous cast when it is necessary to overcome problems of drag. Personally, I prefer this one because it is easier to perfect and, except under windy conditions, I find that I can present the fly more accurately and with even more slack between rod and fly. All you have to do is to aim your cast higher—imagine you are casting to the treetops—and then, as the line stops unrolling, lower your rod tip down onto the water. As the back end of the line near the rod is lowered towards the water, the front end of the line and leader in the air collapse, landing in a lovely pile of slack. This amount of slack can be controlled to a certain extent by the upward angle of the cast. This cast allows the fly to alight on the water like a piece of thistledown. However, under windy conditions the bounce cast is to be favoured.

THE STEEPLE OVERARM CAST (Figure 39)

This is an extension of the well-known steeple cast and was first shown to me by my old buddy Lefty Kreh. The old and popular steeple cast was designed to cover trout rising in front of you when there are very high trees growing along the bank behind you, which makes a normal cast impossible. With this cast you lift the line off the water vertically above your head—which may sound fine but in practice, while you can direct it above your head, it always travels back at a slight angle, often far enough to catch the trees. Apart from this, it is also difficult to lift your head to see where the line is going, as to achieve the cast you have to lift your arm straight up in front of you. With the new steeple overarm cast you twist your wrist as you bring the rod up in front of you to lift the line off the water, which in effect means that the reel is facing upwards instead of down. At the same time it naturally follows that you can turn your shoulder and your head on the casting side, which makes it much easier to direct the path of the line above you. This

Twist arm and wrist so that reel and rod rings are facing up to sky.

Figure 39. The steeple overarm cast

means that not only can you achieve true vertical casts, but you can also direct the path of the cast from side to side to find gaps between the branches of overhanging trees.

THE AIR ROLL CAST

You often find stretches of bank lined with trees behind you and with thick overhanging branches above you, which means you have marginal space to make a normal sideways cast other than for very short distances; neither is it possible to make any sort of steeple cast because of the dense branches overhead. In such situations you often find that the only good trout rising is under the far bank, which may demand a cast exceeding twenty yards or so in length. I have never seen the cast that I have developed for such situations described anywhere else, although I do not doubt that it is known and used by a lot of fly fishers. I have decided to call it the air roll cast. You use a sidearm cast at an angle to the bank, rolling the line behind you off the water. Start the forward cast just as the line is starting to unroll behind you, punching it forward with a very strong wrist snap and at the same time single hauling with the hand holding the line. It takes quite a bit of practice to get it right, the secret being not to let the line unroll too far behind you, where it will snag in the undergrowth. When the cast is perfected you will be surprised at the distance you can achieve with so little backcasting space.

THE STORM OR WIND CAST (Figure 40)

This is a well-known and popular cast used for delivering your fly directly into the teeth of strong winds; a cast that must be mastered if you spend much time fishing big rivers with open banks or when saltwater fly fishing. With this cast you have to double haul, checking your backcast at about one o'clock and on the final delivery punching the rod forward until it is almost parallel to the water, delivering the fly under the wind with a positive snap of the wrist. When fishing in strong winds you will need to shorten your leader, and the stronger wind, the shorter it should be. When you are really competent at this cast, you should be able to push a fly out under the wind at least twenty yards or even more.

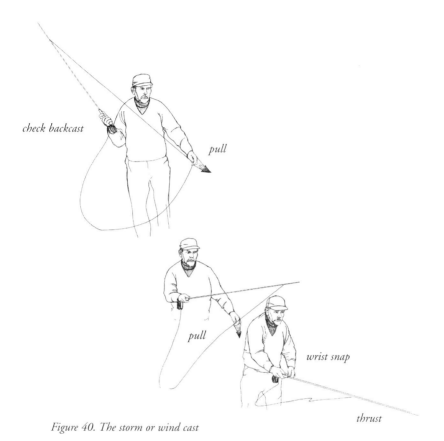

check backcast

pull

pull

wrist snap

thrust

Figure 40. The storm or wind cast

THE ELBOW WIND CAST

This is an alternative to the storm cast for casting a fly directly into the wind. I use it quite a lot where distance is not really required. I have never seen it described in any book on casting; it was shown to me many years ago by an American friend who never did give it a name. For want of a better description I call it an elbow cast. Aerialize the line in the normal way and, when you have sufficient line out to cover the fish you are casting to, make a strong forward cast, punching the rod down parallel to the water at arm height. As you commence this forward power stroke, you lift your elbow up in the air behind you, which, in turn, with a right-handed caster, twists the wrist to the left. For maximum effect the wrist should be strongly snapped as you twist.

THE BELGIAN CAST

A well-known, very simple yet effective cast for fishing heavily weighted flies at distance. Trying to fish such flies at any distance with a normal cast, particularly under windy conditions, is not only difficult but also rather dangerous, as it is very easy to hook yourself. This cast to a very large extent overcomes this problem. It is used extensively by salmon and steelhead fly fishers and also by upstream nymph fishers on the Tongariro River in New Zealand. You make the cast by forming a large oval in a clockwise direction with the rod tip in the air. To put it in simpler terms, the forward cast is made directly overhead, while the return or backcast is made with the rod held sideways at a 45° angle to the ground. This in effect means that the heavily weighted fly passes well away from you out to the side on the backcast, while on the forward cast it passes harmlessly overhead. When making this cast it is essential to wait for the line to extend fully behind you before commencing the forward stroke. If you do not do this, you will find it is difficult to make a good presentation and extend the fly fully in front of you. In practice you will find that, when making really long casts extending the rod well behind you and waiting for the line, leader, and fly to extend fully, they do tend to drop a little, so that when the forward stroke is made the fly whistles forward perilously close to your head. You can always spot the old pros on the Tongariro River—they always duck their head as they make the forward cast. Once you have been hit on the back of the head with a heavy nymph you try to make sure it does not happen again.

THE WIGGLE CAST

This is a useful technique that enables you to obtain long downstream drag-free drifts. It is a very simple yet effective cast to master. The wiggle can be achieved during the casting stroke (see figure 41A), which is to be favoured when you have variable or faster currents between you and your target. In flat water it is even simpler to put the wiggle in after the line has alighted on the surface (see figure 41B). As you make the forward cast and the line starts unrolling in the air, all you have to do is to shake the rod from side to side and it will fall onto the water in a series of S bends. Before casting make sure that you pull off more slack line than you will require to reach your target, as it is necessary to shoot some of this slack through the rod guides to prevent your rod wiggles from pulling the line backwards and shortening your cast. The effect of this wiggle means that while the intervening currents between you and your fly are straightening these bends, your fly will achieve a drag-free float. You can increase or decrease the amount of slack imparted by the number and strength of wiggles. You can also put more slack where it will be of most benefit by wiggling the rod either early or late in the cast.

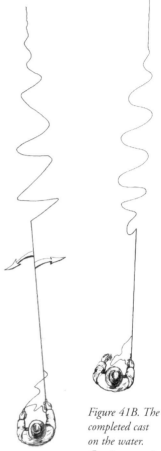

Figure 41B. The completed cast on the water. Continue to wiggle the rod tip as the current takes the fly downstream.

Figure 41A. Wiggles imparted while the line is in the air

THE BOW-AND-ARROW CAST (Figure 42)

This cast is rarely used, but on odd occasions it will be the only way of getting your fly to the fish. It is used to cast to a fish rising beneath very low branches lining the bank for a considerable distance, where it is quite impossible to reach him with any normal cast or even by dabbling or dibbling your fly from beneath the rod tip. It is very simple to achieve as all you do is to pull the fly back against the tension of the rod and then release towards your target like an arrow from a bow. As the rod straightens and projects the fly, you release your finger trapping the slack line against the rod. It is difficult to get much distance, but with a little practice you will find it is possible to reach at least a fair percentage of such fish.

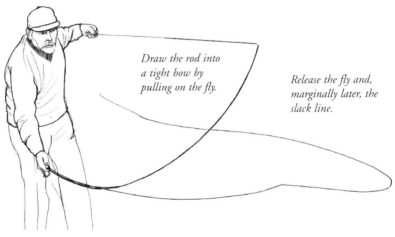

Draw the rod into a tight bow by pulling on the fly.

Release the fly and, marginally later, the slack line.

Figure 42. The bow-and-arrow cast

CURVE CASTS

The final specialized cast is used to present your fly to a fish rising directly upstream without lining him, or for casting around corners or obstructions. It is designed to present the line with a big curve in the leader, to either the left or right, and is known as the curve cast, although in the past it has often been referred to as the shepherd's crook cast. It is accomplished by either overpowering or underpowering a sidearm cast. The former results in the leader and fly swinging around in a positive curve, while the latter results in a weak loop when the fly lands on the surface first. Personally, I have always had difficulty in forming these loops with any degree of consistency, and with an upstream wind find it all but impossible. A few years back Lefty Kreh showed me an alternative method, which he demonstrated with considerable consistency. You merely rotate your wrist as you make the forward power cast. A rotation to the left results in an inward curve to the left, while a rotation to the right throws an outward curve to the right. Like many good casts it is simple to perform, but to obtain a really pronounced curve consistently does require a lot of practice; correct timing is critical.

HOOKING

The successful hooking of a trout has to do with timing; I like to compare it to the timing of a golf swing. Most of the time you instinctively get it right, but on those occasions when you do not the consequences can be most frustrating; and those occasions happen to all of us, no matter how good a fisherman you are. I recall a situation that occurred several years ago when a colleague and I were making a film on trout fishing for BBC television. Now, my friend is a first-class fisherman, yet during the first four or five days of shooting he failed to hook nearly every fish to which he cast. There was no apparent reason for this and the harder he tried, the more frustrated he became. I am sure it was purely due to timing, which has to be adjusted minutely depending upon vagaries of the current and the pace of the stream. To generalize, the faster the current, the more quickly you should strike, while the slower the current, the slower the strike. In fact, on some slow-flowing streams, particularly when fishing large dry-fly patterns such as those representing the green drakes, it is almost impossible to strike too slowly. On stillwater many pundits say you should recite the first lines of the Lord's prayer before striking. On the other hand, you should never be too dogmatic when it comes to fishing; there are nearly always exceptions to any rule. I well remember fishing with Gary Borger a short time ago on a mountain lake in Montana during a colossal damselfly hatch. It was my first experience of fishing such a hatch using a dry, floating damsel pattern, and during the first half hour while Gary was catching fish after fish I was missing fish after fish. I was delaying the strike in the traditional manner, and it took me a long time to realize that these fish were cruising along practically on the surface and therefore I had to strike very quickly.

Apart from timing there are, of course, other factors involved in a successful hookup, such as taking into account the amount of slack line between you and your quarry, and the distance you are casting—at long distance you will need to strike much harder to take up the amount of slack between you and the fish. Conversely, when you set the hook in a fish a short distance away, the strike must be much softer, moving the rod through a much shorter arc. In the past, many times, much to my embarrassment, I have struck too hard and left the fly in the fish.

It is also important to check the hook on your fly, especially if you start missing fish on the strike, or if a fish comes off after you start playing him. Even with top-quality hooks you occasionally get the odd one that is overtempered, which may result in the hook breaking off at either the bend or the point where the barb is cut; if undertempered, the bend will open. This is one of the reasons I always fish with barbless hooks. Without a barb on the hook, the inherent weakness where the barb is cut is removed. Apart from this, a barbless hook nearly always penetrates up to the bend, which is far less prone to opening.

It is good practice to carry a hook sharpener with you at all times, as one of the main essentials in obtaining a good hookup is to keep a razor-sharp point on your hook.

One other factor in obtaining a persistently good hookup rate, rarely if ever mentioned in print, is to offset the hook on your fly. I cannot overemphasize the importance of this, particularly with very small hooks, although I have found it pays to do it with all sizes. I have been offsetting my hooks for many years now and I am convinced that you lose far fewer fish on the strike. It is possible to purchase some makes of hooks with offset points but I prefer to do it myself. I carry with me a small pair of model-maker's pliers with which to offset the hook after I have tied the fly onto the tippet. Very occasionally the hook will break off at the bend when you do this, but so rarely it can almost be discounted.

PLAYING FISH

One of the most important decisions in playing fish, particularly trout, is whether to play them on the reel or by holding the fly line. With fish such as salmon, steelhead, and most saltwater species, you are rarely faced with a choice. They are so strong and powerful that their first run takes up all the slack fly line, so you find you are automatically playing them on the reel. With less powerful species such as trout or grayling, you do have a choice, as more often than not you will find that you have a lot of slack fly line on the ground at your feet after striking. I have always favoured playing these fish with the fly line running between finger and thumb. It is a delicate way of playing a trout and you get much more feel for what the trout is doing. Apart from this, you can concentrate 100 percent on the fish from the moment you set the hook. Over the years I have observed many fly fishers lose trout when trying to spool the loose fly line back onto the reel during those crucial few seconds when the trout is first hooked. If you watch those fly fishers who like to play the fish on the reel, you will notice that their first reaction upon striking is to look down for a second or two to transfer the loose fly line they are holding in one hand to the fingers of the other hand, where it can be trapped beneath the rod so they can start winding the reel to take up the slack. While all this is going on they are not watching the fish or controlling him, and many fish are lost when they suddenly accelerate and dive into a weed bed or around an obstruction, or are given too much slack line. When I am wading, however, I play the fish on the line initially, but as soon as I have control of him, I like to wind in all the slack and finish playing him on the reel; slack line floating on the water can get entangled with the fish as you are trying to land him.

Many authorities advocate winding the slack line onto the reel as quickly as possible after hooking a fish and then playing him from the reel. The argument is that if you play a fish with the line you are more likely to lose him either when you stand on the coils of loose line or when they become snagged on some obstruction. The choice is yours— I can only reiterate that in my opinion you are far less likely to break off a fish when playing him on the line, and in all the years I have been doing this, I have very rarely been broken by the loose line snagging.

When playing fish on rivers that have many obstructions such as large boulders or logjams, and particularly when playing them on limestone or chalkstreams or spring creeks that have thick weed beds, I always feel much happier if I can keep the fish upstream of me. In streams with a fast flow where this may be impossible, I try to keep the fish on a short line and move downstream with him. If you allow a fish to reach an obstruction a long way downstream of you, the harder you pull on the line, the more he will burrow in and when you eventually get there he is usually impossible to extricate. On the other hand, if a fish gets into an obstruction or weed bed upstream of you, by keeping a steady pressure on the rod and not allowing him to bury himself too far, it is usually possible to pull him out the same way he entered.

At times you may find yourself fishing a stream or stretch of river that is full of dense weed beds. If you allow a fish to reach the sanctuary of thick weed he will invariably be lost. I discovered a long time ago that the only solution in such a situation is to lock the reel or loose line as soon as you strike, and hold your hands with the rod as high above your head as possible, thereby pulling the head of the fish above the surface and keeping it there. This will disorient the fish, and, providing you can keep his head above water, he will merely move around in large circles, splashing and exhausting himself. You need a tippet of at least four-pound test. With this method I have over the years successfully landed large trout, including many in excess of seven pounds. Some of these have been rainbows, which normally take off in a sizzling run as soon as you hook them, so you have to be quick on the draw to prevent this.

LANDING FISH

Probably more fish are lost when they are about to be netted than at any other time. Most fish, even when they are seemingly played out, are capable of producing that last surge of adrenaline and making that final strong run for freedom when they see the net or the angler looming over them. Few big trout surrender the first time they are brought to the net, and for the unwary fly fisher this can result in a lost fish and a broken leader or tippet. To minimize the reaction of the fish, always crouch down when netting, as you will present a less menacing silhouette. Never try to net a fish in very shallow water; choose a landing area where the water is deep enough to hold the net well below the surface where he is less likely to see it. The fish can then be drawn over the net, and the net lifted to envelope him. How often I see inexperienced fishers stabbing at the fish with the net and frightening him into the last surge. One other little point: If you are going to use a net, use one with a large enough capacity to land the largest fish you expect to catch from the water you are fishing.

Personally, I never use a landing net, and have not done so for over twenty years except when boat fishing on stillwater. Landing nets are a nuisance to carry and always seem to snag on any bushes or trees that you have to pass through. They are rarely if ever necessary, as, even where there are high banks and deep water, you can usually walk the fish downstream to an area where it is possible to reach down. Incidentally, once the initial runs of a freshly hooked fish have been overcome, you will find that if you keep the line very tight it is possible to lead a fish either up or down the river rather like a dog on a lead. This is a very useful ploy when it is necessary either to find a suitable landing area or to move from an area where there may be many obstructions or weed beds where the fish may seek sanctuary. Apart from the nuisance of carrying a net, if, like me, you return most of the fish that you catch, a net should not be used anyway.

There may, however, be the odd occasion when you want to kill a fish for the pot or to lift him out of the water for photographing. If you are fishing a river or stream that has any shallows adjacent to the bank, the simplest way is to beach the fish once he is played out. This is acceptable on those rivers with soft banks, but on freestone rivers or streams with hard or gravelly banks this should not be attempted unless you are going to kill the fish, as he will slap about on the stones and injure himself. On water with no shallows, find an area out of the main current close to the bank where the fish can be lifted out by hand. Where possible, get into the water to do this—it is much easier than leaning out over the bank. Grasp the fish across the back nearer to the head than to the tail and, as you start to lift, twist your hand so that the belly of the fish is upwards. For some strange reason, if you do this the fish will not struggle at all, and can be lifted carefully onto the bank for photographing. With big fish—over about five pounds—this can be difficult to achieve due to the sheer width of the fish across the back. Try to manoeuver a big fish close into the bank, drop the rod, and use both hands to grasp the fish, one above and one below.

RELEASING FISH

Since the early seventies I have practiced catch and release on those waters where it is allowed, and I am a firm believer that this is absolutely essential on those rivers that hold wild fish if we are to preserve them for future generations. However, I do have certain reservations regarding catch and release; unless such waters are carefully monitored and the rules strictly adhered to, it may do more harm than good. If a fish has fought too long, been handled badly, or had a barbed hook torn from his mouth, he is unlikely to survive and releasing him will do little but help pollute the water to which he is returned. Therefore, I feel very strongly that, on those waters where catch and release has been established, the following rules should be strictly enforced.

- Barbless hooks should be mandatory.

- The minimum breaking test of any tippet material used should be at least four pounds.

- No nets should be used and no fish should be touched with the hand or removed from the water.

It is impossible to remove a hook with a barb from a fish's mouth without causing considerable injury. If you are going to release a fish, it is essential to play and release him quickly. If you fight a fish for too long his chances of survival are pretty slim as lactic acid builds up in the bloodstream and starves the fish of oxygen; the warmer the water temperature, the more quickly this occurs. Therefore, using tippets with a minimum breaking strain of four pounds allows you to play the fish hard and bring him into the point of release quickly. All fish have a coating of slime to protect them from infection, and the more they are handled, the more likely this is to be removed. We are all guilty of removing fish from the water to photograph, but try to do this quickly and handle them gently with wet hands to cause the minimum of damage. Nets should never be used, as this removes the slime more quickly than anything else.

With barbless hooks it is not necessary to remove the fish from the water, as it is a simple matter to slide your hand down the leader and tippet, and grasp the fly to release the fish. If you are on a high bank where it is impossible to reach down to the fish, try this method, which I discovered years ago and have since shown to many fly fishers. Use the tip ring of the rod rather like a disgorger. As soon as the fish is within reach of the rod, and providing you can see the fly in the lip or the scissors, pull on the fly line and slide the rod down the leader and tippet until the tip ring is hard up against the fly in the fish's mouth. Give the rod a very quick short, sharp stab forward down or away from the mouth, and hey presto, the fly is removed. I now release all my fish this way, but you should never try it with a barbed hook or with a large fly where the shank of the hook will not go through the top ring, and never even think of trying it if the fly is inside the mouth of the fish, or you will end up with a broken tip. I have released thousands of fish this way and only ever broken one rod tip, and that was my fault, as I stumbled as I jabbed the rod forward.

8

STILLWATER FISHING

D URING THE EARLY PART of this century, English fly
fishers of the great chalkstream era, such as F. M. Halford and
G. E. M. Skues, led the world with their new patterns and innovative
techniques, but in the intervening years the Americans have leapt
ahead in fly-dressing techniques, in the use of synthetic materials and
in the development of very small dry flies fished on extremely light tippets. However, when it comes to fly fishing on stillwater the English
are once again world leaders and have developed this particular branch
of the sport to a very high degree.

All water authorities throughout Britain must now, by law, allow
leisure pursuits on their reservoirs. One of the easiest ways to comply
with this regulation is to stock the reservoirs with trout and open them
up for fly fishing. By the early seventies, stillwater fly fishing had become
so popular that it created a tremendous demand for more waters, which
led to the stocking and opening of countless small lakes and ponds.
Enterprising landowners dammed streams to form lakes or landscaped
gravel pits containing water, stocked them with trout, usually rainbows,
and sold day or season tickets to fish them, in line with most of the big

reservoirs. Today there are well over a thousand stillwater trout fisheries in Britain, including many large reservoirs such as Chew Valley Lake, Rutland Water, Grafham Water, Bewl Bridge, and Pitsford Reservoirs, which provide some of the best trout fishing to be found throughout Europe. It is therefore not surprising, with the number of fly fishers involved, that many new techniques have been developed both from the bank and from boats. New methods have led to a proliferation of new fly patterns, many of which have proved very effective indeed.

While boat fishing or float tubing on stillwater is quite popular and widely practiced in the States, rarely do you observe any of the more productive English techniques being used. Nor do you see many Americans fly fishing from the bank. I am convinced that if at least some of the following methods were adopted on American stillwaters, catch rates would increase tremendously. In certain situations fishing from an anchored boat or the bank can be very productive, but most of the time the opportunities offered from the controlled drift of a boat are far greater and certainly much more exciting. In my experience there are few thrills in fly fishing to equal the sight of a large trout surging at your surface-fished fly and, in some cases, following it almost to the side of the boat before taking. I have had trout take so close to the side of the boat that it has been impossible to get the line tight enough to set the hook.

Your first visit to a large body of stillwater can be a daunting experience—where to start fishing, which patterns to use? Unlike rivers, where fish can be seen below the surface or located when they rise to surface flies that can be identified by observation, there is little to tell you where the trout are likely to be or on what they are feeding. Much of the time they will be feeding below the surface on fauna you cannot see. Fortunately, with a little experience these problems can be overcome.

First of all, you will have to decide whether you are going to bank or boat fish; this will to a large extent depend upon weather conditions and also on how you want to fish. On rough, windy days you will certainly be better off fishing from the bank, as you will on cold days, or during periods when hatches of flies are poor. Under these conditions the trout are far more likely to be feeding well below the surface, where it is easier for the bank angler to reach them. The bank is also to be favoured if conditions suggest a team of nymphs or midge pupae, as from the bank these can be fished much more delicately and slowly than from a boat, even when it is at anchor.

When I was younger, I much preferred bank fishing—in those days there were more options open to you in the presentation of your flies from the bank than from a boat. Today, with many new boat-fishing techniques available, the odds are more equal. However, there is little doubt that bank fishing is much more physically demanding. Most of the time you are standing in water up to your waist and having to cast long distances. The peaks for bank fishing are just before sunrise as it is getting light, and again just as dusk approaches after the sun sets, which in the height of the summer can result in a very long day indeed. These days I must admit I prefer the comfort of a boat and the shorter hours involved. You seldom start much before nine in the morning and rarely find it necessary to fish very late in the evening.

BANK FISHING

There are many different factors to be taken into account when bank fishing. Early in the season, seek out the deeper areas of the lake or reservoir, as the water temperature is likely to be higher in these areas, which will therefore hold more fish. Once the summer is well under-way, the fish are more likely to be spread out, but will usually favour the shallow areas during the early mornings and late evenings when the sun is off the water. During very hot weather, from late morning to early evening again expect the fish to be in the deeper water, where the temperature will be lower. Avoid fishing from a bank with the wind directly behind you. While the casting may be easier, fewer fish are likely to be present, as the wind will be drifting any surface food out into the body of the water. The only exception to this will be along banks that are heavily bushed or treed, where the wind may be con-stantly blowing tasty morsels out onto the surface.

On very deep lakes and particularly on reservoirs, bear in mind the effect that constant strong winds from the same quarter will have on the current and thermocline. The surface current flowing to the far side will double back below the surface, causing water from deep down in the lake or reservoir to well up along the shore from which the wind is blowing. The temperature and oxygen content of this water will probably be much lower than those of the surface water, and it is likely to be devoid of fish. Under most circumstances the best bank to fish is the one onto which the wind is blowing, as any food on the surface will be concentrated along this shore. However, this will not appeal unless you are an exceptionally good caster, particularly as it is often necessary to cast quite a long line to reach trout that will probably be moving away from you upwind. It is therefore probably best to choose a shoreline along which the wind is blowing to the right, if you are a right-handed caster, or to the left if you are a left-handed.

If the wind is fairly light you can fish almost anywhere, but it will pay you to take into account the topography of the water you are fishing. (See figure 44.) Most reservoirs are formed by flooding agricultural land, so beneath the surface of the water may be old roads, footpaths, ditches, hedgerows, clumps of bushes, or other obstructions. These form natural underwater lanes up which the trout are likely to approach the shore, or holding areas where trout are likely to congregate. Even in natural lakes there will be channels or depressions formed by the contours of the land. Seeking out such areas will pay dividends, as these are often hot spots that will hold trout, while long stretches of water along the shoreline may hold only a few. Other areas where trout are likely to be found are by promontories of shoreline, where trout may be passing either off the tip of land or down either side. These also provide you with a 180° arc in which to fish, which can be very useful on those days when the wind is constantly changing direction. (See figure 45.)

Other hot spots are to be found where streams or rivers enter or leave the lake, and in reservoirs where water is being pumped in. Trout will often frequent these areas in large numbers during very hot weather, as the pressure under which the water is pumped also aerates it very considerably. In hilly or mountainous country, when fishing from the bank either very early in the morning or late in the evening, try to select an area of shoreline that is shielded from the rising or

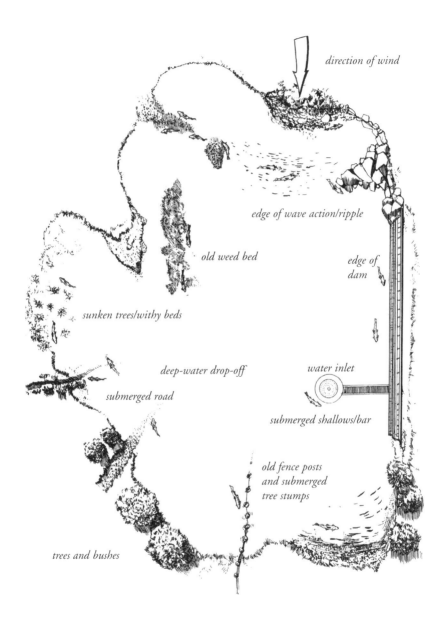

direction of wind

edge of wave action/ripple

old weed bed

edge of dam

sunken trees/withy beds

deep-water drop-off

water inlet

submerged road

submerged shallows/bar

old fence posts
and submerged
tree stumps

trees and bushes

Figure 44. Likely holding areas for trout on a reservoir

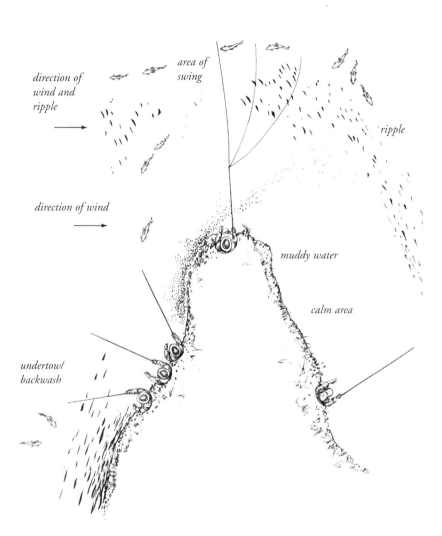

Figure 45. The ideal wind for fishing a promontory for a right-handed caster, showing where the trout are liable to be holding. The reverse would apply, with the wind blowing in the opposite direction, for a left-handed caster.

setting sun. The trout will be more active in these shaded stretches and will provide better sport later in the morning or earlier in the evening than areas that are catching the sun.

Techniques

In the spring and early summer, a team of unweighted nymphs or midge pupae fished deep and very slowly on a floating line is probably as effective as any other method. As the summer progresses, various items of food become available on or near the surface, such as midge pupae, caddis pupae and adults, and damsel nymphs. Later in the summer you may come across snails floating in the surface or even numbers of daddy longlegs being blown onto the surface, both of which are much appreciated by the trout.

In the past, fishing lures with deep-sunk lines used to be very popular and also effective. Today lure fishing—except later in the summer when shoals of fry are vacating the shallows—is far less effective, possibly due to the modern breeding techniques that have been adopted, at least by most UK fish farmers. Rainbow trout used to be susceptible to fast-fished lures, but the rainbows being bred and supplied today are triploids, incapable of reproduction. The elimination of sexual desire seems also to have eliminated much of their natural aggression so that at present, at least on British waters, while rainbows will often follow a lure for a short distance, they are much less inclined to attack it than they used to be.

While it is possible to use similar methods and techniques from bank and boats, there are a few interesting and often very productive methods that are best employed from the bank. In early summer, once the water has warmed up, trout will often frequent the shallow margins of stillwaters, so during the warmer summer months if you can find a length of deserted shoreline try fishing along it, rather than out into the body of the water. You will be surprised how close trout will come into an undisturbed section of bank, and will often take a fly with much more confidence than they will in open water. Approach the shoreline very stealthily and fish along it without entering the water. I have found that the most productive way to fish is to make four or five casts, fishing each in an arc out from the bank, and take four or five paces and repeat the process. I normally fish a team of three attractor-type flies, such as a Peter Ross, a Mallard & Claret, and an Invicta, although as the summer progresses I often vary the point fly according to what may be hatching at the time, such as caddis pupae or even damsel nymphs.

Later in the summer, when the fry start to venture away from the very shallow water along these margins, try using one of the fry-imitating lures that are available. At this time, watch out for trout splashing on the surface, which is usually caused by the taking of floating injured or dead fry. When you see this, a floating fry pattern should be mounted on the point on its own, cast out in the vicinity of the rises and fished static.

During August, when other forms of aquatic food are in short supply, corixae, small beetlelike creatures of the Hemiptera family, will be found in large concentrations in the vicinity of patches of weed along the shoreline. These tiny creatures have to visit the surface constantly to replenish their air supply, and because of this they are only to be found in shallow areas—that is, three feet or less in depth—close to shore. At this time of the year many trout will come into the shallow water, particularly as dusk approaches, to feed upon them. There are many corixa patterns and these should be fished in the sink-and-draw style to simulate the natural as it ascends to the surface.

Many small stillwaters, such as ponds and gravel pits, as well as some large lakes are blessed with crystal clear water, which can provide great sport by stalking cruising trout from the bank. Many years ago I developed a killing pattern called a Gerroff. The body of this pattern is dressed on only half the length of the hook shank, which presents a very small silhouette, and, as it is unweighted, it sinks very slowly. When a cruising trout is spotted, cast this pattern a short distance ahead of the fish, and as he approaches give the fly a slight draw. More often than not you will see the trout turn or lift as he takes the fly, or you may even see the white blink as he opens his mouth to take it.

Another equally exciting tactic is to look for what I term patrolling trout. These are usually the larger, well-established trout that patrol defined areas along the bank, nearly always returning to the same spot. These trout can often be successfully ambushed, but it does require considerable patience. Try to find a bush or tree or some other obstruction on the bank that will provide background cover to make it difficult for the fish to see you. Stand or, better still, sit in front of such an obstruction and wait for a trout to pass by. After several passes it is usually possible to establish his favourite route. Cast your fly into his path, either a Gerroff or a small nymph, allow it to sink and settle on the bed of the water, and wait for him to return. When he approaches the area where your fly is lying on the bottom, slowly lift it to the surface; if he spots it a confident take is usually assured, but if he does not, do not panic; wait for his next pass and try again.

The strategy has also proved very successful on large lakes that have extensive shallows with scattered weed beds, where you can wade out carefully and take up a stance close to a clear channel among the weeds. This ploy has provided me with many large trout on clear American and also New Zealand lakes. Incidentally, when wading from the shore on big lakes and reservoirs, many fly fishers make the mistake of wading out as far as possible before starting to fish, driving any trout that may be present farther out. Start close to the shore and slowly work your way out until the fish are found.

Leaders

Leaders are probably even more important on stillwater than they are on rivers, both from the bank and from a boat. The composition, length, and position of the flies on your leader are of the utmost importance. The butt end is less critical, and for this you can use one of the custom-made tapered leaders, or even one of the braided tapered leaders if you prefer them. The butt should be about nine or ten feet in length, tapering to a nylon point of eight- to ten-pound test, onto which a length of level nylon of six- to eight-pound test should be knotted. The length of this will depend upon the length of the leader that you wish to fish with. Prior to the seventies most stillwater fly fishers used leaders about ten to twelve feet long, similar to those used on rivers. In 1970 I started to experiment with longer leaders on stillwater, as it seemed to me you could unknowingly line an unseen trout between you and the one to which you were fishing, spooking him and also your intended quarry. As a direct result of the longer and longer leaders, my catch rate improved dramatically, and after two years of carefully monitored experiments I published the results in an article in 1973 for one of the leading angling magazines of that time. Shortly after this longer leaders quickly became the norm for stillwater fishing, and today some expert fly fishers use leaders nearly thirty feet in length. Personally, I seldom use a leader much over twenty-five feet in length, and the norm would be eighteen and twenty feet. Long leaders will certainly increase your catch rate, but can be most frustrating and cause much agony unless you are a competent caster, particularly if you are fishing with a team of flies. My advice is to start off with a shorter leader, gradually increasing the length as you become more competent.

Most British stillwater fly fishers use a team of three flies, and these should be set up on droppers with at least four to five feet between each fly. Be careful not to make the droppers so short that after relatively few changes of flies there is no room to tie on another. A new leader will then have to be made before you can continue fishing, which can be most annoying in the middle of a good rise of trout. For this reason and also because the longer the dropper, the less chance the trout has of seeing your leader or of it getting in the way when he takes your fly, I believe in making the dropper as long as feasible, at least eight to nine inches. Do not forget to grease or degrease your leader and flies as the situation demands.

BOAT FISHING

First of all, let us look at the equipment needed for a successful day's boat fishing. When fishing a big lake or reservoir, most fly fishers tend to take their lunch out with them, which means a long day on the water, so comfort is of the essence. If you are not comfortable it becomes very difficult to concentrate, so make sure you have a decent seat. Hire boats often have no room for a proper chair, so you have to sit on the thwarts. It is possible to purchase custom-made, comfortable, padded seats with backs to clamp onto the thwart, but they are quite expensive, so many fly fishers make up their own from thick foam. If the foam is thick enough these are reasonably comfortable. Another tip is to use a car's small-diameter inner tube, which is very comfortable indeed.

Even if the weather is fine when you set out, always take a set of good waterproofs with you, and a sweater in case the temperature drops. Always wear glasses of some sort to protect your eyes from a badly cast fly. While some people like to fish on their own, many like to fish with a buddy. If you are going with a companion make sure it is someone you get along with well as, believe me, there is nothing worse than to be isolated for many hours with someone who may be bad tempered, uncooperative, or, worse still, a bad caster. In a small boat this can be a lethal combination.

The only time I ever use a landing net is from a boat, as I prefer to beach my fish or hand-lift them. To hand-lift a trout from over the side of a boat can be very difficult, so a long-handled, big-diameter net is really essential when boat fishing.

Most boats are provided with one anchor but never two, so I take a spare one with a length of rope in case I want to anchor and fish. With a single anchor the boat yaws all over the place even in very light winds; with an anchor at either end of the boat you will be provided with a secure platform from which to fish by almost any method. Another item rarely provided is a drogue, so again I take one with me. A drogue is a large square piece of canvas with a hole in the centre and ropes secured to each corner. When lowered over the side of the boat on a long length of rope, it acts like a sea anchor to slow your rate of drift when fishing loch style. A drogue is an extremely useful item of equipment, as not only can it slow your rate of drift but it can also, to a certain degree, control your direction of drift according to where it is secured to the boat. Drogues are a mixed blessing, though, as they have to be taken inboard at the end of every drift and reset before you commence your next one. Therefore, in light winds I rarely use them.

So far as rods are concerned, I normally take two with me, but which two will depend upon the methods of fishing I intend to participate in. For loch-style fishing, I prefer a lightweight rod to take a 6- or 7-weight line, ten feet in length or, better still, eleven feet if you can obtain it, as the longer the rod, the better you can control the top dropper. For fishing lures, attractor patterns, or deep-sunk nymphs on heavy sinking lines, you will need a nine- or nine-and-a-half-foot rod to take a 9- or 10-weight line. For fishing surface nymphs, midge pupae, or dry flies, I prefer an eight-and-a-half- or nine-foot rod to take 5- or 6-weight line.

When it comes to fly lines, I only take three reels, one loaded with a No 7 floating line for loch-style fishing, another with a No 5 floating line for nymph or dry-fly fishing, and finally a No 6 or 7 intermediate line for fishing nymphs or pupa patterns just below the surface. I prefer to fish on or near the surface, but during adverse weather conditions the trout may only be feeding on or near the bottom. At this time you will need extra reels, one loaded with a No 7 or 8 sink-tip line, one with a No 8 or 9 slow-sink line, and another with a No 9 or 10 fast-sink or even an extra-fast Hi-D. With these sinking lines many fly fishers prefer to use shooting heads to obtain the extra distance when casting.

Loch-Style Fishing

Drift fishing in the old Scottish loch style is not only one of my favourite methods on big lakes and reservoirs, but also one of the most productive and exciting, especially when the trout are rising or near the surface. Inexplicably, I rarely see it practiced on American stillwaters. The slashing rise as a good trout takes your fly or top dropper can really start the adrenaline pumping, and when, as often happens, a bow wave follows your fly into the side of the boat, and the trout explodes out of the water as he takes almost beneath your rod tip, it is not for fly fishers with a weak heart.

On the Irish loughs and Scottish lochs, fly fishing from boats has been practiced for several centuries. From the early days it was quickly established that the most productive method of catching trout was to fish flies just on or below the surface. Most of the water was of a rather acid nature and, as bottom food was at a premium, most trout were forced to rely on either surface-hatching flies or various terrestrial species that were blown onto the surface.

Although it is not known exactly when drift fishing commenced, it was undoubtedly the canny Scots who first realized that a greater area of water could be covered from a boat drifting downwind. They also must have appreciated that the longer your flies remained in the water, the better your chances of taking a fish. This must have led to their choice of a long rod fished in conjunction with a relatively short fixed length of line. With this method the rod fishes the flies, which never leave the surface of the water apart from the split second or so that it takes to flick or roll them back downwind, which can hardly be termed a cast. Rods varied in length from ten to twelve feet and during the last century it was not uncommon to find these Scottish loch fishers mounting upwards of a dozen flies on droppers on their leaders. The traditional loch boats were heavily built in wood of a clinker construction so that they floated low in the water and drifted quite slowly, even in strongish winds. If the wind was very strong, a sea anchor was used to slow the drift, and this was often a large stone on a length of rope lowered over the windward side of the boat. Usually there would be two anglers, one sitting in the bow with the other in the stern, both fishing their team of flies downwind on quite a short line. Towards the end of the last century this form of loch fishing had become an established art, with a large dry fly on the top dropper being dibbled along the surface as the rod was lifted and the flies retrieved. The art was, and still is, to retrieve this dry fly with the hackles just feathering the surface, forming a slight wake that is most attractive to the trout—not so easy in a strong wind with big waves.

Towards the turn of the century competitive fly fishing became popular, most of the larger competitions taking place on Loch Leven, which was even then famed for the quality of its trout and its fishing. In 1904 the authorities running these competitions decided in their wisdom to restrict the number of flies that could be used on a leader to four. Today most loch-style fishers use three flies, which is also the maximum number you are now allowed to use in competitions.

When loch-style fishing, it is important to keep the top dropper well dressed with flotant, as it will not feather nicely over the surface if it becomes waterlogged. It is equally important to keep the leader and the other flies below the dropper well degreased, so that these always fish just below the surface without leaving any discernible wake. There is a very wide choice of flies that can be used on the top dropper. Traditionally, palmer-type flies have been favoured, and even today one of my personal favourites is a good old Soldier Palmer dressed on a size 10 or 12 hook, although early in the season I prefer a darker pattern such as a Zulu. Under very calm conditions with little wind it is better to use a much smaller fly, size 14 or even 16.

Patterns that can be used on the point and first dropper are legion, varying from traditional wet-fly patterns to the more modern dressings representing various stages of caddisflies, midges, or the nymphs of many species of upwinged flies. I try to use patterns that have at least some resemblance to those species of naturals that are most likely to be present on the water at the time of year I am fishing. On the other hand, I must admit I do have one or two favourite combinations that have been kind to me over the years, such as a Mallard & Claret on the dropper with a small midge pupa on the point, or, later in the season, an Invicta or Dunkeld on the dropper with a Sedge Pupa or Damsel Nymph on the point.

On rivers I tend to fish catch and release most of the time, but on most of the big UK reservoirs you are obliged to kill all the trout you catch with a bag limit of six or eight. Therefore, I always spoon out the first trout that I catch to ascertain on what they may be feeding. At times during the day in the height of the summer, the trout will be stuffed to the gills with small midges (chironomids), and when this occurs I dispense with the large top dropper and mount a team of small midges. In the evenings on the big lakes and reservoirs, you may encounter an extensive surface rise, although unfortunately these are far less common now than they used to be. During this rise, particularly from midsummer onwards, the trout will start off feeding on caddis pupae as they are transposing into the adults in the surface, then suddenly switch to taking the adult, and then switch again to taking midge pupae. It is important to take note of what is going on as, if you do not change your patterns accordingly, you are likely to have a most frustrating evening.

When fishing loch style, I still like to keep at least five feet between each of my flies but tend to use a much shorter leader, usually a maximum of around fourteen feet. If the leader is much longer than this you will find you have a problem dibbling your top dropper correctly.

Tactics

First of all, although you are basically casting downwind, you should try to cover as much water as possible—an arc in front of the boat and as far out to the side as possible.

To the observer, loch style may appear to be a very casual way of fishing, but in fact it requires a lot of concentration. All the time you should be looking for rising fish, which if covered quickly will often result in a positive take. Some of these rises are very subtle indeed, the trout swirling and taking a fly just beneath the surface. The only indication you will have of this is a mere crinkle of water, which can be easily missed unless you know what you are looking for. If you hit the ideal weather conditions and you are lucky, you may encounter a good surface rise, and then you have no problem about where to fish. However, on most days surface rises of any consequence are at a premium, and there is little indication of where to start fishing.

In my experience, particularly on the larger stillwaters, trout are rarely spread out all over the water but tend to congregate in certain areas, depending on the weather conditions and available food. Many times I have had a blank day only to find upon my return to the boat dock that other fly fishers have had limit bags. It is therefore important to do a little research before starting. If other fly fishers are present when you start, do not be afraid to ask them where the current hot spots are likely to be found. Failing this, it often pays to observe the water carefully for signs of any birds working, such as swallows or swifts, which means there will be flies hatching and, hopefully, trout present. If, as often happens, there are no indications at all, choose a likely looking area and try a drift. Before commencing any drift always

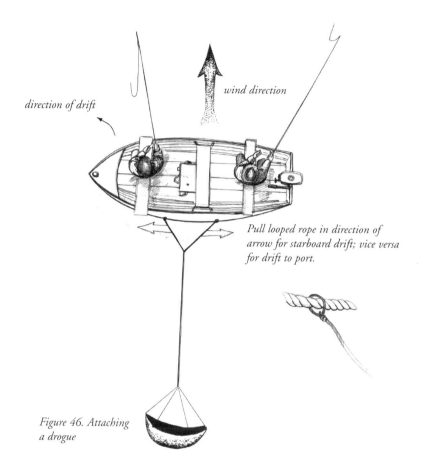

direction of drift

wind direction

Pull looped rope in direction of arrow for starboard drift; vice versa for drift to port.

Figure 46. Attaching a drogue

take cross bearings from marks on the shore so that if you do hit any fish on the drift you can always return to the same spot for another drift. If the drift is negative, do not waste time repeating it but move to a completely different area and try again.

In windy conditions wind lanes often form. These are long channels of slick water often favoured by the trout, which always work up them against the wind. It pays therefore to drift down them, as they will sometimes produce the odd fish. In very windy conditions, seek out bays or other sheltered areas, as trout are more likely to be found in these calmer areas of water.

As already mentioned, in light winds a drogue offers little advantage, but in winds of about force four or over it really is an essential item in the loch fisher's armoury. Not only does it slow the rate of drift to enable you to work your flies better, but it can influence the direction of your drift and also ensure that your boat holds steadily directly across the wind. All boats seem to have a mind of their own, and without a drogue some will drift with the bow slightly upwind while others may drift with the stern a little upwind. The drift will also be affected by the position of the anglers in the boat. These problems can be overcome by attaching your drogue to a long loop of rope, which enables you quickly to adjust the drogue towards bow or stern and so control the drift. This loop is made up using two metal rings to which ropes are knotted, one being tied to the bow while the other is tied to the stern. The drogue is knotted onto the middle of the loop, which can be pulled on one side or the other to adjust the drogue's position. (See figure 46.) Alternatively, a less sophisticated but equally effective method is to use a longer length of rope on the drogue, take this underneath two of the thwarts in the boat, and knot it back on itself to form a big loop, which can be moved from side to side in the same manner.

Additional Techniques

In very heavy winds when the water is very rough with big waves, it is extremely difficult to control the top dropper well enough to produce that tantalizing wake that so often attracts trout to your flies. Under these conditions try fishing a small Muddler Minnow on the top dropper; a size 10 or even 12 is ideal. No fly produces a better wake than a Muddler fished on the surface. Under normal conditions the amount of wake produced by a Muddler would scare rather than attract the trout, but quite often in very rough water trout will charge after it as if it is the last meal they are going to get.

During periods of fairly light winds there are two other techniques you can try that often prove very effective. When you have dibbled your top dropper halfway back to the boat in a straight line, try slowing it down and dibbling it from side to side. This erratic movement will often excite and tempt a reluctant trout into rising. The other technique that may be productive under reasonably calm conditions is to fish sink-and-draw. This may sound alien to a hardened loch fisher, but it can often prove to be a very useful method to try when few, if any, trout appear to be anywhere near the surface. Most stillwater anglers appreciate that trout are particularly attracted to any flies rising to the surface—which is the basis of this method. You still fish three flies with a large palmered fly or a bushy Caddis on the top dropper, but on the point you mount a nymph buzzer or other pattern of your choice, either weighted or dressed on a heavy wire hook, so that it sinks quickly. This format means

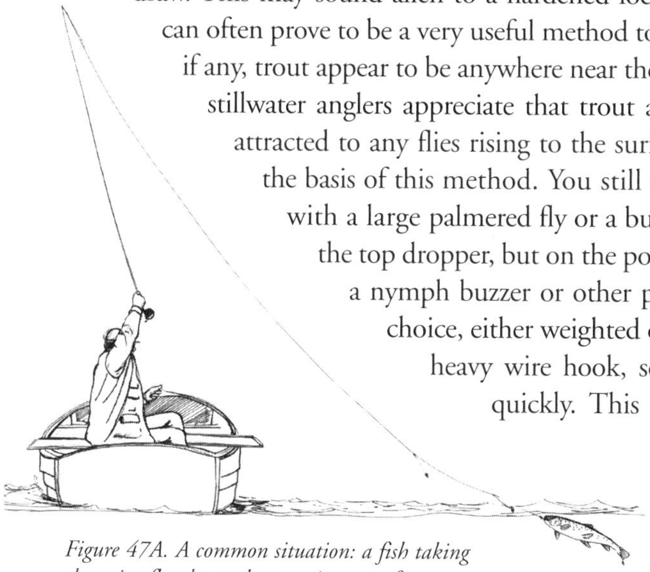

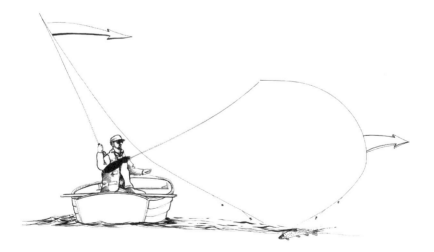

Figure 47A. A common situation: a fish taking the point fly; the angler running out of arm.

Figure 47B. Making a roll cast is usually sufficient to set the hook.

that the point fly and also the fly on the first dropper will sink to some depth, provided that the retrieve rate is very slow. When you reach the point when you would normally lift the rod to dibble the top dropper, stop for as long as possible, depending upon the rate of drift. Then when you do commence to lift, the flies should be ascending towards the surface, often deadly to fish that cannot make up their minds.

Finally, I'd like to suggest a solution to a problem that has always bedevilled loch fishermen. How often have you had a trout follow your flies right into the side of the boat and then decide to take? When this happens, sod's law nearly always operates, which means your arm is fully extended behind you so that it is impossible to strike. When this occurs, providing you train yourself to do it in the heat of the moment, snap the rod sharply forward as you would in a roll cast; this is normally sufficient to set the hook. (See figures 47A and B.)

FISHING THE DRY FLY ON STILLWATER

Within the past five or six years, fishing a team of dry flies has revolutionized sport on most big stillwaters. It is generally accepted that this is now probably the most killing method of all. Prior to this, dry-fly fishing was only ever attempted with a single dry fly and seldom proved very productive. No-one seems to be sure why the technique is now proving so effective, although it may well be due to the fact that over this same period aquatic flies have declined and are now nowhere near so prolific on most of the big waters as they used to be. The trout are therefore having to look more to the surface for their food. Unfortunately you rarely encounter the extensive surface rises to midges and caddis that were once such a feature on the big stillwaters. Four years of semidrought in the UK with a lot of sun and little rain produced an explosion of algae and consequently the water authorities were forced to introduce chemicals into most of the big reservoirs to combat it. One current theory is that some of these chemicals may have led to the destruction of much of the aquatic life, although this does not explain why over the same period many of the big lakes in Ireland, where chemicals have not been introduced, also seem to have suffered from much reduced hatches.

With this method of dry-fly fishing, you fish downwind from a drifting boat in a manner similar to loch-style fishing, using a drogue in wind in the same way. Here, however, the comparison ends; in this style of fishing you will not be constantly casting and retrieving your flies, nor will you be using a long fly rod. In fact, a typical dry-fly outfit for this style of fishing would be an eight-and-a-half- or nine-foot rod with a No 5 or 6 floating line mounted with an eighteen- or twenty-foot leader. Again three flies are mounted, one on the point and the others on long droppers, five to six feet apart. If you are fortunate enough to encounter a heavy surface rise of trout where you are constantly covering rising fish, it is better to position the flies much closer, about two to three feet apart. The dry flies used for this style of fishing are very simple and sparsely hackled, as the secret of success is to fish them in the surface film rather than on top as with a normal dry fly. They should be dressed on small hooks, size 14 or 16 or even size 18 in flat calm conditions. The bodies can be formed from seal's fur or similar material, and the most killing colours seem to be hot orange, red, and claret, in that order, with two turns of brown or grizzly hackle. At times I have also found that a dubbed body of hare's ear or mole's fur seems to be effective, particularly if any upwinged flies are seen to be hatching. I normally mount a much larger pattern on the top dropper as an attractor. This can be dressed on a hook, size 10 or 12, in colours and materials similar to the smaller patterns; the current favourite is an Amber Hopper. This is dressed with three or four turns of hackle and an amber seal's fur body, plus three long trailing legs on either side formed from the knotted flue of pheasant tail fibres.

The top of the leader down to the top dropper should be kept heavily greased, and the flies should be constantly anointed with flotant. In rough conditions the monofilament between the flies should be lightly greased, but in calm conditions it often pays to degrease the nylon. The team of flies is always fished on the dead drift—that is, static. They should be cast downwind on a fairly long line, and the line retrieved with a figure-of-eight movement, just fast enough to keep pace with the drift of the boat without moving them. As in loch fishing, any rise or even the slightest indication of a rise or crinkle in the water should be immediately covered.

This style of fishing requires even more concentration than loch style; apart from looking for rising fish, you must also try to keep one eye on the dry flies on the surface, as takes are often very gentle, in fact almost imperceptible. While it is seldom necessary to strike instantly, a good firm strike should be made after a second's hesitation to take up any slack in the line. As in loch fishing, an arc in front and out to the side of the boat should be covered, and just before retrieving for the next cast, I like to move the flies along the surface very slowly for a few feet before lifting them off. I have found that this movement will often tempt a reluctant trout in the vicinity to take. Many top stillwater dry-fly fishers have discovered that it pays dividends to re-cast the team of dry flies several times as you drift, rather than fishing the drift out without moving them. As you drift, every fifteen or twenty seconds re-cast the flies to a different area. This in effect not only means you will be covering a bigger area of water when drifting, but also increases your chances of attracting trout to your flies, as the disturbance they make each time they alight on the surface will often attract any trout in the vicinity.

While dry-fly fishing is now one of the most popular and effective methods of fishing big stillwaters, it is rarely very effective under rough conditions, where it is best to employ other methods. It is the favoured method in light winds with a nice ripple and can also be reasonably effective in a good breeze, but it is generally accepted that the calmer the conditions, the better the dry fly fishes. Therefore, most experts tend to seek out areas of flat calm where they can be found. This is, of course, directly opposed to other forms of drift fishing, where in light winds areas of calm are to be avoided. Before dry-fly fishing was widely practiced, the worst times for fishing on big stillwaters were considered to be during hot, sunny, calm weather when the water appeared like a sheet of glass. These conditions are no longer feared, as the dry fly can often by very effective at these times.

DAPPING

This is probably the original way of fly fishing on stillwaters, practiced before the traditional style of loch fishing was refined early in the nineteenth century. It is still a popular way of fishing many of the big loughs in Ireland, where they very often dap with a live mayfly early in the season, and with a live daddy longlegs later in the season. Within the last few years it has also become reasonably popular on many of the large English reservoirs, and under the right conditions can be a very pleasant manner of fishing. (See figure 48.)

To dap either a live insect or an artificial fly, you require a long, light rod about fourteen or fifteen feet in length mounted with a floating No 7 fly line. Onto the end of the fly line, splice a length of silk floss, narrow silk ribbon, or machine crimplene a quarter of an inch or less wide. This should be slightly shorter than the rod being used. Onto the end of this, splice a short leader and tippet. You need to fish an artificial that will float well, such as a bushy caddis pattern or one of the many palmered patterns available, and this should be well treated with flotant. Patterns in sizes from 10 to 14 may be used; the calmer the conditions, the smaller the fly. Dapping can be restful as well as enjoyable, as casting is not necessary; you merely hold the rod in a near-vertical position with a yard or so of fly line extending beyond the tip of the rod, the floss, silk, or ribbon streaming

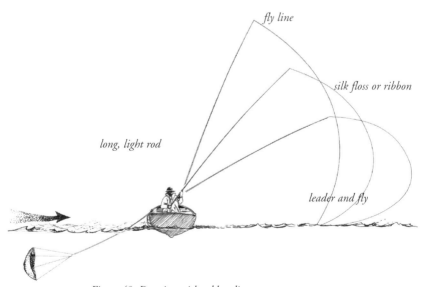

Figure 48. Dapping with a blow line

out in the wind. The length of fly line extending beyond the tip will depend upon the strength of the wind, as the secret of successful dapping is to keep the fly tripping around on the surface, creating a slight wake. Dapping is not possible in flat calm conditions, nor in very strong winds, as it is almost impossible to keep the fly on the surface for long enough.

In a stiff breeze it is a good idea to mount the bushy dapping fly on a dropper about two feet from a small weighted nymph on the point. In such conditions the weighted nymph sinking below the surface will help you control the dapping fly on the surface and will also be an added attraction for the trout.

GENERAL DRIFT FISHING

Apart from loch-style and dry-fly fishing, there are several other methods you can employ from a boat drifting downwind. Use a nine- or nine-and-a-half-foot rod in conjunction with a No 7 or 8 forward-tapered floating line and as long a leader as you can handle. The farther you cast downwind from the boat, the better, and the rate of retrieve will depend upon the pattern or patterns of fly you are using. In rough weather try fishing a single Muddler Minnow on the point and strip this quickly through the waves. Later in the season when the fry of other fish are likely to be found in open water, replace this with a white Baby Doll or similar lure. During hot weather, when the water is like pea soup with green algae, try fishing a shocking pink Baby Doll, or, if the algae is of a brownish colour, try a Viva. This is a black fly with a lime green tail. Another very effective pattern on stillwaters throughout the world is a damsel nymph pattern dressed on a long-shank hook in sizes from No 8 up to 12. The natural nymphs vary tremendously in colour and tend to take up the basic colours of their environment. There are many different species but the three most common throughout the world in the adult form are blue, green, and red, respectively. Where the green and blue are present, use basically green-coloured nymphs, and in those areas where the red variety are predominant use a brown-coloured nymph. Two of the best patterns I know are Cliff Henry's Damsel Nymph, and Gary Borger's Damsel

Nymph. In late summer keep an eye open for daddy longlegs. These are the largest members of the Tipulidae family, which are often blown out onto the water under windy conditions. A big artificial daddy dressed on an 8 or 10 long-shank hook well treated with flotant and fished static among the waves can often prove very killing indeed. From midsummer on, during the late afternoons or early evenings, a team of three caddis pupae in different colours can be well worth trying, with a change later in the evening to a hatching caddis pattern on the top dropper.

Throughout the season midges are one of the main sources of food on most stillwaters throughout the world. There are hundreds of different species, varying in size; some of the adults are less than an eighth of an inch (two millimetres) in length, while others, are over three-quarters of an inch (two centimetres). They also vary in colour from black through brown to green, while some species are distinctly red. While the wings of all the different species are transparent, they often briefly take on an orange colour while they are hatching in the surface. While it is possible to fish patterns to represent both the larvae on the bottom and the adults on the surface, it is when the fully mature pupa leaves the bottom and ascends to the surface to hatch that both fish and fishermen are presented with the best opportunities. During the early stages of a hatch the trout will commence feeding upon them as they ascend to the surface, and at this stage a team of my own Hatching Midge Pupae is very effective. These should be well degreased and cast downwind as far as possible from a drifting boat, and then allowed to sink as far as possible before retrieving them in the sink-and-draw style. Another very effective method is to mount a large dry floating caddis pattern on the top dropper and use this as a strike indicator for the Midge Pupae patterns hanging below.

If the hatch is a fairly heavy one the trout will gradually move nearer and nearer to the surface until they eventually concentrate on taking the pupae hanging in the surface film preparatory to hatching into the adult. When this occurs, the riseform to the larger species is very distinctive, as the trout cruise along just beneath the surface and suck in the pupae with a lazy head and tail rise. The smaller species that usually hatch during the day are taken with a less distinctive rise, the trout feeding upon them in a straight line upwind or along wind lanes. In calm conditions the trout have an odd habit of feeding in circles.

When the trout are feeding upon pupae in the surface film they become very selective and will only accept a pattern presented in the film. Ever since the early part of this century when Dr Bell of Blagdon experimented with midge-feeding trout and launched his Black Buzzer, which as far as I know was the first pattern dressed specifically to represent midge pupa, fly fishers have had problems trying to present pupa patterns in the surface film. When I first started stillwater fly fishing in the early fifties, hatches of midges were often prolific with so many trout rising you did not know which one to cast to. Despite this, more often than not few trout were caught. In those days the only known method of presenting your pupa patterns in the film was to grease the whole leader very heavily in order to hold the pupae there. In practice, they did not hang vertically like the naturals, and apart from this they would only remain on the surface for a few seconds before sinking the length of the dropper, which even if only two or three inches was too far. The problem was not solved until the early eighties when a couple of friends and I developed a pattern, now extremely popular, called a Suspender Midge Pupa. This pattern is formed by securing a small ball of white foam enclosed in a nylon mesh over the eye of the hook. This floats the pattern in the film with the body and hook hanging vertically below in a manner similar to the natural pupae. Furthermore, from below the surface the base of this white ball looks like the white breathing filaments on the head of the natural pupae.

When midges are hatching and surface rises visible, I mount three of these in different sizes and colours in the same manner as I do my Hatching Midge Pupa patterns, cast them downwind, and fish with little or no movement. I always spoon out the first trout I catch, which shows the colour and size of the naturals hatching. I can then mount corresponding suspenders. It is worth noting that most of the larger species of midges usually hatch in the early morning or late evening when the surface is calm. A heavy surface film is often present, through which the pupae find it difficult to emerge and transpose; they therefore spend considerable time hanging vertically in the film. Every few seconds they will adopt a horizontal position and swim along under this film looking for a crack or weak spot through which they can emerge. During a heavy hatch there will be thousands of pupae hanging in this film at the mercy of the trout, so at this time there will be heavy and widespread surface rises—unfortunately far less common today than they used to be. When fishing a team of suspenders during such a heavy surface rise, I mount them much closer together, between eighteen inches and two feet, and cast into the path of any rising trout. When trout are head and tailing in the surface, their vision to either side is restricted to little more than twelve inches, so when flies are mounted close together at least one of them is likely to been seen by the trout. They should be fished static, although an occasional tweak on the line will lift the artificials from the vertical into the horizontal position and move them a few inches in a manner similar to the naturals. This slight movement also helps to draw the attention of any trout in the vicinity.

When drifting broadside with the wind, as in loch-style fishing, it is rather unusual to consider fishing with a sinking line. However, there is an effective method of fishing a team of nymphs if the wind is not too strong, using a nine or nine-and-a-half-foot stiffish rod with a No 7 or 8 Hi-D line. The secret of its success to a large extent lies in using a shortish leader and positioning the fly on the top dropper very close to the tip of the fly line, so that it sinks very quickly and to the same depth as the fly line. Mount three or four nymphs, one on the point and the others on droppers, which should be no longer than two to three inches to avoid tangles. The flies should be spaced about three feet apart, with the top dropper no more than two feet from the tip of the fly line. Use a variety of nymphs, such as a Pheasant Tail, a PVC, or a Hare's Ear, or intersperse these with various Midge Pupa patterns. The team of nymphs should be cast as far downwind as possible, and allowed to sink as quickly as possible. Watch the end of your fly line, as trout will often take one of the nymphs on the drop. The line can be retrieved with a figure-of-eight movement, but only as fast as the drift of the boat downwind, as at this stage you do not want to move the flies. By the time you are actually ready to retrieve the nymphs, the fly line should be hanging almost vertically down into the water, and the nymphs should be hanging in a big loop close to the bottom. As you start to bring the nymphs up, great concentration is needed, as takes are likely to occur at any stage. They can be quite savage but more often than not the only indication will be a slight heaviness in the line, or the loop of line hanging down from the rod tip will not sag back as normal under its own weight when you pause between retrieves.

This form of fishing depends almost as much on the feel of the line in your hands as it does upon your eyesight, and can be very rewarding when you strike into a trout that has given you only the faintest indication of a take through your fingers. It is most effective in water between twelve and twenty feet in depth, and where possible try to arrange a drift that is taking you towards the shore, where the water is gradually shallowing off in front of you. This sunk-line method is only effective in calm conditions or with light winds. In big winds or even in a strong breeze it is not practical, as the boat will be drifting too quickly for the nymphs to sink deep enough before you have to retrieve.

FISHING AT ANCHOR

Many fly fishers prefer fishing from an anchored boat, particularly those who are happier fishing with sinking lines, while others, myself included, who prefer the mobility of a drifting boat only resort to fishing at anchor when other methods are not viable. If you are forced to find shelter in high winds and big waves, always moor the boat from the bow and never use more than one anchor. (See figure 49.) Anchored in this fashion it is possible to fish lures, or other sinking-line techniques, despite the fact that moored this way the boat will tend to yaw a lot from side to side. If the waves are not too big this yawing can be minimized by securing the anchor from one corner of the stern. (See figure 50.) If you wish to use sensitive techniques such as fishing nymphs very slowly, you will require a stable platform, which can only be achieved by using two anchors. (See figure 49.) When using two

Figure 49. Anchor position 1 is the safest in high winds with big waves. In calm conditions, when you require a stable platform for fishing nymphs, use two anchors in positions 1 and 2.

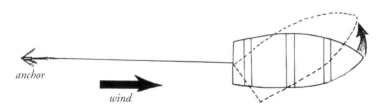

Figure 50. To minimize yawing when at anchor in windy conditions, secure the anchor rope to the centre of the stern, wait until the boat stops swinging, and then transfer it to the corner.

anchors in this fashion, moor the boat with the bow facing into the wind. Under calm conditions, if two anglers are fishing it is better to anchor the boat broadside to the wind.

There are many methods that can be employed from an anchored boat. You will see a lot of fly fishers fishing lures or attractor patterns on fast-sink lines and stripping these back at a very fast pace. Another method is to fish a team of nymphs on a floating line, letting the wind swing these around while at the same time retrieving them very slowly indeed. You can alternate this with fishing them sink-and-draw. The method of fishing a team of nymphs on a Hi-D line from a drifting boat—as detailed in the last section—can also be used in some cases very effectively from an anchored boat. There is one other relatively new technique, which has proved to be very successful over the past three or four years. This involves a rather revolutionary pattern called a Booby, which is loosely based on our Suspender pattern except that it is dressed on much larger hooks and is basically a lure-type pattern. Instead of one ball of white foam enclosed in a nylon mesh, it has two, mounted on each side of the eye of the hook. It is normally dressed with highly coloured bodies such as lime green or hot orange. The body is mounted on the point of a very short leader—four to five feet in length—and is fished on a fast-sink line. When fishing with Boobies, allow plenty of time for the fly line to sink to the bottom, and then retrieve a yard or so at a time, with long pauses in between. This in effect means you will be fishing the Booby in a reverse sink-and-draw style, which trout obviously find very attractive. The end of the fast-sink line will be lying on the bottom with the very buoyant Booby floating above it. As soon as you start to retrieve the line it will pull the fly towards the bottom, and then as you pause it will start floating back towards the surface. An extremely effective option is to mount the Booby on a short dropper about twelve inches from the end (point) of the leader, and then mount a small nymph or midge pupa on the point. Retrieve the fly line in the same fashion, but with this combination the trout invariably take the small fly hanging below and moving up and down with the Booby.

ALTERNATIVE DRIFT-FISHING METHODS

Within the last two decades or so several new methods of drifting and fishing have been developed. Two in particular offer some distinct advantages, although they do have some disadvantages, over the old traditional style of loch fishing, drifting broadside to the wind.

The first of these involves the use of a drogue trailed over the stern of the boat. (See figure 51.) In this position there is a much smaller area of the boat for the wind to push against, so the boat will drift much more slowly. With the boat drifting downwind bow first, the two

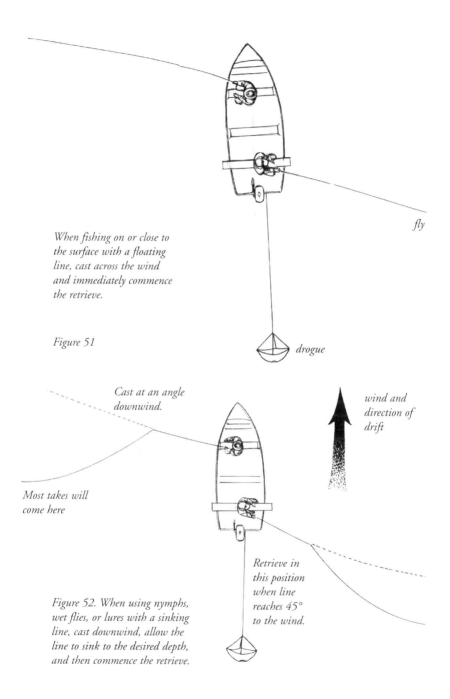

fly

When fishing on or close to
the surface with a floating
line, cast across the wind
and immediately commence
the retrieve.

Figure 51

drogue

Cast at an angle
downwind.

wind and
direction of
drift

Most takes will
come here

Retrieve in
this position
when line
reaches 45°
to the wind.

Figure 52. When using nymphs,
wet flies, or lures with a sinking
line, cast downwind, allow the
line to sink to the desired depth,
and then commence the retrieve.

anglers fishing must cast on opposite sides of the boat. The advantage here is that you will be retrieving across the ripple and also covering a much greater area of water. The only disadvantage is that the trout may see the boat at a greater distance. This way, and also with the following method, it is possible to fish lure-type flies or attractor patterns on various types of sinking fly lines from sink tip to Hi-D. (See figure 52.) Cast out at right angles to the boat, or even a little downwind, and allow the flies to sink until the line is pointing upwind at about a 45° angle before starting the retrieve. The speed of the retrieve will depend upon the types of flies being used. Most takes will occur soon after the retrieve commences as the fly line and leader begin to straighten out.

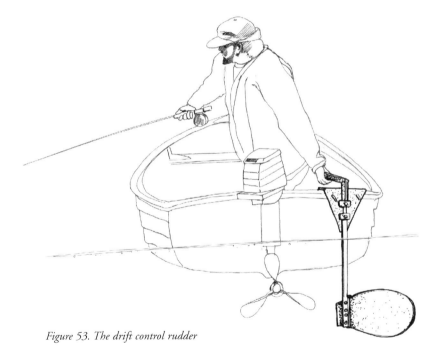

Figure 53. The drift control rudder

The second method involves the construction of a fairly simple rudder (see figure 53), the post of which is secured to a metal plate that can be clamped to the stern of the boat. This is called a drift control

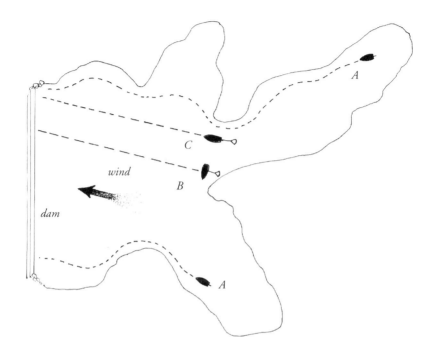

Figure 54. The advantage of using a drift control rudder. The rudder-controlled boat A can follow the contours of the shore, while the drogue-controlled boats B and C are at the mercy of the wind.

rudder and takes the place of the drogue. Although the drogue results in a much slower drift, the big advantage of the rudder is that the direction of the drift can be controlled to some degree. Rather than having to drift in a straight line, across or down the lake, the undulations of the bank may be followed, thus providing a much better and more interesting drift. (See figure 54.) The two anglers should fish to either side, as before.

With the previous method and also from float tubes it is possible to fish most of the techniques described in this chapter. Personally I love fishing from a float tube and always try to get in at least a few days fishing from one whenever I am offered the opportunity. Unfortunately, in

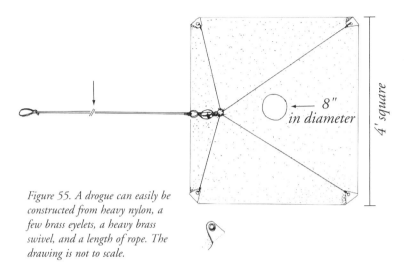

Figure 55. A drogue can easily be constructed from heavy nylon, a few brass eyelets, a heavy brass swivel, and a length of rope. The drawing is not to scale.

England they are banned on most of the big stillwaters. The big advantage of float tubes is that they sit very low in the water, so drift much more slowly than a boat, which needs a drogue to slow it down in anything other than very light winds. Drogues are generally available in fly tackle shops in England, but where they are not available it is perfectly possible to make one with the aid of a sewing machine. Figure 55 shows

Figure 56. A good alternative to a drogue is a thirty-foot length of one-inch link chain. This can be suspended from bow to stern and provides a slow, broadside, downwind drift.

how one is constructed. If you do not wish to go to this trouble there is a very reasonable compromise. Buy a thirty-foot length of one-inch metal anchor chain from your nearest boat chandlers, and either hang this in a big loop from stem to stern (see figure 56) or just hang it from the stern. Using the second method you can, up to a point, regulate the speed of the drift by adjusting the length of chain hanging over the stern. This also alerts you to any shallow areas—when the chain starts to drag along the bed of the lake, the boat slows down. (See figure 57.)

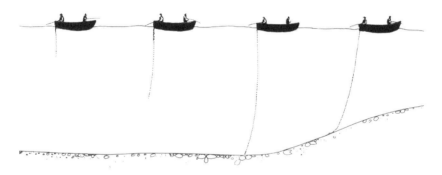

Figure 57. For drifting downwind bow first, a similar length of chain may be used. The longer the length of chain hung over the stern, the slower the drift. An added advantage is that shallows can be detected, as the boat slows down or even stops as more chain is grounded.

9

FLIES

The History and Development
of the Author's Most Popular Patterns

FLY DRESSING—ART OR CRAFT?

Wherever fly dressers gather, this is a subject that provokes heated debate. Many practitioners look upon it as a pure art form, while just as many see it as a traditional craft. My own view has always been that it is a little bit of both.

First of all, I think we must look back into the history of fly fishing and consider how fly patterns have developed over the centuries. The true history of fly fishing can be traced back at least to the late fifteenth century with the publication in 1496 of *A Treatyse of Fysshynge wyth an Angle,* attributed to Dame Juliana Berners. In this now famous book she gave a list of twelve artificial fly patterns, and it is from these humble beginnings that we have arrived at the proliferation of patterns that are available to the fly fisher today. For well over a century there were few if any additions to the list until, during the latter half of the seventeenth century, several important books on angling were published. The first, in 1653, was that great classic *The Compleat Angler* by Izaak Walton, closely followed in 1662 by *The Experienc'd Angler* by Robert Venables.

Both of these gave vague descriptions of a few new patterns. In 1676 the sixth edition of *The Compleat Angler* included a second book entitled *Being Instructions How to Angle for Trout or Grayling in a Clear Stream,* and in 1681 another now familiar title appeared—*The Angler's Vade-Mecum* by James Chetham. The publication of the sixth edition of *The Compleat Angler* heralded the arrival of more than sixty new patterns, and in the appendix of Chetham's book there appeared an even longer list of more modern patterns.

Art is usually associated with an original concept or creation, while craft is a special skill that is taught. Therefore I have little doubt that, at least during the first few centuries, fly dressing was a craft that was handed down from father to son or from fisherman to fisherman. None of the above-mentioned books gave precise details of all the dressings, so they could only have survived over this long period of time through the passing on of skills and personal knowledge. Even today the basic skills required to dress a fly can be learnt from instructional books or by attending fly-dressing classes. There again, the dictionary description of art is "the making of things that have form and beauty," and I am sure that even nonanglers would agree that many artificial flies have both of these attributes, particularly many of the larger fully dressed salmon flies. You could make a very good case for fly dressing as an art, but not in its basic form where you are copying the ideas of the originators of the patterns. Art is also defined in the dictionary as any branch of creative work, and this most certainly applies to the thousands of fly dressers over the years who have been responsible for creating original patterns. In support of this point I can do no better than quote the following from *Northern Memoirs,* written in 1694 by Richard Frank:

> Among the variety of your fly adventurers, remember the hackle, or the fly substitute, formed without wings, and drest up with the feather of Capon, Pheasant, Partridge, Moccow, Phlimingo, Paraketa or the like, and the body nothing differing in shape from the fly, save only in ruffness and indgency of wings.

Apart from all this, due to the proliferation of new synthetic fly-dressing materials in the last three or four decades, there now exists a pure art form of fly dressing. This is practiced by a relatively small body of very skilled fly dressers, particularly in the USA, who specialize in producing patterns not necessarily to fish with but to copy as closely as possible some of the natural flies, nymphs, pupae, and larvae upon which the fish feed. In many cases the patterns produced are so lifelike that it is virtually impossible to tell them apart from the naturals. Despite this it has been my experience that few if any of them are very successful when it comes to catching fish.

FLY PATTERNS

When I started fly dressing in the late fifties, I was fishing the river Itchen in Hampshire, one of the premier chalkstreams. At Abbot's Barton the river is full of the pickiest trout, as I mentioned earlier. I still consider the Itchen to be one of the most demanding trout streams in the world, and it is one of the few that really does require a pretty close copy of the species of fly that is hatching. I took up macrophotography so that I could provide my own magnified colour pictures of the indigenous insects to help me tie lifelike patterns in silk, fur, or feather. At least two of these patterns—the PVC Nymph and the Last Hope, dressed to match the small pale watery duns that were one of the more important hatches on this stream—are still in use regularly to this day.

My views on what constitutes a successful pattern have changed over the years, and since the early seventies I have concentrated on what I now consider to be the two most important aspects—simple designs that are quick to tie and trying to single out trigger points, which means emphasizing a particular feature of a natural fly that I think the fish may be looking for. Three good examples are the colour and position of the wings on my Poly May Dun, the size of the body in relation to the hook size in my Gerroff, and the pale gold tag representing the partially empty shuck on my Super Grizzly Emerger.

There follows a selection of my most popular patterns.

The Last Hope

This is the first pattern that I developed. It became popular on the streams of southern England during the late sixties and seventies, and still has a following on some rivers. At Abbot's Barton during the early part of the summer we would regularly experience good hatches of a very tiny upwinged dun commonly referred to as a pale watery. Members of the *Baetis* genus, they have a very pale, watery, olive-coloured body less than a quarter of an inch (five millimetres) in length. Later in the summer this would often be replaced by hatches of another member of this same genus, the small dark olive, which was even smaller and had a very dark, greyish olive body. When the trout were rising and feeding upon these, usually to the exclusion of any other species, they were extremely difficult to tempt with any of our standard patterns. Eventually, in desperation, I decided to attempt a pattern of my own and, after much trial and error, settled upon a dressing that proved to be reasonably successful—at least it fooled some of the trout some of the time. When we came across trout feeding upon these tiny duns, we would still offer them a variety of patterns usually to no avail, and then as a last resort we would mount one of my new creations; hence the name we bestowed upon it—the Last Hope.

It is essential to dress this pattern with a good-quality honey dun hackle very short in the flue, so that it fishes low down on the surface. It is far less effective with a normal-length hackle floating high on the surface. To assist flotability I dress it with very long tails; originally I used fibres from a blue dun cock hackle, but now I use nylon filaments, as introduced in the late seventies by that innovative American fly dresser, John Betts. To represent the body of the pale watery dun I chose the buff-coloured fibres from the breast feather of a Norwegian goose, and for the Small Dark Olive those with a greyish colour.

For the Last Hope, in fact for any dry flies with tails, I build up a small ball with the tying silk on the shank at the bend of the hook, and when I tie in the four or five tail filaments I snug them down behind this little ball, which gives them a good spread like the tails of the natural. Providing you have the correct materials, this is a very quick and simple pattern to dress.

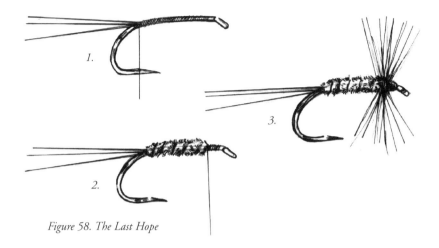

Figure 58. The Last Hope

Hook: Partridge arrow-point barbless, 16 or 18

Tails: nylon filaments

Body: fibres from Norwegian goose breast feathers, buff or greyish

Hackle: three turns from hackle of honey dun cock, short in flue

1. Tie in nylon filaments for tail, positioning to give exaggerated length.

2. Form tapered body with Norwegian goose feather herl.

3. Tie in honey dun cock hackle, short in flue, and wind to complete fly.

The PVC Nymph

At the time I developed this pattern in the midsixties, I was a member of the Piscatorial Society and we had just taken on some new water on the Upper Kennet at Axford. It was late June and, as on much of the Kennet in those days, hatches of surface flies from midsummer onwards were often rather sparse. This particular stretch had not been fished for a couple of years and consequently there were a lot of large trout, most of which were very dark and in poor condition. Our water warden was keen for these to be removed before restocking took place. They were very dour fish and the best chance of removing them was by nymph fishing. The nymph of the time was Sawyer's Pheasant Tail and, as I had recently become friendly with Major Oliver Kite, who was largely responsible for popularizing this then relatively new pattern, it was hardly surprising that it was my favourite. During early July I took a lot of the big trout on this pattern but as the summer progressed I found the fish were becoming even dourer and certainly much more wary. The Pheasant Tail Nymph, with its large thorax of wound copper wire, is fairly heavily weighted, and it could be fished either on the dead drift or with an induced take. Initially I always like to present a nymph on the dead drift and only resort to the induced-take method, if the trout consistently refuses. While this induced take is certainly a most deadly method, particularly early in the season or on lightly fished waters, there is little doubt in my mind that on a hard-fished water, particularly later in the season, the sudden acceleration of the nymph to the surface will spook a trout quicker than anything else. By the end of July it was all but impossible to take any of these larger Axford trout using the induced take, so I was limited to the dead-drift method and I was getting an awful lot of refusals, even using other patterns.

It was at this point that I began to consider the possibility of a new pattern. The next visit to the water was spent dredging the bottom with a net and collecting as many different species of nymphs as I could. While some of these were quite dark in their overall colouration, an even larger proportion, particularly the agile darters of the *Baetis* genera, were very light indeed, pale to the point of being almost translucent. Most of the various nymph patterns I had tried, including the Pheasant Tail, were quite dark, so I decided to try to develop a similar but olive-coloured pattern with a translucent look. After much experimentation with strips cut from various plastic sheets or polythene bags, all of which were useless, I was given a small sheet of opaque PVC material by my late friend David Jacques, who had connections with manufacturers of synthetic materials.

This material was a little thicker than most other plastics of a similar nature; it had a rubbery feel and stretched very well when cut into narrow strips for winding over the body. The sheet I was given was a natural colour but I found this could be given a fine olive tint if immersed for a short time in Picric acid. I have since found out that many shower curtains are made from this material, so if you can find an old one of these in an olive or light green colour you will have enough material to last you forever. This new pattern proved to be an instant success and accounted for a lot more big Axford trout before the end of the season. It is now an established and popular pattern, but be warned that many commercially tied patterns do not use the correct PVC material.

The PVC Nymph is not a particularly easy pattern to dress. Apart from obtaining the correct PVC, it is essential to apply the various materials in the correct proportions to obtain the desired silhouette. First of all, take a length of copper wire and build up a substantial thorax as in a Pheasant Tail Nymph; wind this wire down to the bend and break off. Then tie in with silk thread the three tails of olive-dyed golden pheasant tippets. Next tie in at the bend the cut strip of PVC, and leave it hanging while you tie in a length of olive-coloured polypropylene yarn. Wind this along the shank and over the thorax to form the body, and tie off behind the eye. Then wind the tying thread back over and just behind the thorax, and wind the PVC strip along the body, and tie in with the thread just behind the thorax. Finally, take the thread back to the eye and tie in a length of herl from any black feather. Tie over, double back, and tie in at the eye to form the wing case.

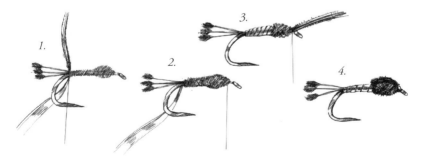

Figure 59. The PVC Nymph

Hook:	Partridge arrow point, 12 to 18
Silk:	brown
Underbody and Thorax:	copper wire
Tails:	three golden pheasant tippets
Overbody:	one strand of olive-coloured polypropylene yarn
Body covering:	¹⁄₁₆"- to ⅛"-wide strip of clear PVC, dyed olive
Wing pads:	three strands of dark pheasant tail or black cock

The Hatching Midge Pupa

This is another one of my very early patterns still regularly in use on lakes and reservoirs, for which it was designed. It is dressed with different-coloured bodies and in a range of sizes to represent the pupae of the many different species of midges (chironomids) as they ascend to the surface to hatch. When I developed it the only other pattern available was a Black Buzzer, originated by Dr Bell during the early part of the century for fishing on Blagdon Lake. Dr Bell was a well-known fly fisher of his time. While his pattern proved to be very successful and popular during the early days of stillwater fly fishing, I felt it could be improved because it bore only a passing resemblance to the natural. It had a black silk or wool body thickening towards the eye with a silver rib and a small bunch of white wool tied in sloping back over the body at the eye. At the time I was making a study of stillwater midges, and over a period of several months reared many different species in my own specially constructed tanks. When the pupae hatched and started their journey to the surface, I noticed two outstanding features on all of them—the startling white, breathing filaments on top of their heads and the white caudal fins at their tails. I therefore incorporated these two features in my new pattern. So as far as I am aware, I was the first person to develop and popularize a series of patterns in different sizes and colours incorporating white nylon filaments tied around the bend of the hook to represent caudal fins and a short strand of white fluorescent wool or marabou sloping forward over the eye of the hook to represent the breathing filaments on top of the head of the natural. Since then dozens and dozens of patterns have appeared with minor differences incorporating these features under different names, so now fly fishers are spoilt for choice. I use this pattern to represent the naturals ascending to the surface, but not to represent the pupae hanging in the surface film ready to hatch. For this stage in their life cycle I use a more recent pattern, the Suspender Midge Pupa (see page 207–210).

The Hatching Midge Pupa is a fairly straightforward pattern to dress. Start by tying the white nylon filaments and rib as far around the bend as possible. Then take the body material two-thirds of the way along the shank and rib, leaving room to tie in the herls of either peacock or turkey to form the thorax. The strand of white wool should be tied in over the eye and then, when you wind the thorax, take the last two strands under the white wool so that this slopes forward and up over the front of the thorax and the eye.

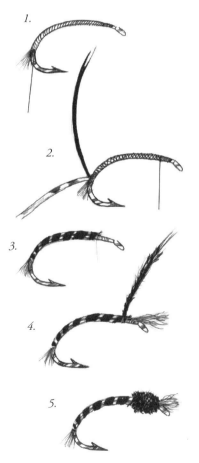

Figure 60. The Hatching Midge Pupa

Hook:	Limerick bend, 10 to 14
Silk:	as body colour
Tag or tail:	strands of white nylon filaments projecting ⅛″ below body
Body:	black, red, brown, green, or orange marabou silk or polypropylene yarn wound as far around bend as possible
Rib:	flat silver tinsel
Thorax:	three strands of peacock herl or brown-dyed turkey
Head filaments:	short strand of white fluorescent wool or marabou

1. Starting behind the eye, take the waxed tying silk down the shank and well around the bend of the hook. Tie in small strands of white nylon filaments.

2. Follow this with a length of flat silver tinsel or Lurex and a length of marabou silk. Return the tying silk to the point shown.

3. Wind the marabou up the shank into a tapered shape and tie it in. Trim off waste and follow up with the tinsel rib in neat, even turns. Tie in and trim off waste.

4. Tie in a tuft of white wool and then two or three strands of peacock herl.

5. Make a rope of the herl by twisting it together anticlockwise, then wind around the hook shank several times to form the thorax, the last two turns under the wool tuft. Make a neat head with the tying silk. Complete with a whip finish and then varnish.

The Sedge Pupa

This was developed for fishing in big lakes and reservoirs where from July onwards one of the main items in the trout's food chain is the sedge or caddisfly. With nearly two hundred different species in the UK alone, varying in colour and size from a few millimetres to well over an inch, the demand for good patterns to represent both pupal and adult stages was paramount. There were literally dozens and dozens of patterns available representing the adult caddis; there were even wet-fly patterns imitating the hatching caddis, many of which were being used way back in the last century on the Scottish lochs, but there were only one or two rather indifferent pupal patterns available prior to the introduction of my new one. It was designed to represent the emerging pupa swimming to the surface and quickly proved to be a very killing pattern and so very popular. Today, of course, there are many different patterns available, some of them so lifelike that it is difficult to tell them apart from the natural. Despite this my pattern still seems to be fairly popular, taking its share of trout. It is a simple and fairly quick pattern to dress.

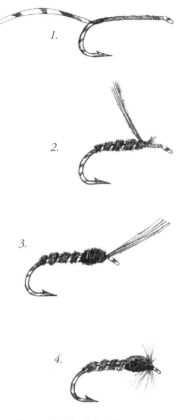

Figure 61. The Sedge Pupa

Hook:	down-eyed long-shank wide-gape, 10 or 14
Silk:	brown
Rib:	narrow silver Lurex or oval tinsel

Body:	cream, brown, orange, or green seal's fur
Thorax:	dark-brown-dyed turkey
Wing cases:	two or three pale-coloured feather fibres, doubled and redoubled
Hackle:	rusty hen (sparse)

1. Narrow silver Lurex tied in.

2. Silk dubbed with seal's fur and wound forward to the position shown, then ribbed. Three fibres of turkey herl tied in.

3. Herl wound to form a plump thorax. Three fibres of pale-coloured feather tied in at the eye.

4. Double and redouble these fibres to form a wing case. Hackle tied in and wound.

The Goddard Caddis (G & H Sedge)

This is one of my most successful patterns. It was developed in the early sixties with the assistance of my very good but sadly late friend Cliff Henry. We gave it the name the G & H after the initials of our surnames, but over the years it has become better known under its other name, coined by Andre Puyance, a well-known fly dresser who owns a large fly tackle shop just north of San Francisco. I first met him in the midsixties when he visited England and fished with me for several days on the chalkstreams. It was fairly late in the summer and one evening there was a particularly good hatch of large sedge or caddis-flies. I took several very nice trout on this relatively new pattern. Eventually I gave him one to try and he also had some nice browns on it. He was particularly impressed as at the time it was a completely new technique to use deer hair to form the wings. Before he left he asked me to tie him several in the larger size as he felt certain they would prove very killing on some of the larger western streams in the States.

They proved to be so effective that he decided to sell them commercially through his shop and mail-order business, and he marketed them under my name. I was completely unaware of this until I visited Montana three or four years later and, to my amazement, found them being sold in large quantities in every fly shop I visited. By this time they were apparently one of the two most popular caddis patterns in the western part of the USA, mainly for fishing on the larger rivers. Since then, as with a lot of things that become popular in the States, the name filtered back to England.

When Cliff and I first designed the pattern we never dreamt it would one day become so well known in the States for use on rivers; we originally developed it for fishing specifically on large lakes and reservoirs. During the early sixties, Cliff and I used to spend a lot of time in the late summer, when the best of the river fishing was past, in the west country fishing Blagdon and Chew Valley Lakes. In those days there used to be some marvellous hatches of big sedges at that time of the year, and we spent hours at the fly-tying bench trying to develop a pattern that would float well. This was about the time that the Muddler Minnow first appeared from America, demonstrating the excellent floating qualities of deer hair. So we tried tying a sedge with the traditional type wings behind a large Muddler deer hair head, with a modicum of success; but when we extended the deer hair right along the shank and clipped it to shape, the problem was solved. It floated fantastically well and with one application of flotant could be fished all day without sinking. Since then it must have taken thousands of trout. We used to fish it on Chew during the day along the margins by casting it as far as possible from an anchored boat and then giving it the occasional twitch. It was also very effective indeed fished loch style from a drifting boat on the top dropper. Another killing method was to skate it very fast along the surface from a drifting boat as dusk approached.

Eventually we dressed some smaller patterns on size 12 and 14 hooks for use on rivers, but it is basically a pattern for fishing the larger stillwaters and big, brawling rivers. In many fly shops in the States they sell the pattern dressed on hook sizes as small as 18, and I have even seen some dressed on size 20, mainly for fishing on the smaller streams. How they spin the deer hair on such tiny hooks amazes me, as I have found it all but impossible.

Providing you have mastered the technique of spinning deer hair on a bare shank, this is a relatively simple pattern to dress; however, it is very time consuming, as many turns of hair have to be applied to obtain the correct silhouette. The first stage is to apply the deer hair and clip it to shape. Wind on a substantial hackle behind the eye and in front of the deer hair wing, leaving the stalks of the two hackles used to project in front of the eye to represent the antennae of the natural sedge fly. Finally, spin seal's fur of the desired colour on a strong thread from the eye, pull this taut underneath the body, and secure at the bend. In fact, I now dispense with this last somewhat tedious operation, as I have found it much easier to colour the underpart of the deer hair wings with a waterproof felt-tip pen.

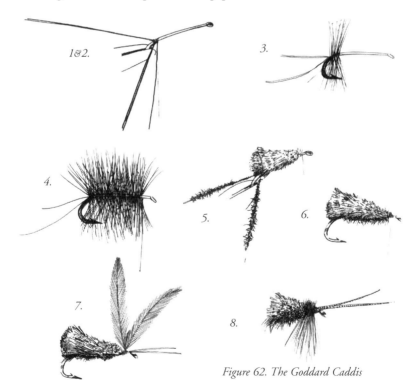

Figure 62. The Goddard Caddis

Hook:	down-eyed long-shank, 8 to 14
Silk:	green
Body:	spinnings of deer hair
Underbody:	seal's fur of desired colour
Hackle:	two rusty dun cock hackles

1. Tying silk tied on at the bend. Separate length of tying silk, about 8 inches, tied in at its midpoint at the bend of the hook.

2. First spinning of deer hair placed at the bend.

3. Spinnings of deer hair all the way along the shank. Silk secured with a half hitch after the final spinning. Deer hair trimmed as close as possible under the shank.

4. Rear view of trimmed body—note the triangular section. Pair of silk strands each dubbed with underbody fur.

5. Dubbed silks brought down and twisted into a rope, taken underneath the shank, and secured with tight turns behind the eye. Waste dubbed silk trimmed.

6. Matching hackles selected, good proportion of butt fibres stripped away to leave long quills (which form the fly's antennae). Hackles tied in with quills forward over the eye. Wind the hackles and tie off. Trim waste.

7. Hackles with upper fibres trimmed off, leaving downward-facing "legs."

The Persuader

This was developed in the late sixties when I was fishing a medium-sized reservoir, Hanningfield in Essex, on a regular basis. When I first started to fish it in the early sixties it was very rich in terms of food for the trout and in those days used to produce rainbows of exceptional quality with flanks like a newly minted silver dollar. Hatches of various species of chironomids throughout the year were phenomenal, and in the latter half of the season various sedge flies and perch fry predominated. At this time the surface fishing for rainbows was so good that few if any of the rods bothered with the brown trout on or near the bottom. However, towards the end of that decade not only did the insect hatches deteriorate, but the perch disease that was prevalent at that time struck the reservoir and the perch were all but wiped out. Due to these twin calamities the surface fishing for rainbows deteriorated, so many of the rods turned to fishing from boats with sinking lines for the browns. We quickly found out that these Hanningfield browns could be very selective, some days feeding upon sedge pupae or fry, other days feeding on damsel nymphs, snails, or midge pupae, so consequently a lot of time was wasted in trying to find out on what the fish were feeding that day. I thought that a general pattern that would look vaguely like some of the fauna that the trout were taking might be the answer. I decided on a white body, which might appear frylike; an orange thorax, as for some strange reason this colour in stillwater seems very attractive to trout, particularly from midsummer onwards; and a long-shank hook to give it a silhouette similar to a sedge pupa. This quickly became established with many of the regular rods and accounted for many fine brownies. It also proved to be a very good point fly fished from a boat just below the surface, particularly on the bigger reservoirs later in the summer when many of the naturals took on that greenish colour due to algal bloom. I still use this pattern with confidence on the odd occasions when I fish any of the larger reservoirs, and I am led to believe that in recent years it has become quite a popular pattern on many small stillwaters, where it is mainly fished as a nymph.

Hook: Partridge down-eyed long-shank, 8 to 12

Silk: orange

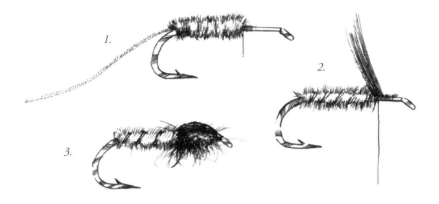

Figure 63. The Persuader

Body:	five strands (twisted) of white ostrich herl
Rib:	round silver tinsel No 20
Thorax:	hot orange seal's fur or substitute
Wing pads:	several strands of dark brown turkey herl

1. Tie in round silver tinsel and five strands of white ostrich herl. Twist ostrich herl and form body to position shown.

2. Rib body and attach dark brown turkey herl for wing pads.

3. Shape thorax with orange seal's fur or substitute. Bring turkey herl forward and secure to form wing pads.

The Gerroff

This may appear to be a very odd name for a fly, yet the explanation is really quite simple. At the time I developed it, in the great drought of 1976, I was fishing the chalkstreams. By the middle of the summer the flow of the river had been reduced from over 500 million gallons an hour to little over 50 million gallons, and the normal river weeds had been covered with a blanket of silkweed. In the extremely hot weather the trout were hugging the bottom and refusing to rise, so the only way to tempt them was with a well-presented nymph. This was very difficult, as the normal weighted nymph patterns sank too quickly and often disappeared into the silkweed before the trout could reach them. The trout under these unusual conditions were very choosy and would not accept any large nymphs. During the next couple of weeks I played around with various ideas and dressings with little success, until I eventually hit upon the idea of dressing an unweighted pattern on a biggish hook that would sink very slowly to give the trout plenty of time to intercept it before it disappeared into the silkweed. The body of this pattern was dressed on less than half the length of the hook shank, which solved the problem of size; tied this way it presented a very small silhouette.

This is an extremely simple pattern to dress, and for the body I used the same mixture of furs that I use for my very successful shrimp or cress bug pattern; for some odd reason this mixture, with a touch of fluorescent pink in the dressing, seems fatally attractive to trout. Shortly after I designed this pattern I presented one to my good friend Brian Clarke to try out. I was lingering over coffee when he took off downriver and started fishing. Within a couple of minutes I heard him shout, "Get off," repeated again and again as he fished his way up towards me—this was reduced to "Gerroff" by the time he reached me, so that was how the fly was christened. The reason for his exasperation was the fact that every time he cast the new pattern to a decent trout, a small one would appear out of nowhere and grab it.

I now always carry a few of this pattern in my fly box, as it is very effective fished in any slow-flowing sections of clear water. Cast it out in front of the fish and let it sink slowly; most trout seem to take it as it is sinking. I have also found it to be lethal for cruising trout in small clear lakes, as well as in some big lakes when the water is clear enough. Over the past few years, dressed on a size 10 or 12 hook it has proved to be one of my most killing patterns, particularly on large New Zealand lakes.

Figure 64. The Gerroff

Hook:	wide-gape, 10 to 14
Silk:	brown
Body:	seal's fur or substitute; 50% olive, 40% midbrown, and 10% fluorescent pink. Blend well and dub onto a little less than half the length of hook shank
Back:	a strip of olive PVC or latex stretched along the top of dubbed body and secured at the eye

1. Halfway along shank tie in PVC or latex up to eye. Dub seal's fur or substitute body.
2. Stretch PVC over top of body and secure at eye.

The Mating Shrimp

This is a pattern I developed to imitate the mating shrimp (*Gammarus* sp) or cress bug. The basic colour of these small crustaceans is a pale watery olive, but in the latter half of the summer when they take on their mating colours there are tinges of red. When I was experimenting in an effort to produce an effective pattern to represent these mating shrimps, I was fishing a deep and fast river with many pools holding trout that were hugging the bottom. Normal weighted nymphs would just not get down to these trout, so I really wanted a larger heavier nymph. While it was no problem to dress a nymph on a larger hook, it was impossible to add sufficient weight due to the slim silhouette and relatively small size of the natural nymph. It was then that I realized it would be a simple matter to dress a pattern to represent the shrimps on a large hook with plenty of lead, as the average shrimp is much larger and bulkier than most of the more common nymphs. The deep-lying trout accepted this new dressing very readily. Since its inception the pattern has accounted for a lot of large trout and also grayling when they have been lying in deep water.

For the body of the pattern I mix seal's fur or substitute, 50 percent olive, 40 percent midbrown, and 10 percent fluorescent pink. This touch of pink in the dressing seems to act as a catalyst, as the trout are fatally attracted to it. It is a simple but not speedy pattern to dress. Start by winding the brown tying silk down the shank of the hook to the bend, and leave it hanging by the bobbin. Next cut a thin strip—about an eighth of an inch wide—from a thin lead sheet (the lead capping from the top of a wine bottle is ideal). Lay the end of this on top of the shank just short of the bend and secure with the silk almost up to the eye, then lap the strip back and forth, reducing its length on each lap, until eventually it is too short to lap anymore. If it is lapped evenly, you should finish up with the lead almost in a semicircle on top of the shank, which not only adds a lot of weight, but also provides the finished dressing with an excellent silhouette to match the strongly arched back of the naturals. After the laps of lead strip are completed, I use the blade of a screwdriver to smooth the edifice down before whipping over it with the silk. I then secure a fairly wide strip of olive-coloured PVC at the bend, followed by a length of oval silver tinsel, before winding on the dubbed mixture of seal's fur up to the eye and securing. Next rib the oval tinsel up to the eye and also secure, followed by the PVC (this should be wide enough to extend at least halfway down each side of the body). Finally, tease out the fur below the body to simulate the legs of the natural.

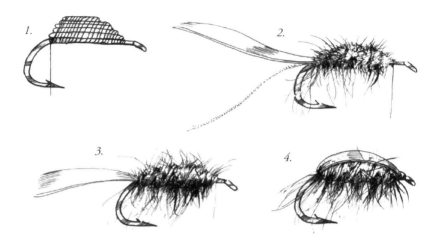

Figure 65. The Mating Shrimp

Hook:	wide-gape, 8 to 12
Silk:	brown
Body:	seal's fur or substitute; 50% olive, 40% midbrown, 10% fluorescent pink
Rib:	oval tinsel
Overbody:	cut strip of olive-dyed PVC

1. Form shaped underbody using continuously decreasing lead foil strip on top of hook shank.

2. Attach olive PVC strip and oval tinsel. Dub body using seal's fur or substitute.

3. Rib body to eye.

4. Bring forward olive PVC strip and secure at eye to form back. Tease out dubbing below body to simulate legs.

The Suspender Midge Pupa

During the writing of *The Trout and the Fly*, Brian Clarke and I developed several new artificial patterns; one of these was the Suspender Nymph. At the time we were trying to develop a pattern to represent the olive nymphs hatching through the surface film on many of the rivers we fished, and we discussed this problem at some length with Neil Patterson, a most accomplished fly fisher and a very good friend. A couple of weeks later Neil showed us an article he had found in an American book describing a hatching pattern developed by Charles Brooks called the Natant Nylon Nymph. The original concept must therefore be credited to him. His pattern incorporated a small ball of polypropylene yarn enclosed in some nylon netting and mounted on top of the body. We dressed some of these but found that, even when treated with floatant, they did not provide as much buoyancy as we required. A short time later, Neil came up with the idea of enclosing a little ball of plastazote (which he found used as outer packing in a postal envelope) in a section of nylon stocking. This seemed to solve the problem of flotability but we could not find the source of these little balls. The problem was solved by cutting little squares of the desired size from sheets of closed-cell ethafoam, which I was using at the time for the lining of a fly box being produced by my company. Trimming these cut squares with a sharp pair of scissors produced the required ball. These, however, were white—quite the wrong colour—and I think it was Brian who suggested we use a waterproof felt-tip pen to colour them to the desired shade. We now had an excellent Hatching Olive pattern that proved to be very effective; all it lacked was a name. Neil solved this problem for us by suggesting the Suspender.

Some months after this I was sitting at my fly-tying desk dressing some of these Suspenders when I accidentally tied in the ball far too near the eye of the hook. Removing it from the vise, I tossed it onto the desk. While dressing another pattern I idly glanced at the discarded one from some distance and it suddenly struck me that the white ball sitting almost over the eye of the hook closely resembled the bunch of white breathing filaments on the top of a natural midge pupa. Now, for years I had been wrestling with the problem of trying to perfect a midge pupa pattern for use on stillwater that would hang head up in the film where the trout expects to find them, with a marked lack of success. Could this be the answer? I tied in a green floss body with a silver wire rib and a thorax of dark brown condor herl. Brian and Neil both thought it was a great idea, and during the remainder of that season I tried the Suspender Midge Pupa out on many stillwaters with great success. Later I modified the dressing and materials quite considerably, reverting fairly closely to the earlier and very successful Hatching Midge Pupa pattern. The Suspender Midge Pupa has over the years become very popular with stillwater anglers and, dressed with various-coloured bodies to match the hatch, accounts for a lot of trout.

In the early morning or late evening on stillwaters when there is a good surface rise to the natural pupae, I usually fish three of these patterns tied on size 12 or 14 hooks on droppers about three to four feet apart on a long leader. Present them in the path of a rising trout, occasionally giving the fly line a slight tweak to pull the artificials up from the vertical to the horizontal position, simulating the natural midge pupa when it adopts this horizontal position as it swims along beneath the film looking for a weak spot through which to emerge. In a very heavy surface rise I cast the team of artificials onto the surface and leave them for the trout to find naturally—this often proves very effective. However, sometimes even in a quite heavy evening rise, trout can be very difficult to tempt. This may be due to the relatively short distance that a trout can see with his binocular vision when cruising along only just below the surface, and it is worth mounting the midge pupa patterns much closer together. I have found this to be most successful and have had very encouraging reports from other stillwater fly fishers who have tried it.

During the last three or four seasons I have undertaken some interesting research on natural midges on rivers and have come to the conclusion that they are generally far more numerous than the Ephemeroptera or upwinged flies. Despite this, until quite recently they have been largely ignored by river fly fishers. As a result of autopsies I soon found out that, in many cases, trout lying very close to the surface sipping down flies, including those infuriating smutting trout, were often full of small, dark-coloured midge pupae as well as other small flies such as reed smuts. I consequently discovered that Suspender Midge Pupae dressed with dark green or brown bodies and tied on size 16 or, better still, 18 hooks proved to be amazingly successful for any trout lying close to the surface, including those that were apparently smutting. Even when dragging in an adverse current, the flies would often be taken by the trout; the fish would turn and follow them and yet still take in a most confident manner. In this case it may be that the fly resembles a pupa adopting the horizontal position and swimming prior to emerging.

One other useful ploy when fishing these small Suspenders on rivers can be used late at night when the evening rise is coming to an end. At this time it is often all but impossible to see your dry fly on the surface in the fading light, so when a trout rises you do not know whether it is to your fly or not. Fishing with a Suspender, lay your fly hard down on the surface. The plop as it enters the water can usually be seen, so you will know where your fly is in relation to the trout to which you are casting. Trout will often feed avidly on midge pupae late in the evening but, as the takes are very gentle, I have found it pays to keep in very close touch with your fly by lifting the rod as the fly is brought towards you with the current. This keeps a fairly tight line. This is easily done as you are usually fishing at very close range late in the evening.

Hook:	down-eyed, 10 to 18
Silk:	to match body colour
Head:	ball of plastazote or ethafoam wrapped in small piece of nylon stocking mesh
Tail or tag:	white fluorescent wool or filaments
Rib:	fine silver wire or Lurex

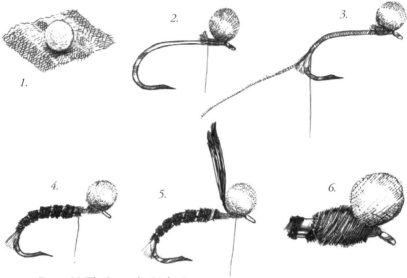

Figure 66. The Suspender Midge Pupa

Body: seal's fur of required colour

Thorax: pale-brown-dyed turkey herl

1. Plastazote "head" trimmed to sphere of approximately
   ³⁄₁₆″ diameter or large enough to support size of hook
   used, then wrapped in nylon stocking mesh.

2. Head whipped to hook shank behind the eye.

3. Silk taken well around the bend, tail fibres and silver rib
   tied in.

4. The silk is then dubbed with the seal's fur and wound
   forwards to the point indicated, secured, and ribbed.

5. Silk is taken forwards and thorax of herl is tied in behind
   the head.

6. Thorax is wound and secured.

The Super Grizzly

This is a dressing I developed in the late seventies. Tied on different-sized hooks, the pattern represents the many species of olives *(Baetis)* found on my local rivers. Up to that time I had been using Ollie Kite's Imperial, an excellent and popular general pattern that was, however, sometimes refused by trout feeding upon the darker olives due to the pale colour of the honey cock hackle. My modified pattern had the same heron herl body, but longer tails for greater flotability, for which I used nylon filaments in a pale brown colour. For the hackle I tied in together a brown and a grizzly hackle of good quality, sharp and short in the flue. When the very small olives are hatching, I use a further modification—my Super Grizzly Emerger —which I only dress on hook size 18 (see page 220-221).

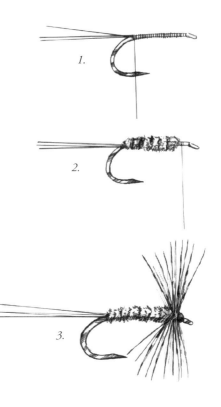

Figure 67. The Super Grizzly

Hook:	Partridge arrow-point barbless, 12 to 16. No CS20
Silk:	brown or purple
Tail:	long, pale brown nylon filaments
Hackle:	three turns of matching grizzly and Rhode Island Red cock hackles
Body:	heron herl

1. Tie in nylon filaments for tail, noting extended length.

2. Form tapered body with grey heron herl.

3. Tie in back to back and wind simultaneously one Rhode Island Red and one grizzly cock hackle.

The Poly Caddis

If you are looking for a caddis pattern that is both simple and quick to dress, this is for you. In the early eighties a new material appeared on the fly-dressing market called polypropylene yarn. It is extremely buoyant and available in many colours. It comes carded and is quite simple to separate into three strands. For the smaller patterns—dressed on hook sizes 14 to 18—I use one of the twists and for larger patterns, two twists. If wetted before using, the yarn snugs down much better to give a smoother finish. For the basic pattern, tie in the yarn—any colour—required at the bend of the hook and wind up to the eye, forming a cylindrical body; then take the yarn back over the top of the body and splay it out to form the wings. Tie in two or three turns of a cock hackle of the chosen colour to complete the fly. I often require the wings to be of a different colour from the body, in which case I tie in a separate section of different-coloured yarn over the top of the body. While this pattern floats extremely well, it is even more effective in fast, broken water dressed palmer fashion with a hackle wound over the body from the bend to the eye. With this modification it is better to tie in the wing separately, sloping back over the hackle.

Hook:	down-eyed wide gape, 10 to 18
Silk:	as body colour
Body:	polypropylene yarn of the chosen colour
Wings:	as body
Hackle:	two or three turns of a cock hackle of desired colour tied in behind eye, or wound along body palmer fashion

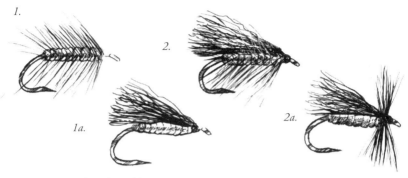

Figure 68. The Poly Caddis

1. Form cylindrical body with polypropylene yarn and palmer with cock hackle.
2. Tie in wing using material as for body.

   1a. Form cylindrical body and wing with polypropylene yarn.

   2a. Tie in cock hackle and wind two or three turns to cover base of wing.

THE POLY MAY DUN, THE GODDARD WESTERN DRAKE, AND THE POLY MAY SPINNER

This was developed in the early eighties specifically to represent the dun (subimago) of the mayfly *Ephemera danica* or *E. vulgata,* the largest of the upwinged flies, commonly referred to as the green drake. Prior to this I had relied on several well-known patterns such as Jacques' Mayfly, the Fore & Aft Mayfly, and, one of the most effective of all, the Grey Wulff, but none of these had a very high success rate against the more educated trout. The basic idea for the new dressing came from a fly a friend of mine was fishing on the Kennet during a heavy hatch of large green drakes. This had a split hair wing rather like a Wulff pattern and a strongly dubbed body of cream seal's fur. It was a rather nondescript pattern but took a lot of trout that day as it was very durable, although it was less effective later in the week when the trout became more selective.

For my new pattern I retained the split hair wings but aimed for a closer representation of the natural. After considerable trial and error I finished up with a pattern that bore little or no resemblance to the original. It was dressed to represent the emerging mayfly on the surface. This was achieved by tying the tips of the bunch of calf's tail used to form the wings, as a tag, about half the shank length of the hook beyond the bend; this represented the partly empty shuck of the emerging mayfly. The calf's tail was then bound along the top of the shank almost to the eye, where it was turned up and divided into the required V shape with a figure-of-eight tying, pointing slightly forward over the eye. For maximum flotability I decided upon cream polypropylene yarn for the body, and also a substantial hackle with at least a couple of turns on each side of the hair wings. I now had a pattern that was very durable, floated very well, and was simple to dress. Over the next two or three seasons I experimented with different-coloured wings and hackles. I soon found that a black hackle was most effective and finally decided upon pale gold wings, as I had noticed that on bright days the naturals, when hatching, seemed to transmit a golden glow despite the fact that the wings, when closely examined, appeared greenish blue with dark patches. While the final pattern close up seemed to bear little or no resemblance to the naturals, on the water surface it was extremely difficult to tell them apart. Trout must have the same difficulty, as it has proved to be a phenomenally effective pattern. I am sure it is equally effective along the eastern half of the United States, as the big green drakes found in this area are very similar in appearance, size, and colour to the UK species.

As a regular visitor to the western states, particularly Montana, I soon became acquainted with several similar species of large upwinged flies generally referred to as western green drakes, which emerge during June and early July. The Poly May Dun, modified to match their very different colours, has had quite spectacular results and seems to be particularly effective on many of the more difficult spring creeks. These western green drakes are considerably smaller than their British counterparts so I use smaller hook sizes, No 12 and even No 14. I call this dressing the Goddard Western Drake. Two big pluses with both these patterns is that they are quick to dress and durable.

The Poly May Dun

Figure 69. The Poly May Dun

Hook: Partridge-wide gape, 10 or 12. No GRS2A

Silk: strong white

Shuck and wings: bunch of white calf's tail dyed pale gold

Body: cream-coloured polypropylene yarn

Hackle: black cock, two turns on each side of wing root

1. Tie in calf's tail for wings and leave tips protruding over bend of hook to represent shuck.

2. Divide wings with figure-of-eight tying.

3. Using cream polypropylene yarn, tie in and form body.

4. Tie in black cock hackle and take two turns behind wings and two turns in front.

The Goddard Western Drake

Hook:	Partridge wide-gape, 12 or 14. No GRS2A
Silk:	strong green
Tag or shuck:	six to ten strands of pale gold Krystal Flash, a little over half body length
Body:	olive green polypropylene yarn
Rib:	thick yellow Naples silk
Wings:	bunch of white calf's tail dyed pale grey, tied in V shape over eye
Hackle:	olive green saddle hackle, two turns on each side of wing root

The complementary Poly May Spinner, which represents the imago of the mayfly, is basically of the same design except it has long tails, a white body, and a mixture of black and white calf's tail for the wings. These Wulff-style V-shaped wings are tied in with a much wider V so that, when the fly lands on the water, one wing lies flat on the surface while the other is cocked vertically. Most other mayfly spinner patterns are tied with horizontally dressed wings so that they both lie flat on the surface. Next time you are present during a large fall of natural mayfly spinners, look to see how many dead and dying spinners are floating along with one wing cocked vertically. These days when I am fishing during a mayfly spinner fall, I use only two patterns, either this new pattern of my own or an equally killing pattern developed by Neil Patterson called the Deerstalker, which is dressed with both wings lying flat in the traditional manner. I dress my spinner pattern with a hackle a little shorter in the flue than in the dun pattern, as this allows it to fish a little tighter in the surface and also facilitates the desired cocking to one side or the other.

The Poly May Spinner

Hook:	Partridge arrow-point, 10 or 12. No CS20
Silk:	black
Tails:	three long nylon brush filaments coloured black with waterproof felt-tip pen
Wing:	black and white calf's tail fibres, well mixed, tied in wide V
Body:	white polypropylene yarn
Hackle:	black cock hackles short in flue. Two behind wing and two turns in front

The Goddard Smut

This pattern is very simple and quick to tie, developed specifically for those infuriating trout taking smuts or similar tiny flies that are prevalent on many chalkstreams. Ever since the inception of dry-fly fishing towards the latter half of the last century, these very tiny reed smuts have been referred to as the black curse, and trout feeding upon them used to be considered uncatchable. Even the doyen of dry-fly fishermen, the great Frederick M. Halford, dismissed them as impossible, although in his later years he did introduce two patterns to represent them—but apparently these were rarely successful.

The main problem is, of course, the tiny size of the natural reed smut, which means that to represent them it is necessary to dress your artificial on extremely small hooks; even sizes 24 and 26 are barely small enough. It is extremely difficult to set such small hooks successfully, and, even if this is accomplished, your chances of landing a trout of substantial weight are poor due to the very fine nylon point you have to use. For many years I experimented with tiny dry flies for smutting trout, but with lamentable lack of success. I failed to hook most of the trout that accepted the fly, and on those very odd occasions when I was successful, I would be broken on the 7X point if the trout was much over two pounds.

A few years ago I took a rod on a stretch of the middle Test where one of the main beats was on a rather slow-running carrier. Although this stretch of water held many good trout, they were extremely difficult to catch, as most days they would be feeding exclusively upon those wretched smuts. They say that necessity is the mother of invention, and eventually I looked more closely at the basic problem of how to produce a pattern that would appear very small yet be capable of hooking and holding relatively big trout. The Gerroff (see page 202-204) had proved very successful for taking trout in clear, shallow, slow-running water, when even small weighted nymphs sank too quickly and disappeared in the silkweed on the bottom. It was unweighted, the body dressed only halfway along the shank to produce a small silhouette on a relatively large hook, to make it sink slowly. Could the basis of this pattern solve the problem for smutting trout? It seemed such a simple solution that I could not understand why no-one had thought of it before. I dressed some size 18 wide-gape hooks with a very sparse black body and hackle halfway along the shank from the eye. Armed with these, I achieved spectacular success with the smutting trout on the carrier and by midafternoon had landed and released over a dozen trout, most of which were well over two pounds.

During the remainder of that season I caught many more and killed some of them in order to examine their stomach contents. To my surprise, not only did I find many reed smuts and other small

Diptera, but I also found considerable numbers of small chironomids, mostly green or dark brown. Towards the end of the season I therefore decided to try, in addition to my new smut pattern, some small midge patterns, eventually discovering that my own Suspender Midge tied on size 18 hooks was even more successful. These two patterns now form the basis of my armoury for tackling smutting trout. Dressed on size 18 hooks, they not only provide a good percentage of hookups, but also allow the use of much thicker nylon on the point of the leader, which with a modicum of luck allows you to grass even the largest of trout you are likely to catch. After you have tied the fly on the leader, always offset the hook a little with a pair of pliers. This is particularly important on the smaller-sized hooks, sizes 16 and upwards, and results in a much higher hookup rate.

Figure 70. The Goddard Smut

Hook:	Partridge arrow-point barbless, 18 or smaller. No CS20
Silk:	fine black
Body:	three or four turns of black ostrich herl halfway along shank
Hackle:	two turns of very small black cock hackle short in flue

1. Attach black ostrich herl halfway along shank and form body.
2. Tie in very small black cock hackle and wind two turns only.

The Super Grizzly Emerger

During the summer of 1988 I spent some time fishing in Montana and discussed fly patterns with Craig Mathews, who owns the celebrated fly tackle shop Blue Ribbon Flies in West Yellowstone. Craig and John Juracek, both excellent and innovative fly dressers, had just perfected a new pattern that they called a Sparkle Dun, which was proving to be very killing when any small olives were hatching. These were all dressed on very small hooks with a splayed deer hair wing and different-coloured bodies, varying from pale cream through olive to dark grey, but the most novel feature was a small bunch of pale brownish sparkle wool tied in at the tail to represent the empty shuck of an emerging olive. These proved to be exceptionally effective, and during the remainder of my stay I took many nice trout on them.

Halfway through the following season I was fishing on the Kennet one day when I chanced upon one of those difficult rising trout that ignored all my usual offerings. Rather nonplussed, I was looking through my fly box wondering what to offer him next when I chanced upon several of Craig's Sparkle Duns left over from my Montana trip. Mounting one of these on the leader, I was mildly surprised when the trout, a lovely wild Kennet trout of just over three pounds, accepted this the first time I covered him. For the remainder of that season I found the pattern very effective indeed for both brown and rainbow trout when any of the small summer olives were hatching. It was even more effective for the grayling and is now my favourite grayling fly. That winter I was tying up a Super Grizzly on smaller hooks than usual and, noticing a resemblance to the Sparkle Dun, wondered if it would prove more effective dressed as an emerger pattern. Having no pale brown sparkle wool to represent the empty shuck, I decided to use some pale gold Krystal Flash, and this looked so good I dressed a dozen or so to try during the coming season. I have used this Super Grizzly Emerger pattern for the past few seasons and, from late June onwards, when the small olives are hatching, it has proved to be fantastically successful. I dress it in one size only, a Partridge arrow-point size 18, and during the past two seasons it has accounted for well over two hundred trout, most of which were returned. Recently I

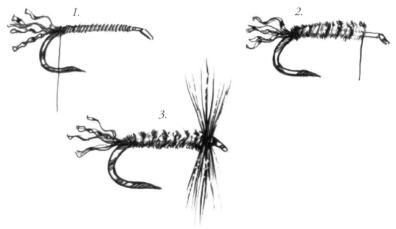

Figure 71. The Super Grizzly Emerger

have found this pattern dressed with a hot orange seal fur or substitute body very effective in the late evening.

Hook:	Partridge arrow-point, 18. No CS20
Silk:	fine nymph, brown or purple
Tail or shuck:	pale yellow or gold Krystal Flash, half a dozen strands three-quarters the length of the body
Body:	grey heron herl
Wing:	one Rhode Island Red and one grizzly cock hackle, short in flue, tied in together

1. Tie in Krystal Flash for tail, three-quarters the length of the body.
2. Form tapered body with grey heron herl.
3. Tie in back to back and wind simultaneously one Rhode Island Red and one grizzly cock hackle, each short in flue.

The Shrymph

Since it was developed in 1993, this pattern has proved to be very effective indeed for large grayling, for which it was originally intended. It is equally killing for large, deep-lying trout.

I may only fish the nymph to trout later in the season on those occasional dour days when there is no surface activity at all, but not so grayling. Although your average grayling is a free riser, very large grayling tend to hug the bottom in the deeper holes, and the only way to reach them is with a heavily weighted deep-sunk nymph. While I have had a certain amount of success with large weighted Pheasant Tail and PVC Nymphs and Sawyer Grayling Bugs in the faster and deeper sections of the river that really big grayling seem to love, I have found it difficult to get any of these patterns down to them quickly enough. I tried tying some of the patterns on larger hooks and/or with more weight but they looked out of character, and obviously the fish formed the same opinion, as they were not very successful. I did have quite a lot of success with my own Mating Shrimp pattern, which was originally developed for deep-lying trout grubbing on the bottom for shrimps, but I was not completely happy with this for grayling. What I really required was not only a heavily weighted pattern that would sink very quickly, but also one that I could fish off the bottom with the induced-take method as with a traditional weighted nymph.

Eventually it occurred to me to try a pattern that looks vaguely like a nymph but has the colours and weight of the Shrimp. I am sure that one of the main reasons for the outstanding success of my Mating Shrimp pattern is the blend of furs—which includes a judicious amount of fluorescent pink—so I decided to use this same mixture for both the body and the thorax of the new pattern. I also ribbed the body with the same heavy silver ribbing material that I use on the Shrimp. Using lead wire, I built up a substantial thorax to add as much weight as possible and finished the pattern with flue from a black crow feather doubled and redoubled over the top of this thorax. The finished creation at a quick glance appeared to be a shrimp, but in silhouette was certainly more like a nymph, so what other name could I possibly give it? I am delighted to report that this pattern has not only proved to be phenomenally successful for big grayling—it has provided me with over two dozen grayling of over two pounds apiece—but has also fooled some very large trout. Towards the end of last season it was instrumental in deceiving what is to date the largest rainbow trout ever taken from a UK river. This rainbow, which was in superb condition, came from the river Test and weighed in at fifteen and a quarter pounds.

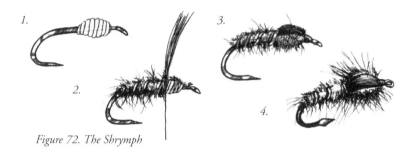

Figure 72. The Shrymph

Hook: wide-gape, 8 to 12

Silk: brown waxed thread

Body and thorax: seal's fur or substitute; 50% green, 40% brown, 10% fluorescent pink

Rib: rib the body up to the thorax with heavy silver ribbing material

Wing cases: the flue from a black crow feather doubled and redoubled over the top of the thorax

1. Form pronounced thorax with lead wire.

2. Tie in silver ribbing and make dubbed seal's fur or substitute body. Rib body with tinsel and tie in herl for wing case.

3. Dub thorax, double and redouble herl for wing cases.

4. Pick out seal's fur on each side of thorax with dubbing needle to simulate legs.

The Black Gnat

When black gnats are blown onto the water surface, trout will often take these tiny terrestrials in preference to upwinged duns that may be hatching at the same time. There are many patterns available to represent them but I have not found one that I have been completely happy with. One of the key features of the natural is the translucent wings, which, when viewed from underwater, particularly in sunny conditions, seem to sparkle and reflect all the colours of the rainbow. The wings of my new pattern are formed from rainbow-coloured Krystal Flash, which I am sure is the major factor in its success. It has accounted for a lot of trout and also grayling over the last season. It is a very simple and easy pattern to dress.

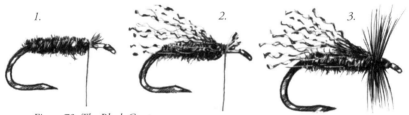

Figure 73. The Black Gnat

Hook:	Partridge arrow-point, 16 or 18. No CS20
Silk:	black
Body:	black or dark grey sparkle wool
Wing:	a dozen or more strands of rainbow Krystal Flash, sloping back over body
Hackle:	black cock, short in flue

1. Tie in black or dark grey sparkle wool and make body.

2. Secure Krystal Flash sloping back over body.

3. Select black cock hackle short in flue. Tie in and wind hackle.

INDEX

INDEX 229